Navigating
Differences

Navigating
Differences

Integration in Singapore

EDITED BY

TERENCE CHONG

ISEAS YUSOF ISHAK
INSTITUTE

First published in Singapore in 2020 by
ISEAS Publishing
30 Heng Mui Keng Terrace
Singapore 119614
E-mail: publish@iseas.edu.sg
Website: <http://bookshop.iseas.edu.sg>

The responsibility for facts and opinions in this publication rests exclusively with the author and his interpretations do not necessarily reflect the views or the policy of the publishers or their supporters.

ISEAS Library Cataloguing-in-Publication Data

Names: Chong, Terence, editor.
Title: Navigating differences : integration in Singapore / editor: Terence Chong.
Description: Singapore : ISEAS – Yusof Ishak Institute, 2020. | Includes bibliographical references.
Identifiers: ISBN 9789814881265 (soft cover) | ISBN 9789814881616 (PDF) | ISBN 9789814881623 (epub)
Subjects: LCSH: Social stratification—Singapore. | Social integration—Singapore. | Singapore—Social conditions.
Classification: LCC HN700.67 A8N32

Typeset by Superskill Graphics Pte Ltd

Contents

Acknowledgements

This book was mooted in 2017 by then Director of ISEAS – Yusof Ishak Institute, Mr Tan Chin Tiong, as a contribution to Singapore's Bicentennial Commemorations. The aim of the book was to take stock of Singapore's socio-cultural progress through the decades and to offer insights into the potential mid- to long-term challenges facing the country. After some deliberation, we decided that the theme of integration would be a highly relevant one. In a multicultural society open to global trends, it is clear that the tensions between different values, beliefs, worldviews, identities, and ideologies will remain with us for the foreseeable future. These tensions have only become more complex, and it is increasingly necessary to understand integration as a multidimensional issue that warrants a multidimensional examination. This volume is an attempt at such an examination.

Such a book will not be possible without key individuals. It has been my privilege to identify local scholars whose work I admire to contribute to this volume. I have benefitted immensely from their learned perspectives. I am grateful to Mr Tan for the opportunity to work on this volume as well as the advice offered along the way. My thanks also goes to ISEAS' Publications Unit and the editorial team for their professional work. My colleagues Daljit Singh, Benjamin Loh, and Hui Yew-Foong helped to sharpen the arguments and ideas in the chapters with their valuable feedback and critical comments. Research Officer John Choo Rong Hui was a very reliable and extremely competent assistant, and was instrumental in the coordination of the project. Last but not least, the kind support of Mr Choi Shing Kwok, the current Director of ISEAS, also went a long way in ensuring this book came out in a timely fashion.

List of Contributors

Ja Ian CHONG is Associate Professor of Political Science at the National University of Singapore. He previously worked with the Center for Strategic and International Studies in Washington, DC and the Institute of Defence and Strategic Studies. He held fellowships from the Harvard-Yenching Institute, East-West Center, and the Princeton-Harvard China and the World Program. His book *External Intervention and the Politics of State Formation: China, Indonesia, Thailand, 1893–1952* (Cambridge, 2012) received the 2013/14 International Security Studies Section Book Award from the International Studies Association. Dr Chong's work crosses international relations, comparative politics, and political sociology, and focuses on security issues in the Asia-Pacific.

Terence CHONG is Deputy Director and Senior Fellow at the ISEAS – Yusof Ishak Institute. He is a sociologist who works on religion and the middle class in Southeast Asia, as well as multiculturalism in Singapore. He has published in journals such as *Modern Asian Studies, Journal of Contemporary Asia, Asian Studies Review, Pacific Affairs, Journal of Southeast Asian Studies*, among others. He has edited books on Singapore, Thailand, and Christianity in Southeast Asia.

Vincent CHUA is Associate Professor at the Department of Sociology, National University of Singapore. He received his PhD in Sociology from the University of Toronto, in 2010. His research areas are in the fields of social networks (and social capital), labour markets, social stratification (gender, race, education and class) and neighbourhoods. His research is featured in journal publications such as *Social Networks, Social Science Research, Current Sociology, Sociological Perspectives, American Behavioral Scientist,* and *Sociology of Education.*

Fang Yu FOO graduated from the National University of Singapore with a Major in Geography (BSc Hons). Her graduating research thesis focused on the Chinese diaspora and new immigrants in Singapore. She also holds a Postgraduate Diploma in Education and is currently teaching Geography and Social Studies at the secondary school level in Singapore.

Daniel P.S. GOH is Associate Professor of Sociology at the National University of Singapore. He studies state formation, postcolonialisms, race and multiculturalism, urbanisms, and religion. His recent co-edited books include *Urban Asias: Essays on Futurity Past and Present* (JOVIS Verlag, 2018) and *Regulating Religion in Asia: Norms, Modes and Challenges* (Cambridge University Press, 2019). His current work focuses on the cultural politics of history, heritage and global city making in Hong Kong, Penang and Singapore. He has published over fifty articles in journals and books; these can be found at www.danielpsgoh.com.

Elaine Lynn-Ee HO is Associate Professor at the Department of Geography and Senior Research Fellow at the Asia Research Institute (ARI), National University of Singapore. Her research addresses how citizenship is changing as a result of multidirectional migration in the Asia-Pacific. She is author of *Citizens in Motion: Emigration, Immigration and Re-migration Across China's Borders* (Stanford University Press, 2018), which received the American Sociological Association's (ASA) award for "Best Book in Global and Transnational Sociology by an International Scholar" in 2019.

Laavanya KATHIRAVELU is Assistant Professor at the Division of Sociology, Nanyang Technological University, Singapore. Her research interests lie in the intersections between migration and citizenship, urban studies, and race and ethnicity. Her first book is *Migrant Dubai: Low Wage Workers and the Construction of a Global City* (Palgrave Macmillian, 2016). She was Fung Global Fellow at Princeton University between 2015 and 2016 and was a Postdoctoral Research Fellow at the Max Planck Institute for the Study of Religious and Ethnic Diversity (2011–14). She is currently working on a series of projects on migration infrastructures, immigrant integration, and invisible privilege in Singapore.

Gillian KOH is Deputy Director (Research) and Senior Research Fellow in the Governance and Economy Department at the Institute of Policy Studies, National University of Singapore. Her research interests are in the areas of party and electoral politics, the development of civil society, state-society relations and state governance in Singapore. Among other things, Dr Koh conducts surveys on Singaporeans' political attitudes, sense of identity, rootedness and resilience and their social networks. She has helmed several scenario-planning projects; written and edited published works on civil society and political development in Singapore.

LEONG Chan-Hoong is Associate Professor at the Centre for Applied Research, Singapore University of Social Sciences. He received his PhD in Psychology (2006) from Victoria University of Wellington, and

MSc in Statistics (2011) and Applied Geographic Information Systems (2019) from the National University of Singapore. His research focuses on social diversity and national narratives. He is the Singapore national representative for the World Association for Public Opinion Research, and elected Board Member of the International Academy for Intercultural Research. Chan-Hoong was consulting editor for the *International Journal of Intercultural Relations* (2013–14), and editor for its 2019 Special Issue, *Viewing Intercultural Adaptation and Social Inclusion Through Constructs of National Identity*.

Joseph Chinyong LIOW is Dean of the College of Humanities, Arts, and Social Science, Nanyang Technological University, Singapore.

Kalyani K. MEHTA is former head of the Master of Gerontology degree programme at Singapore University of Social Sciences. She launched the first PhD in Gerontology in Singapore in 2017. Professor Mehta is an outstanding researcher on ageing issues and she has published six books and more than forty-five articles in highly reputed journals. She has served as Nominated Member of Parliament in Singapore from 2007 to 2009. Her research interests range from ageing-related policies, retirement, mature workers, gerontechnology, family caregivers of seniors and intergenerational relationships.

Irene Y.H. NG is an Associate Professor of Social Work and Director of the Social Service Research Centre in the National University of Singapore. She holds a joint PhD in Social Work and Economics from the University of Michigan. Her research areas include poverty and inequality, intergenerational mobility, and social welfare policy. Her research projects include a study of in-work poverty among the young; an evaluation of a national Work Support programme; National Youth Surveys 2010, 2013, 2016 and 2019; a study of low-income households with debt; and an evaluation of Social Service Offices. She is active in the community, serving or having served in committees in the Ministry of Social and Family Development, National Council of Social Service, Ministry of Manpower, and various voluntary welfare organizations. Her teaching areas include poverty, policy, welfare economics, youth work, and programme planning.

NORSHAHRIL Saat is Senior Fellow and Co-coordinator of the Indonesia Studies Programme at the ISEAS – Yusof Ishak Institute. His publications include *The State, Ulama, and Islam in Malaysia and Indonesia* (Amsterdam

University Press, 2018); *Tradition and Islamic Learning: Singapore Students in the Al-Azhar University* (ISEAS – Yusof Ishak Institute, 2018); and *Islam in Southeast Asia: Negotiating Modernity* (ISEAS – Yusof Ishak Institute, 2018). His articles have also been published in journals such as *Asian Journal of Social Science, Contemporary Islam: Dynamics of Muslim Life, Review of Indonesian and Malaysian Affairs,* and *Studia Islamika.*

TAN Ern Ser is Associate Professor, Department of Sociology; Academic Convener, Singapore Studies, Faculty of Arts and Social Sciences; and Academic Adviser, Social Lab, Institute of Policy Studies, at the National University of Singapore. He received his PhD in Sociology from Cornell University, USA. He is author of *Does Class Matter?* (World Scientific, 2004) and *Class and Social Orientations* (Institute of Policy Studies, 2015). He is also Adviser for Socio-economic Research and Chairman, Research Advisory Panel, Housing and Development Board (HDB). He was appointed a Justice of the Peace in 2013.

Kenneth Paul TAN works at the National University of Singapore's Lee Kuan Yew School of Public Policy. As an expert on Singapore's politics, society, and culture, Professor Tan has written extensively and holistically on the tensions and contradictions around Singapore's transition from a developmental state to a neoliberal global city. His work is critical, qualitative, interpretive, and interdisciplinary. He authored *Singapore: Identity, Brand, Power* (Cambridge University Press, 2018), *Governing Global-City Singapore: Legacies and Futures After Lee Kuan Yew* (Routledge, 2017), *Cinema and Television in Singapore: Resistance in One Dimension* (Brill, 2008), and *Renaissance Singapore? Economy, Culture, and Politics* (NUS Press, 2007).

WALID Jumblatt Abdullah is an Assistant Professor at the Public Policy and Global Affairs Programme, Nanyang Technological University, Singapore. He completed his PhD under the Joint Degree Programme between the National University of Singapore and King's College, London. He works on relationships between Islam and the state, political Islam, and political parties and elections. He has previously published in *Democratization, International Political Science Review, Government and Opposition, Asian Survey, Asian Studies Review, Journal of Church and State, Australian Journal of International Affairs, Commonwealth and Comparative Politics, Indonesia and the Malay World, Japanese Journal of Political Science, Small Wars & Insurgencies, Journal of Muslim Minority Affairs,* and *Journal of Religious and Political Practice.*

Yvonne YAP is a Senior Research Analyst at the Institute of Policy Studies, Social Lab. Her research interests lie in exploring the impact of spatial policies on individual life outcomes, community relations and social stratification. In her Master's thesis, Yvonne examined the effect of ethnic preferences and socio-economic differences on housing patterns in Singapore. At the Institute of Policy Studies, she is currently involved in Youth STEPS, the first national-level longitudinal study of youth in Singapore, as well as a geo-spatial study on attitudes towards immigrants in Singapore. She holds an MSc in Sociology from the University of Oxford, a BSocSci (Honours) in Sociology from the National University of Singapore, and a BA (Double Degree) from Waseda University.

1

Introduction

TERENCE CHONG

Integration in Singapore is becoming increasingly important. While this may sound like a truism today, it certainly was not the case when Singapore was thrust into modernity under the auspices of the East India Company in 1819. Established as a trading port, and later as part of the Straits Settlements Crown Colony in 1867, the island began to see a steady stream of immigrants from South China and South India arrive onto its shores. As indentured labourers, small traders, and farmers escaping droughts, these Chinese and Indian immigrants added another socio-economic layer to the existing network of activities of the Orang Laut, Javanese, and Bugis that had long connected the island to the rest of the Malay World prior to Stamford Raffles' arrival. Integration was not a priority for the colonial administration. Preferring clear and distinct communal divisions, these ethnic communities were, over time, allotted different living quarters near the mouth of the river. Intermediaries from these ethnic communities were appointed to represent collective interests and concerns to the colonial government. Key institutions such as clan associations, guild houses, *kongsis* and temples for the Chinese community, and Hindu associations, merchant groups, and temples for the Indian community served as constellations for their respective cultural universes (Trocki 1990; Rai 2014) from which these communities formed their collective identities. Naturally there was everyday intermingling between the ethnic communities in shared public spaces while economic and business relationships were forged across ethnic divides in the marketplace. However, because there was no overarching common identity and because of the desire for many of these Chinese sojourners to return to their homeland, the idea of social integration in which different social groups incorporate themselves into the existing social structure to function cohesively so as to achieve the collectively desired outcomes was just not in the air.

Integration ceased to be an abstract concept upon separation from Malaysia in 1965. The island's multicultural character made it necessary for Singapore's first-generation leaders to find an equilibrium between two ideological positions. On one hand is the belief that the "nation" is only meaningful because it is made up of local communities. Implicit in this belief are the principles that the cultural and ethnic rights of a community are inalienable and that it is incumbent on the state to protect and accommodate such rights. On the other is the belief that the concept of the nation takes primacy over all local interests. The interests of local communities, be they religious, ethnic, or class, need to be suspended occasionally to allow national interest to transcend identity politics. Indeed, the success of Singapore's integration efforts over fiftey years since independence has depended on seeking an equilibrium between these two positions.

Chasing this equilibrium between national and communal interests has required vigilance and sensitivity. This is because the perennial challenges of race, language, and religion do not always present themselves in the flesh. They may be guised in all manner of disputes, lying just under the surface only to emerge when conflicts are poorly managed. The burning of incense paper or the indiscriminate parking of vehicles on Friday afternoons may appear to be innocuous acts but in Singapore they are loaded with racial and religious meanings. When Singaporeans learn to accommodate these moments of inconvenience they are, by extension, learning to integrate with communities of different races and religions. It may be appropriate to understand what exactly we mean by "integration". A typical functionalist perspective would define integration as a system in which different groups understand their social and economic roles, work in tandem with each other, and contribute to the greater whole whereby the success of the integrative process is measured by how well society functions as a unit or as an economy (Hamilton 1992). Such a perspective, however, has been criticized as too operational or mechanical in its approach, and thus unable to account for the conflict and social negotiations which invariably take place in multicultural settings (Treviño 2001). Others, in attempting to redefine "integration" for an era of global immigration, have called for the assimilation of new immigrant groups and minorities into society (Alba and Nee 1997). The assumption here is that "assimilation has diminished cultural differences that once served to signal ethnic membership to others and to sustain ethnic solidarity" (ibid., p. 841). This has certainly not been Singapore's experience. It is highly unlikely that the country's ethnic minorities will accept an assimilationist model because it goes against Singapore's multicultural ethos. Furthermore, with large numbers of lower and higher skilled workers who are transitionary in nature, such an assimilationist definition of integration is not practical for Singapore. The most conventional model of integration for Singapore was articulated by then Prime Minister Goh Chok Tong who offered the image of four overlapping circles. According to PM Goh (1999),

> The four circles, each representing a community, will never totally overlap to become a stack of four circles. But they are closely linked to one another, forming a clover leaf pattern. This overlapping circles approach to building a nation and common identity is diametrically opposite the melting-pot approach. The melting-pot approach would have meant absorption of the minority communities by the majority community. Our Chinese have no wish to force Malays, Indians, Eurasians and others to speak, dress and eat like them. Nor would the other races want to be like them. The overlapping circles approach maximizes our common ground but retain each race's separate identity.

This overlapping circle model is not too dissimilar to the "salad bowl" model in which there is intermingling and mixing of different groups but each retaining their character, unlike the "melting pot" model of America that requires assimilation (Yang 2000). Singapore's idealized integration may thus be described as a society in which different groups and communities interact regularly and readily for the common good, choosing to highlight their shared characteristics and values while de-emphasizing their differences in order that society at large may reap the benefits of pluralism; meanwhile retaining their separate identities, norms, and ways of life in which cultural boundaries and the Other must always be treated with respect.

Generally speaking, Singapore has had to deal with different integration challenges over four periods in its post-independence history. These different challenges have been shaped by the particular economic, political and socio-cultural milieu of the time. To be clear, these periods are not neatly bound and distinct from each other. These challenges are not limited to these periods but continue to test the integration process even today. Instead, these periods are marked out to demonstrate that distinct challenges become more pronounced and pressing under particular socio-political economic conditions.

During the first period, roughly from 1965 to the end of the 1980s, the main obstacles to the integration of the local population were, as mentioned above, race and religion, and they continue to be so. The country's problematic merger with Malaysia from 1963 to 1965 and the 1964 racial riots were key moments that underlined the importance of integrating a pluralistic migrant society. The three main ethnic groups were the Chinese, many of whom divided themselves up into dialect groups, the Malays who were drawn from different parts of the Malay World, and the Indians who were from various parts of South India. These communities spoke in a variety of languages including English, Mandarin, Chinese dialects, Malay, and Tamil. Underpinning these ethnic and linguistic diversity were religions such as Christianity, Catholicism, Islam, Buddhism, Taoism, Sikhism, just to name a few. From this pluralism the postcolonial state proceeded to construct the national myths of multiculturalism and meritocracy as both principled and practical means to forge a coherent national community. Integration was not left to chance but carefully facilitated by decisive state intervention. Only four official languages were recognized; Chinese dialects were banned from local media with Mandarin promoted as the "mother tongue" of all ethnic Chinese, while the state effectively homogenized ethnic complexity with its "CMIO" categorization of the population. The ethnic quota on public housing later ensured that ethnic groups were evenly distributed across the island. All these have had a streamlining effect on Singapore society. This reductionist approach to cultural complexity allowed diverse interests to be shaped and crystallized for more efficient administration. Such a reductionist approach has suited the nation-building project over the years.

The second period from the early 1990s to early 2000s was a time when class distinction emerged as a key obstacle to integration alongside race and religion. The Singapore middle class had come into its own during the 1980s and had begun to display signs of conspicuous consumption in the 1990s. Pithy phrases like "the 5 Cs" (cash, condominium, car, credit card, and country club) encapsulated the relentless drive to achieve class distinction and societal recognition. This drive for class distinction amongst Singaporeans was in tandem with the country's journey towards global city status as the government sought to relax regulations in several sectors such as banking and the arts in order to be an attractive node in the network of global cities. Regionally, the decade also sparkled with exuberant economic growth in Malaysia, Indonesia and Thailand. This growth saw the beginnings of a regional middle class that defined a "Southeast Asian modernity" through its particular political consciousness, consumption patterns and relations with the state until the Asian Financial Crisis came along in 1997 (Robison and Goodman 1996). Nevertheless, in the case of Singapore, class politics had by then become such a common feature in everyday life that it became a fecund theme for local films and dramas. Class differentiation also entered political discourse with then Prime Minister Goh Chok Tong popularized the terms "heartlander" (to denote the "average" Singaporean who lived in public housing) and the "cosmopolitan" (to denote higher income and globally minded Singaporeans) as a means of simplifying and, indeed caricaturing, the complex class politics that was entrenching itself society. After all, the drive to become a vibrant and culturally exciting global city was fuelled by the need to attract highly talented foreigners to work in the country while retaining globally mobile Singaporeans who may be tempted by greener pastures elsewhere. Over the years the economic maturity of society has resulted in the self-renewal of class which, in turn, has led to the hardening of class strata. Income inequality has created different economic worlds in Singapore prompting commentators to assert that class has now replaced race and religion as the most divisive fault line in the country today (*Channel News Asia*, 1 October 2018).

The period from the early 2000s to 2011 saw tensions between locals and foreigners as the most pressing challenge to integration. In the bid to take advantage of favourable global economic conditions, the government had adopted liberal immigration policies to encourage both cheap labour and skilled talent to work and live in Singapore. From 2000 to 2010, the percentage of permanent residents increased from 7 per cent to 11 per cent, while "non-resident" foreigners working and living in Singapore rose from 19 per cent to 25 per cent (see Koh, Soon, and Yap 2015). Unfortunately, this steady influx of foreigners was not matched by existing infrastructure in the areas of public housing and transport. Trains and buses were constantly overcrowded, resulting in frequent breakdowns. Private property prices skyrocketed while the limited availability of public housing triggered anxiety and resentment within the local population, particularly amongst young families in the lower and middle-class strata. Unsurprisingly, anti-foreigner sentiments began to surface. Such sentiments were a heady mix of class resentment and racism (see Tan 2015; Lim 2015; Chong 2015). Singaporeans vented their anger at the 2011 General Elections which saw the ruling People's Action Party (PAP) winning their lowest share of the popular vote since independence. At stake was not just the occasional vitriol spewed at Indian nationals who were perceived to be overrepresented in the banking and financial industry or at Filipino nationals in the service industry but the greater global city project. With national survival so intimately tied to globalization, how could the country afford to be perceived as anti-foreigner by the rest of world? With typical responsiveness, the government took immediate steps to tweak the offending policies. Quotas on foreign workers were tightened, the public transportation system was overhauled and received a large injection of state investment. Meanwhile public housing was no longer built only when there was demand but in anticipation of demand in order to avoid long waiting times. The decisiveness of government action succeeded in lowering the temperature of anti-foreigner sentiments to the point of insignificance when the general elections was next held in 2015. However, this is not to say that local-foreigner integration is no longer an issue. Non-residents in Singapore have increased from 1.63 million in 2015 to 1.68 million in 2019, with citizens increasing only from 3.38 million to 3.5 million during the same period (*Channel News Asia*, 25 September 2019). Coupled with dipping number of Singaporean marriages and the population's low fertility rate which fell to 1.14 in 2018 (*Today*, 25 September 2019), Singaporeans are living cheek and jowl with foreigners, and it would not take much for anti-foreigner anxieties to be aroused once again.

The period from 2011 to the present can be argued to have been marked by increased complexity. Not only do race, religion, class and foreigners continue to be clear and present fault lines in Singapore, they are now influenced by cultural and political developments on these issues in other societies. How we speak about race and racism, for example, is now informed by the cultural and political vocabularies from elsewhere. Take for instance the Preeti and Subhas saga. In July 2019, Preeti Nair, a social media personality popularly known as "Preetipls", and her brother, Subhas Nair, a local rapper, were reprimanded for making a profanity-laced rap video. In the video entitled "K. Muthusamy" the duo rapped about how "Chinese people always out there f**king it up" and that "No matter who we choose, the Chinese man win" [*sic*]. The government's response to the rap video was swift. Law and Home Affairs Minister K. Shanmugam said that the video "crosses the line" and that it "insults Chinese Singaporeans with vulgarities" (*Straits Times*, 31 July 2019). The siblings were made to apologize though not without first issuing a spoof apology (*Channel News Asia*, 2 August 2019). The siblings had made the video in response to a print advertisement by NETS, an e-payment platform in which local Chinese actor, Dennis Chew, portrayed a Malay woman in tudung; an Indian man; and cross-dressed as a Chinese woman, to presumably show that people from different walks of life could use e-payment. The Nair siblings' rap video accused Chew of "brownfacing" himself with visibly darker skin to portray an Indian character. "Brownfacing", of course, is a local derivation of the American experience of "blackfacing" which dates back to nineteenth century minstrel shows where white actors painted themselves with black polish to mimic African-Americans. However, blackfacing is not merely the act of impersonation. It is the purposeful and calculated physical and cultural caricature of African-Americans as lazy, dim-witted, and ultimately, undeserving of equal treatment or rights; thus echoing historical justifications for slavery (Johnson 2012). Hence blackfacing is not just about darkening one's skin but, more potently, the specifically racist agenda for doing so.

In juxtaposing Chew's "brownfacing" with the American "blackfacing" experience, local commentators were drawing moral equivalency between the ethnic minority experience in Singapore and the African-American experience in America. This moral equivalency was never explicitly argued by commenters but, rather, implicitly suggested by placing the Singapore ethnic minority experience and the African-American experience side-by-side and pointing to the act of darkening one's face as a shared experience (Lim 2019). This way moral equivalence could be drawn without any overt comparison of trauma. While "blackfacing" is clearly racist because it is the purposeful caricature of African-Americans, it is unclear if Chew's impersonation of the Indian man or Malay woman was done to mock or caricature the ethnic minorities. His impersonations did not come with exaggerated gestures such as Indian headshaking or embellished Malay accent for comic relief; and if they had, the advertisement could be rightfully deemed racist. Certainly, the "brownfacing" advertisement can be justifiably criticized for being lazy and gimmicky for using a well-known impersonator to portray different ethnic groups instead of, say, ethnic minority celebrities to do the job. To be sure, there needs to be a local conversation over the implications of "brownfacing" in Singapore, and why it is deemed offensive by ethnic minorities but to associate it with "blackfacing" in America is not the way to kick-start it.

Another example of adopting foreign vocabularies is the growing popularity of the term "Chinese privilege" in Singapore (*Straits Times*, 15 February 2018). Generally speaking, the term is used to describe the obvious and hidden advantages enjoyed exclusively by the Chinese majority vis-à-vis other ethnic minorities. As yet, it is a vaguely defined concept though this has not prevent it from being bandied about freely. Some see it as the predominance of Mandarin, the array of Chinese cuisine available, and not being discriminated against for jobs (Wee 2017), while others "define Chinese privilege similarly to white privilege" (Sangeetha Thanapal, quoted in Tan 2017). As with "blackfacing", American terminology is used to frame local experience. In America, the term "white privilege" gained popularity in the field of education and was used to connote the "unacknowledged privilege" of white men such that "much of their oppressiveness was unconscious" (McIntosh 1992, p. 31). Since then the concept of "white privilege" has been criticized for simplifying white racial identity, indulging in confessional politics, and not addressing systemic injustices (Lensmire et al. 2013). Likewise, "Chinese privilege" is a clumsy concept because it makes no distinction between different types of privilege such as economic or political. It also makes no distinction between privileges enjoyed by majority communities in all societies, and privileges that stem specifically from being from a particular ethnic community. Furthermore, because it is an "unconscious oppression", "Chinese privilege" is an accusation that can be levelled at any Chinese individual by virtue of his or her ethnicity. In turn, this Chinese individual will have to confess his or her "unacknowledged privilege"—something that members of the Chinese underclass or working class will find incongruent to their own everyday experience.

Terms like "brownfacing" and "Chinese privilege" demonstrate that integration in Singapore is increasingly influenced by cultural politics elsewhere. The appropriation of such terms may, in some cases, offer new ways of looking at age-old issues such as Chinese chauvinism or casual racism by bringing to bear the experience of other societies. Indeed, there are three reasons why the appropriation of these terms are becoming more commonplace. First and foremost is the connectivity that the Internet offers. This connectivity ensures that identity politics in different parts of the world, particularly Western societies such as the United States in which such politics are most developed, are well known across the globe. Secondly, this connectivity allows for moral empathy to develop across boundaries. People of different cultures and histories may identify with each other by virtue of their shared experience of injustice, exploitation, or persecution. Such moral empathy is especially forthcoming for identity politics that revolve around ethnic minorities and sexual orientation, thus encouraging the adoption of vocabularies, responses, and solutions. Thirdly, using such well-known terms helps to draw attention to local agenda. Local activists or scholars may leverage on such terms to lend some novelty or creativity to their causes. Nevertheless, there are clear pitfalls for the uncritical appropriation of such terms. As critical concepts, these terms are designed to describe politically and historically specific struggles and injustices. As such, there is always the danger of Singaporeans assuming moral equivalence between "blackfacing" and "brownfacing" or "White privilege" and "Chinese privilege", thus resulting in a skewed reading of the local situation or arousing disproportionate indignation and anger. It is clear that issues of race, language, religion, class, and immigration will not be going away anytime soon. The adoption of vocabularies and identity politics from elsewhere may either elucidate or muddy these issues, depending on whether activists and commentators are judicious enough with the specific politics and histories of their borrowed concepts.

This book is divided into four parts to cover the different types of challenges to integration in contemporary Singapore. The first part, entitled "Religious Communities", delves into issues that have arisen from within the Muslim and Christian communities in Singapore. Joseph Liow provides a broad introduction to the cultural and religious diversities on the island. Liow begins with a useful historical overview to underline why religious and ethnic harmony have been so jealously guarded by the state, and proceeds to offer key events that have shaped the policies and regulations that now govern ethnic and religious relations. He concludes by noting that while such policies and regulations may have their critics, they are necessary a necessary feature of a small multicultural society. Terence Chong's chapter looks at Christian activism and public morality in Singapore. He asserts that Christian activism only began in earnest after 1990s when the government began to liberalize not just the banking and financial sectors, but also the arts and entertainment industry in order to turn the island into a culturally vibrant global city. The need to attract global talent and to dissuade globally mobile Singaporeans from immigrating to greener pastures made it necessary, among other things, to relax censorship regulations and allow more risqué forms of entertainment, much to the dismay of religious conservatives. Another turning point came in the 2007 parliamentary debate in which Prime Minister Lee Hsien Loong observed that the government would only lead on issues like the economy, technology, education, but when it came to moral values, "we will let others take the lead, we will stay one step behind the front line of change". Both conservatives and liberals alike took this as their cue to become more vocal when it came to championing their causes lest they allow themselves to be outflanked by other groups. Chong goes on to look at public expressions of Christian identity and suggests how these may unfold in a multicultural society. Norshahril Saat's chapter examines rising piety amongst Singaporean Muslims. He begins by observing that there have been signs of increased religiosity amongst Malay-Muslims. He asserts that the spectre of terrorism and national security has loomed large over the local Malay-Muslim community and this has, in fact, eclipsed instances of non-violent extremism. Norshahril argues that while the Malay-Muslim community rightfully condemns all types of religion-inspired violence, this alone is not proof of the community's moderate character or ability to integrate. Instead, he contends that participation in communal activities or sharing perspectives on key national issues are just as important for integration. For example, while a Muslim may reject violence as a means to an end, what if the same Muslim similarly rejects secularism or the principle of a secular state? What if Muslims reject terrorism but also believe that Islam is a better alternative to secular governance and that the Islamic concept of *shura* is superior to democracy? Norshahril tackles these difficult questions and concludes that there "is reason for concern over the Malay-Muslim community's ability to integrate into broader society" because the expression of its religious beliefs among some remain strong, resulting the desire for differentiation.

The second part—National and Ethnic Communities—covers integration issues from an ethnic perspective. Elaine Lynn-Ee Ho and Fang Yu Foo's chapter looks at "new" Chinese immigrants in Singapore and their reception from "local" Singaporeans. They note that PRC immigrants who came to Singapore in the 1990s were more willing to work at integrating with the local-born Chinese Singaporean community, while those who came later in the 2000s were less likely to do so, preferring to live and work amongst themselves. However, both sets of PRC immigrants were less likely to integrate with the rest of multicultural Singapore because of their perceived inability to converse fluently in English. In addition to linguistic barriers, Ho and Fang found that vocation and class have emerged as obstacles for the integration of PRC immigrants and non-Chinese Singaporeans, and conclude that this may lead to the social alienation of the latter.

Walid Jumblatt Abdullah looks at the state of integration between the Malay community and the rest of society. Walid begins by addressing the so-called "Malay problem" that sees the community lag behind the rest in terms of education and income, and proceeds to unpack the obstacles to integration. Among other things, he notes that the position of Singapore Malays is influenced by the fact that they are a minority in the country and a majority in the region. This has ensured that the government makes special accommodation for the community such as recognizing the community's indigenous status and making Malay the country's the national language. However, the spectre of Islamic extremism in the region has also meant that the community feels that it is under scrutiny. As such, Walid asserts that some in the community feel, on the one hand, infantilized because of their position vis-à-vis other ethnic communities, while on the other, constantly under suspicion for their religious affiliation.

In her chapter, Laavanya Kathiravelu delves into the relationship between new Indian immigrants or non-resident Indians (NRIs) and broader Singaporean society. She argues that the friction between NRIs and the rest of society is not indicative of any deep-rooted racism within

Singapore because of the country's multiethnic make up and its recent immigrant history. Instead, the cause of this friction is down to class and notions of civilizational heritage. Laavanya notes that not only do NRIs generally belong to the higher income professional class, thus measuring favourably against local-born Indians, these NRIs also believe that Singaporean Indians have lost touch with their heritage and culture. This in turn has sparked resentment amongst Singaporean Indians. Laavanya concludes that more spaces for intermingling must be carved out for mutual understanding to emerge.

The third part is "Political Divides and a Divided Polity" which provides readers with an overview of the political and ideological issues that are running through contemporary Singapore. It is taken for granted that the economic maturing of society will usher in greater political and ideological pluralism. The higher income and educational levels enjoyed by the polity, as well as its broader cosmopolitan outlook nurtured through wider travel and exposure to different norms have laid the grounds for this pluralism to emerge. Whether this pluralism is manifested in the desire for greater political party contestation; personal freedoms such as human rights or freedom of expression; or cultural values regarding sexual orientation, it is clear that this pluralism is here to stay. Equally clear is that this pluralism will come into conflict with conservative communities who may believe in the continued importance of the dominant one-party state. Such communities may value the concept of a traditional family unit and believe in the merits of trading the unpredictability of political contestation for stability. The larger question then is how Singapore society will achieve a grand modus vivendi to accommodate the pluralistic and conservative impulses in society without sacrificing national cohesion and civility.

Daniel P.S. Goh's chapter looks at how protest and the so-called "culture war" have developed in Singapore. Using examples from politics and the arts, Goh observes that opposition politicians and artists who adopted non-established modes of engagement such as street protests and forum theatre, respectively, were often met with state suspicion. However, he notes that the Singapore state is a responsive one, constantly assessing and adapting to such modes of engagement, resulting in more comprehensive regulations and policing. On the culture war front, Goh notes that groups such as the LGBT (lesbian, gay, bisexual and transgender) community have learned to adopt the vocabulary of conservative groups. Instead of demanding greater personal freedoms or calling for rights, the LGBT community is calling for greater inclusivity, respect, but most radically, declaring their love for the "family" unit.

Kenneth Paul Tan's chapter examines political inclusion and the state of the PAP. Tan asserts that while the ruling party has been successful in its dominance, it will need to embrace diversity to be a "big tent" party in order to remain relevant. This means drawing talent from more diverse corners of society lest it indulges in group think and old formulas. He cites four broad factors for the PAP's success—performance legitimacy; moral authority; electoral advantage; and the fear factor—and argues that there are other developing issues that need to be monitored. They include an overly rigid style of pragmatism that discourages risk-taking and creativity, the unintended consequences of a singular interpretation of "meritocracy", and the rise of populism.

In his chapter, Ja Ian Chong surveys one of the more pressing issues of our time—the ideological attraction that China holds for sections of the Singapore Chinese community. China's economic rise has been accompanied by the lengthening of its geopolitical reach, in part, through various forms of engagement with Chinese overseas who are now citizens of nation-states in the region. Chong notes how the United Front Work Department has made clear its intentions of reaching out to Chinese overseas to advance China's interests. Chong observes that profound implications for Singapore's foreign policy are but one of the many complications that may arise from China's allure for Singaporean Chinese. For example, Malaysia and Indonesia, both with histories of anti-Chinese sentiment, may view Singapore as a "Chinese fifth column", and thus impact bilateral relations as well as the country's domestic multicultural complexion.

The final part in this volume is entitled "Diverging Economic Worlds". As the title implies, the part looks at how the economic and material circumstances for different communities are deviating, and what this means for integration in Singapore. Irene Y.H. Ng's chapter looks at the issue of income inequality and the ideological factors that surround the phenomena. She begins by observing that Singapore does not fare too badly in the Gini index compared other developed countries. However, this is because of government tax and transfers; without which local income inequality will remain high. Ng proceeds to identify the government's stance against welfare policies for handouts to improve personal economic well-being and its corresponding emphasis on self-resilience as ideological narratives which shape the debate over income inequality in Singapore. Ng concludes by offering two scenarios. On one hand, if Singaporeans decide to tackle social inequality seriously, then a comprehensive ideological review of many of our main institutions will be needed. On the other, if we accept inequality as part of life, then we will see such social and economic inequalities as unavoidable consequences of the economic model of development we have chosen for ourselves.

Gillian Koh, Tan Ern Ser, and Vincent Chua focus their chapter on the Singapore middle class. They observe how middle-class anxiety was been one of the unintended consequences of rapid economic growth. The combination of rising cost, stagnating incomes, and ever-expensive markers of material affluence, young Singaporeans from the 1990s have long feared that they may not be able to enjoy the trappings of middle-class success. With an array of data, the authors suggest that even older Singaporeans already in the middle class may feel insecure over the possibility of falling behind their peers. This group would be senior PMETs (professionals, managers, executives and technicians) who would have been most vulnerable to global recessions and economic restructuring. Koh, Tan and Chua conclude that if left to market forces and non-state intervention, Singapore's middle class will shrink. The result of which will be the erosion of social solidarity and egalitarianism.

Leong Chan-Hoong and Yvonne Yap examine one of the most iconic markers of integration in Singapore—public housing. The Housing and Development Board (HDB), set up in 1960, provides homes to over 80 per cent of the population. However, by 1989, there were signs of ethnic enclaves emerging with certain ethnic groups found to be clustering together. The Ethnic Integration Policy (EIP) was introduced to impose a quota on the maximum number of households from the same ethnic background at the block and neighbourhood. While not without unintended consequences such as impacting ethnic minority sellers negatively, the policy has been responsible for preventing ethnic enclaves from forming and is recognized as a signature policy when it comes to managing integration. Thirty years after the EIP there are now signs of different types of segregation emerging. Using housing data Leong and Yap show that different neighbourhoods are becoming more exclusive because high-income earners are converging there. In addition, these neighbourhoods such as Tanglin, Bukit Timah, Novena, Marine Parade and Bishan are more likely to have families who speak English frequently at home. The icing on the cake is the clustering of prestigious and desirable schools in these areas. Leong and Yap conclude that the key challenge to public housing is no longer ethnic integration but class segregation.

The final chapter in this book, penned by Kalyani K. Mehta, deals with the need to better integrate Singapore's rapidly ageing community into the rest of society. Addressing the stress endured by caregivers from caring for the elderly, the anxiety from the elderly in navigating an increasingly cyberconnected world, and their need for emotional and physical attention, Mehta assesses the array of policies that address the elderly from home to workplace. In light of the increasing elderly population, Mehta concludes that the challenges will only become more acute unless we change the way we see the elderly and create more age-inclusive spaces.

References

Alba, Richard and Victor Nee. 1997. "Rethinking Assimilation Theory for a New Era of Immigration". *International Migration Review* 31, no. 4. Special Issue on "Immigrant Adaptation and Native-Born Responses in the Making of Americans" (Winter): 826–74.

Channel NewsAsia. 2018. "Class—Not Race Nor Religion—Is Potentially Singapore's Most Divisive Fault Line". 1 October 2018. https://www.channelnewsasia.com/news/cnainsider/regardless-class-race-religion-survey-singapore-income-divide-10774682 (accessed 15 August 2019).

———. 2019a. "Preetipls, Subhas Nair's Statement 'A Mock, Insincere Apology': MHA". 2 August 2019. https://www.channelnewsasia.com/news/singapore/preetipls-subhas-nair-statement-a-mock-insincere-apology-mha-11777108 (accessed 15 August 2019).

———. 2019b. "Singapore's Population Grows to 5.7 Million, Boosted by Increase in Foreign Workers". 25 September 2019. https://www.channelnewsasia.com/news/singapore/population-number-singapore-foreign-workers-new-citizens-11941034 (accessed 27 September 2019).

Chong, Terence. 2015. "Stepping Stone Singapore: The Cultural Politics of Anti-Immigrant Anxieties". In *Migration and Integration in Singapore: Policies and Practice*, edited by Yap Mui Teng, Gillian Koh, and Debbie Soon. London and New York: Routledge.

Goh, Chok Tong. 1999. "Whither Singapore?". Address by Prime Minister Goh Chok Tong at the PM's Forum organized by the Nanyang Technological University Students' Union, 11 May 1999.

Hamilton, Peter, ed. 1992. *Talcott Parsons: Critical Assessments Vol IV*. London: Routledge.

Johnson, Stephen, ed. 2012. *Burnt Cork: Traditions and Legacies of Blackface Minstrelsy*. Boston: University of Massachusetts Press.

Koh, Gillian, Debbie Soon, and Yap Mui Teng. 2015. "Introduction". In *Migration and Integration in Singapore: Policies and Practice*, edited by Yap Mui Teng, Gillian Koh, and Debbie Soon. London and New York: Routledge.

Lensmire, Timothy, Shannon McManimon, Jessica Dockter Tierney, Mary Lee-Nichols, Zachary Casey, Audrey Lensmire, and Bryan Davis. 2013. "McIntosh as Synecdoche: How Teacher Education's Focus on White Privilege Undermines Antiracism". In *Harvard Educational Review* 83, no. 3: 410–31.

Lim, Selina. 2015. "Images of the New Citizen and Permanent Resident in Singapore's

Mainstream News Media: Prospects for Integration". In *Migration and Integration in Singapore: Policies and Practice*, edited by Yap Mui Teng, Gillian Koh, and Debbie Soon. London and New York: Routledge.

Lim, Sun Sun. 2019. "Why Depicting 'Brownface' Characters Is No Joke". *Straits Times*, 3 August 2019. https://www.straitstimes.com/opinion/why-depicting-brownface-characters-is-no-joke (accessed 15 August 2019).

McIntosh, Peggy. 1992 (1988). "White Privilege: Unpacking the Invisible Knapsack". In *Multiculturalism*, compiled by Anna May Filor, Chair of Research and Development Committee, New York State Council of Educational Associations. New York: New York State United Teachers.

Rai, Rajesh. 2014. *Indians in Singapore 1819–1945: Diaspora in the Colonial Port City.* Oxford: Oxford University Press.

Robison, Richard and David S.G. Goodman, eds. 1996. *The New Rich in Asia: Mobile Phones, McDonald's, and Middle Class Revolution.* Abingdon, Oxon: Routledge.

Straits Times. 2018. "Being Chinese in Multiracial Singapore: A Framework to Check One's Ignorance". 15 February 2018. https://www.straitstimes.com/opinion/being-chinese-in-multi-racial-spore (accessed 17 August 2019).

———. 2019. "Rap Video by Local YouTuber Preetipls on Racism Not Acceptable: Shanmugam". 31 July 2019. https://www.straitstimes.com/politics/local-youtubers-rap-video-on-racism-not-acceptable-shanmugam (accessed 15 August 2019).

Tan, Kenneth Paul. 2015. "Images of the Migrant Worker in Singapore's Mainstream News Media: Prospects for Integration". In *Migration and Integration in Singapore: Policies and Practice*, edited by Yap Mui Teng, Gillian Koh, and Debbie Soon. London and New York: Routledge.

Tan, Cheryl. 2017. "What Privilege Looks Like in Singapore". *Vice.com.* https://www.vice.com/en_asia/article/gvqa59/what-privilege-looks-like-in-singapore (accessed 17 August 2019).

Today. 2019. "Number of Citizen Marriages in Singapore Lowest since 2013". 25 September 2019. https://www.channelnewsasia.com/news/singapore/number-marriages-singapore-population-birth-rate-11940734 (accessed 27 September 2019).

Treviño, A Javier, ed. 2001. *Talcott Parsons Today: His Theory and Legacy in Contemporary Sociology.* Oxford: Rowman and Littlefield Publishers, Inc.

Trocki, Carl A. 1990. *Opium and Empire: Chinese Society in Colonial Singapore, 1800–1910.* Ithaca: Cornell University Press.

Wee, Vanessa. 2017. "12 Signs You Have Chinese Privilege and Don't Even Know It". MSNews, 16 January 2017. https://mustsharenews.com/chinese-privilege-singapore/ (accessed 17 August 2019).

Yang, Philip Q. 2000. *Ethnic Studies: Issues and Approaches.* New York: State University New York Press.

Part I

RELIGIOUS COMMUNITIES

2

Managing Religious Diversity and Multiculturalism in Singapore

Joseph Chinyong Liow

According to the Pew Research Centre, Singapore is the most religiously diverse country in the world on grounds that its population claims to be followers of at least eight religions including Christianity, Islam, Buddhism, Taoism, Hinduism, Sikhism, and several Chinese "folk religions".[1] In 2012, Forbes ranked Singapore the third richest country in the world.[2] In 2015, ValuePenguin, a prominent New York consultancy firm, ranked Singapore the second safest country in the world.[3] Taken together, these figures suggest that in an age where religious tension and conflict is said to be on the rise, Singapore has managed to maintain multiethnic and multireligious harmony whilst achieving a level of development which has been the envy of many a developing country.[4] This record is all the more remarkable when one considers the trying circumstances of Singapore's independence in 1965, or the number of intrastate conflicts that had afflicted so-called Third World countries during the Cold War, many of which were triggered by issues related to the assertion of differences between communal identities. In fact, many countries continue to be bedevilled by communal and sectarian conflicts today.

The peace and stability that Singapore has enjoyed however, has not been the result of chance, serendipity, or circumstance. To the contrary, it has for a large part been the consequence of carefully calibrated policies on the part of the state, with the endorsement of the leadership of respective religious and ethnic communities in the multicultural nation-state. That the state has had to proactively intervene in order to head off the risks of tension, discord, and conflict between religious and ethnic groups has been explained by Home Minister K. Shanmugam in the following manner:

> The Government has an important role. It has to be vigilant. There are tough laws to prevent race and religion being used to create divisions … We will do our best to keep Singapore safe, and ensure equality of opportunities, fairness and a fair stake for all in Singapore. We will also ensure everyone has the freedom to practise his or her religion.[5]

The government's stance as articulated by the minister corresponds with a general view amongst the population that accords to the state a major role in building and managing peaceful coexistence of different faiths. For instance, a recent survey by the Singapore-based Institute of Policy Studies registered a view that it was incumbent upon the state to monitor, and where necessary, police the public expression of religious beliefs: "consistent state policy and action over the decades has ensured that Singaporeans of different faiths live in peaceful coexistence. The survey found strong support for the state to deal firmly with religious bigotry and to check insensitive comments levelled against any religion."[6]

By way of these observations as a point of entry, the purpose of this chapter is to unpack the dimensions of security as they relate to the matter of religion, and more specifically, interreligious harmony and resilience as reflected in the concept of multiculturalism.[7] Rather than provide a general survey of religion(s) in Singapore, something which has already been comprehensively done in other volumes, it will endeavour to outline the policies designed to manage the expression of religious faith and practice of religion, the collaborative relationships between the state and (religious) civil society that underpin these policies, and the historical and ideational contexts and circumstances that shape them. In doing so, this chapter argues that even as the state considers religious identities to be a source of cultural strength, the historical record impresses the point that multireligious societies tend also to be given to the "primordial" pulls of identity markers that emphasize difference, and thence, are potentially more fragile and volatile. As this renders the state acutely cognizant of religion's potential as a centrifugal force that could pose a security threat to the country by way of undermining social trust, eroding social capital, and fomenting disharmony, it follows that the state has concomitantly adopted a proactive approach since independence to manage the expression of religious faith in the wider framework of the national narrative of multiculturalism, today widely accepted as a core organizing principle of Singapore society.

RELIGION AND MULTICULTURALISM

The point has already been made that Singapore is the most diverse country in the world. Equally important is the fact that religion is featuring prominently in narratives of identity and social activism as well. Recent statistics indicate that the awareness of religious identity and affiliation among Singaporeans has increased over the years. Not only has statistical research identified growing trends of religiosity; they also suggest correlation between Singaporeans' religious identity with race, legal rights, personal identity, and perceptions of morality. To that effect, statistics reveal that Muslims, Protestants, Roman Catholics, Hindus and those who profess to be followers of several other smaller religious movements ranked religion as "important" or "very important" to their identity as compared to Buddhists and Taoists. Parsed further, more Muslims (67.6 per cent) reported religion as "very important" to identity construction in relation to 26.9 per cent of Roman Catholics and 44.1 per cent Protestants.[8] In addition, amongst those who declared no affiliation to organized religion, a portion still claimed religion to be important in their lives, indicating that not subscribing to an organized religion does not necessarily negate the significance of religion to the wider outlook of an individual. Overall, this points to the salience of religion's continuing function as a potent force in shaping identities in Singapore.

The theme of multiculturalism has been a subject of growing policy and scholarly interest in Singapore. Multiculturalism has been an organizing principle of Singapore society since independence in 1965. From the perspective of the state, the primary assumption behind this has been the belief that the tension evident among ethnic groups in Singapore in the immediate post-war years could only be defused by efforts to stress the uniqueness of the cultural identity of each ethnic group, which nevertheless would be encompassed within a larger societal edifice constructed on merit and not favouritism towards any given group. At the same time, scholars have argued for the need to expand the discussion beyond the "security" and "social stability" domains to interrogate hardened categorization of ethnicity and culture to accommodate hybrid realities.[9] Of course, given this chapter's focus on religion, it is interested in a more specific expression of multiculturalism—that which relates to religious allegiances—as opposed to broader expressions of cultural identity.

The centrality of multiculturalism in the national narrative, particularly its emphasis on cultural heterogeneity and endeavour to manage and accommodate the stresses associated with it, is captured in the opening lines of the Singapore pledge which all citizens have committed to memory: "We, the citizens of Singapore, pledge ourselves as one united people, regardless of language, race, or religion." By this measure, to understand the role and place of religion, religious identities, and the expression of religiosity in Singapore society, it is necessary to first consider the multiethnic and multicultural character of the island-state's population. This is predicated on the belief that culture, of which religious faith is a constituent element, continues to be a key feature of both individual as well as communal identity.

Ethnic, religious, and linguistic heterogeneity has been the defining feature of Singapore society since the establishment of the island as a British port in 1819, which occasioned large influxes of people from all over the region and beyond, including Europeans/Eurasians, Arabs, Chinese, Indians, and non-indigenous Malays. Chinese, South Asians, and to some extent Malays/Indonesians, are also further split into dialect groups although these differences have receded with time and national curricula in common languages, leaving only the religious differences intact. This is because ethnic and religious identities are intertwined to considerable extents in Singapore. For instance, the vast majority of ethnic Malays are Muslims, while adherents to the Hindu faith comprise mostly those classified in the national system as Indians. There is a further correlation between language and religion as well. Consider, for example, the fact that 75 per cent of Tamil speakers profess to be Hindu. The religious identities and allegiances of the ethnic Chinese community, however, tend to be more heterogeneous, covering a range of traditional "Chinese" religions as well as Buddhism and Christianity. Ethnic and religious identities are to a degree further reinforced by socio-economic factors. This is most evident with Christianity, which has strong correlation with upper middle-class, tertiary-educated households.[10] Their adherents tend also to be predominantly English-speaking, as opposed to followers of the other main religions.

At this juncture, it is important to stress that in Singapore multi-culturalism does not merely describe social demographies; it also speaks very much to deliberate, conscious government policy pursued on the understanding that harmony between various communal groupings is neither organic nor to be taken for granted. This perspective is captured in the following remarks of Prime Minister Lee Hsien Loong:

> But you must remember that what we have here is not something natural, nor something which will stay there by itself. It is the result of very hard work, a lot of toil and sweat, and the gradual education and bringing together of people. It was also because of the gradual inculcation of

shared values and attitudes that we came to have the confidence, trust and mutual respect to make us one people. We brought people together and consciously created common spaces and opportunities. We used English as our common working language, while ensuring a place for our mother tongues. We mixed all races together in HDB (Housing and Development Board) estates, so that there are no enclaves or ghettos in Singapore. In schools, we recite the Pledge every day. We created GRCs (Group Representation Constituencies) so that in Parliament we will always have minorities represented. We came down hard on extremists—regardless of whether they were Chinese chauvinists or Malay, Indian or Hindu extremists—because they have to understand that this is what Singapore is, and this is how Singapore will act when racial chauvinists try to stir up sentiments against others. Sometimes we think we have arrived, and that we can do away with these provisions and rules which feel like such a burden. But in fact, it is the other way around. It is precisely because we have these provisions and rules, that we have achieved racial and religious harmony.[11]

To say then that multiculturalism has been the dominant lens through which the state has conceptualized and approached the issue of religious diversity is hardly an exaggeration.

The Singapore government's views on—and approach to—multiculturalism has been shaped by an acute understanding of the historical experience of nation-building. Following the end of the Second World War, Britain made plans to grant independence to its Malayan territories, conscious of the declaration of independence made by Indonesia immediately upon Japanese surrender. In the course of deliberation over the terms of independence, the rights of migrants in these territories—the Indians and Chinese populations—proved a contentious issue in their negotiations with Malay leaders. An initial proposal designed to draw the parameters of independence and citizenship was floated in 1946 and provoked much controversy. Known at the time as the Malayan Union experiment, the proposal recommended granting equal citizenship rights to migrant populations, and in so doing catalysed widespread Malay opposition that roundly rejected any attempt to accord non-Malays equal standing in the Constitution of a newly minted independent Malaya. The Malayan Union was soon replaced by the Federation of Malaya Agreement in 1948, which among other things made clear that while Malays and other indigenous groups would be granted full citizenship in an independent nation-state, non-Malays would have to accept a lesser status. From that point on, issues of race and religion weighed heavily on negotiations towards eventual independence in 1957. Singapore's subsequent split with Malaysia in 1965 was also due to questions of racial representation and equality.

Born in the cauldron of Cold War ideological rivalry which nevertheless also saw the Chinese Communist Party leverage ethnic and linguistic affinities to overseas Chinese communities in Southeast Asia, and against the backdrop of regional affairs which witnessed elements from Indonesia and Malaysia periodically instigate the island-state's Malay minority to agitate for a recognition of their indigenous rights following Singapore's acrimonious separation from the Federation of Malaysia, the political leadership in Singapore was mindful of the appeal of issues of religion and race, the volatile nature of pluralism in the fledgling country, and the need for the state to play an active role in mitigating these issues.

With independence, Singapore found itself in a unique position as a Chinese-majority population but with an indigenous Malay population that was predominantly Muslim, as well as large minority groups with different religious affiliations. Given that the population of its neighbours, Indonesia and Malaysia, were predominantly indigenous ethnic groups (the majority of which were also Muslim in religious affiliation) that coexisted in a complex and tenuous relationship with respective Chinese minorities which were devoid of major political influence but nevertheless possessed considerable economic heft, Singapore could not afford to engage in racialized political discourse, or to use issues of language, race, or religion as the basis upon which to construct a national identity. Needless to say, this was an important consideration towards the end of the establishment of a Singapore society that would comprise a Chinese majority, but which would nevertheless not possess a Chinese-dominated political system. In the 1980s, this extended to ensuring racial representation through the GRC system, which typically groups together four to six members of parliament (MPs) one of whom must belong to a minority racial category (including some of mixed descent), although the ruling Peoples' Action Party (PAP) has periodically been criticized for instrumentalizing racial protections to create laws that afford them political advantages come election season.

It is against this backdrop of the trials of nationhood that the management of relations and interaction between religious groups—and indeed the expression of religious faiths and beliefs—has been shaped in order to mitigate its centrifugal effects. Put simply, the state assumes a primary responsibility to foster harmony between adherents of different religions and to restrain any impulse towards exclusion and intolerance. The thinking behind this perspective in terms of risks to Singapore's multicultural social fabric and the need for active state intervention are outlined in the following remarks by S. Jayakumar, former Minister for Home Affairs:

> Non-homogenous societies face unique challenges. In societies that are less homogenous, the rule of law is all the more important, as it makes expectations transparent. In countries that have only recently become nations, and in which people of different ethnic, cultural and religious backgrounds rub shoulders, the rules that prevent friction and which make life in a crowded society bearable have to be stated explicitly and enforced fairly and consistently. Otherwise, there will be constant strife and misunderstanding. Harmony in a diverse society cannot be achieved with a laissez-faire system; or the different ethnic, religious, cultural and language groups will have their own song sheet and the government as conductor will not produce harmony ... For multi-racial and multi-religious societies, where there are several communities with different religious beliefs and values, each community will hold its moral values deeply. Without observance of the rule of law, the individual can and will act according to his conscience as guided by his moral beliefs even when it breaks the law. Each will do his own thing, no doubt sincerely, passionately. The result will be strife and conflict. To avoid this there has to be respect for the law by all on accordance with common ground rules of engagement and conflict resolution, and to secure as large common secular space which belongs to all citizens regardless of race, language or religion.[12]

RELIGION AND INTOLERANCE

That the establishment of laws and institutions to manage relations between different ethnic and religious groups is imperative is evident in the risk of the outbreak of racial and religious tensions. This has been the source of consternation for the island-state's political leaders since independence.

The early thinking of Singapore's founding fathers was shaped by historical episodes of racial and religious tensions, foremost of which was the case involving Maria Hertogh (Nadra binte Maarof), a Dutch Catholic girl who was raised by Malay-Muslim foster parents after she was separated from her biological parents during the Second World War. Articulating the sentiments triggered by the case and its effect on the thinking of Singapore's decision makers, former Chief Justice Chan Sek Keong described: "Although the courts resolved the legal problem, its aftermath was disastrous for race relations between the colonial masters and their Muslim subjects, and brought to fore grievances against the perceived lack of impartiality of British justice."[13] The issue at the time was that in determining the future "best" interests of the child, they determined that custody should be awarded Dutch parents, the biological father being the best determiner of her "interests". Media attention on the case had inflamed anti-colonial sentiment, so both Malay and Chinese gangs participated in riots that attacked European or European-looking people. Chan concludes, "This case may be regarded as the defining event in Singapore's road to the establishment of racial and religious harmony. This tragic episode has informed all of Singapore's post-independence policies on racial, religious, and cultural issues in nation building."[14]

While the Maria Hertogh riots proved to be a defining event in the national narrative of multiculturalism and the fragility of communal relations in Singapore, it is by no means the only such event. Indeed, over the years, Singapore has encountered several incidences where communal tensions threatened to spill over into conflict and violence. These include:

- Prophet Muhammad birthday riots, 1964: Actually two spates of riots in July (on the Prophet's birthday) and September. Dozens were killed, hundreds injured, and over 2,500 arrested in various related offences. Tun Abdul Razak, then Deputy Prime Minister of Malaysia, attributed the cause of the riots to Indonesian/Communist provocateurs, while Lee Kuan Yew laid blame on Syed Jaffar Albar and an ultra-nationalist faction of the Malaysian political party, United Malays National Organization (UMNO). "Goodwill" committees were set up in the aftermath to address rumours and provocateurs.
- Detention of *Nanyang Siang Pau* editors, 1971: Editors were arrested for allegedly stirring up Chinese chauvinism, a charge that had previously been made against Malay agents in previous incidents, having accused the government of suppressing Chinese education and language.
- "Marxist Conspiracy" and Operation Spectrum, 1987: a total of twenty-two people, including Catholic lay workers, were detained for allegedly plotting to subvert the government using tactics from the era of the communist insurgency and the Catholic Church in Singapore as cover for these activities. This event strained relations between the Catholic Church (and the wider community of Christian believers in Singapore) and the government, and saw the personal intervention of then Prime Minister Lee Kuan Yew who met with the Archbishop and several other clergy. While the controversy eventually abated, scepticism towards the veracity of the government's allegations remain.
- Kampong Gelam Malay Heritage Centre Issue, 1999: When the former

Istana Kampong Gelam and neighbouring building were identified as sites for Malay preservation, the residents, descendants of the Johor royal family, were offered compensation to vacate the premises. Malaysian press covered the issue extremely negatively criticizing it as breaking the last historical ties that linked the indigenous Malay community with their ancestral land, as well as with Johor and its royalty. The Singapore government used Malay MPs to explain the situation in the hope of defusing potential tensions. Foreign Minister S. Jayakumar chastised the Malaysian media for trying to destabilize ethnic relations and bilateral ties.

- Tudung issue, 2002: Parents of four Malay Muslim girls insisted on having their children wear tudungs (the Muslim female headscarf) to school, threatening legal action after the girls were suspended for doing so as the tudung was not recognized to be part of regulation uniform in national schools. The issue was further amplified by the Malaysian press as well as emerging social media.

- Jemaah Islamiyah arrests, 2001–2: Thirteen and twenty-one Muslims were arrested in 2001 and 2002, respectively, over terrorist links and plots to bomb American and other diplomatic targets in Singapore. While not cast as an intercultural or interreligious issue, it could have been construed as such against a trend of rising Muslim religiosity. In order to head off the risk of Islamophobia, religious leaders, including clerics from the Muslim community, mobilized to condemn the terrorists and the ideology they propounded.

- In 2005, Benjamin Koh Song Huat, Nicholas Lim Yew and Gan Huai Shi were charged under the Sedition Act for making inflammatory remarks about Muslims and Malays online. They were sentenced to between two years' probation and community service (Gan, a minor), a day (Lim) and a month (Koh) in jail, as well as fined.

- In 2009, Ong Kian Cheong and Dorothy Chan Hien Leng were charged under the Sedition Act for distributing evangelical tracts that disparaged Muslims and Roman Catholics via mass mail. They were both jailed eight weeks and fined.

- In 2010, Pastor Rony Tan of Lighthouse Evangelical Church was interviewed by the Internal Security Department after video clips emerged of him making disparaging comments about Buddhist and Taoist beliefs. The video clips were removed and an apology issued.

- In 2015, sixteen-year-old video blogger Amos Yee was arrested and charged with making provocative remarks against Christians, amongst other things. He was sentenced to time already served and was released at the conclusion of his trial. Charged for a similar offence against Muslims in November, Yee was imprisoned for six weeks. He fled to the United States, where he was eventually granted asylum in September 2017.

- In 2017, two unnamed foreign Christian preachers were denied entry permits to Singapore having made disparaging remarks about Buddhism and Islam in sermons given abroad.

Also in 2017, two Muslim preachers were banned from Singapore for expressing intolerant views of non-Muslims. A replacement Muslim preacher was also barred. The ban was supported by Muslim religious leaders in Singapore. During these incidents, it came to light that "cruise ship teaching" that left Singapore waters was being used to circumvent the regulations. It was clarified that such workarounds would also be deemed illegal.

MULTICULTURALISM AND POLICY

As a crucial paradigm governing social relations in Singapore, multi-culturalism has served as a bulwark against the potential hegemony and dominance of certain communities over others, towards the ends of creating an aspirational Singapore "culture" predicated on the values of pluralism, harmony, and resilience. As K. Shanmugam elaborated:

> Looking at current trends, the kind of centrifugal forces that society is facing, including Singapore, online, there are different pulls and pushes. I think many will agree it is going to be challenging to achieve a homogenous race of Singaporeans, in the near term. What we can realistically achieve is a strong national identity, a Singaporean identity, which will overlay our separate racial, religious identities, and that framework can create a vibrant society.[15]

By virtue of being a secular state, Singapore does not promote or recognize a state religion. That does not mean, however, that religion and religious identities are not recognized. Religious freedoms are enshrined in and protected by the Constitution, and the government has enforced these protections of a citizen's right to profess and practise their religion. Enforcement however, also means that there are, accordingly, laws and policies that restrict the right of religious freedom especially when the exercise of these rights are deemed prejudicial to the rights of adherents of other religions to practice their own faiths and beliefs (such as in the case of aggressive proselytization when such efforts at propagating faith offends others), or are in breach of other laws of the land as they relate to issues of morality, public order, and public health. In accordance with the law, religious groups are required to be registered under the Societies Act.

Even prior to independence, the Inter-Religious Organization had already been constituted (in 1949) and tasked to work "assiduously yet unobstructively in Singapore to create a climate of religious understanding and cooperation in order that religion should be a source of national unity rather than disunity."[16] As suggested earlier, this was largely a contextual necessity since the PAP government would eventually inherit a diverse population and saw the assiduous management of this multiracial and religious population to be pivotal to social and political stability. As such, although the Singapore state considers itself to be secular and religiously neutral in nature, dealing with religious problems attains a bureaucratic dimension and state intervention is exercised where necessary. Again, Singapore's political leadership has been unapologetic in its rationalization of state intervention, for "it is because of provisions and rules that Singapore has achieved racial and religious harmony."[17]

Officially, social policy as it relates to ethnic and cultural identity revolves around the practice of racial categorization inherited from the British colonial administration. Singapore's population are broadly compartmentalized in four "racial" categories known as the CMIO—or Chinese, Malay, Indian and "Others", with "Others" covering a diversity of small groups including people of Arab, Jewish, and European/Eurasian descent. This manifests most apparently in the compulsory teaching of a "mother tongue" in all schools, alongside English, as well as the ethnic community self-help groups: Mendaki (Council for the Development of Singapore Malay/Muslim Community), SINDA (Singapore Indian Development Association), and the CDAC (Chinese Development Assistance Council). To foster greater interreligious understanding, religious education was introduced into the curriculum of national schools as well, although the utility and value of this approach has been somewhat diluted given the tendency for students to study their own, rather than other, religious faiths.

Another key policy is the ethnic integration policy in HDB estates to prevent the creation of enclaves—a common phenomenon in post-colonial societies—of ethnically or religiously defined groups living in heavily racialized segregated communities, which tends to be the case in post-colonial societies. Though highly controversial, enclavement has proven one of the ways in which the modern nation-state manages and regulates religion. Enclaves may be physical, such as the usage of walled spaces, or non-physical, which may take the form of technological surveillance and control. Mindful of the "natural" inclination of communities of believers to gravitate towards each other, Singapore has worked to prevent the creation of such enclaves by enforcing ethnic quotas in public housing developments. Given the country's problem of land scarcity, Singapore has also had to adopt a functional approach to religious territoriality. Each portion of land reserved for religious use in any of the new towns built by the HDB is open for tender for specific religious groups. In other words, land allocated for Christians will not be open for tender for other religions. This is to ensure that all the major faiths in Singapore are equally represented in the nationwide public housing estates.

Singapore has a slew of laws and institutions dedicated to the promotion and preservation of religious harmony, many of which were originally developed during the period of British rule. The guiding principle behind this legislation is not to seek to eliminate local custom but tolerate them so long as they did not contradict common law. Most notably, the Administration of Muslim Law Act (AMLA) permits the parallel functioning of *sharia* courts to govern domestic/social affairs of Muslims, including some laws and practices that apply only to the Muslim community, such as polygamy. Institutions include the Presidential Councils for Religious Harmony and for Minority Rights. The Religious Harmony Council comprises an interfaith group of senior religious leaders of the major denominations in Singapore. It advises the Minister for Home Affairs on matters that might bear on religious harmony. The Presidential Council for Minority Rights comprises representation from government, the religious communities, and the legal fraternity, who scrutinize new bills to ensure that they do not discriminate against particular racial or religious groups. Both are established under the Maintenance of Religious Harmony Act, and demonstrate the close cooperation between the state and religious civil society groups in fostering and preserving harmony among religious groups:

> Our religious groups and leaders are generally very supportive of our efforts to build and maintain religious harmony in Singapore. They know how important it is that our religions co-exist harmoniously and why we need to maintain our common spaces. Religion can, and has been, a source of strength for our society, but we must also watch out for exclusivist, intolerant practices because that can deepen our fault lines and weaken our entire society.[18]

Extremism, Tolerance, and Interfaith Dialogue

The resilience of multiculturalism in the form of values such as interreligious harmony and understanding were tested at the turn of the century when it emerged that a terrorist organization claiming legitimacy in the name of Islam was planning mass casualty attacks in Singapore, including the possible targeting of a public transportation facility in the suburbs. Against the backdrop of global concern for the threat of terrorism following the September 11 attacks in the United States, Jemaah Islamiyah, a terrorist group claiming a regional presence by way of cells in Singapore, Indonesia, Malaysia, the Philippines, and Australia, and with links to the international terrorist organization, Al Qaeda, was identified as a clear and present danger to Singapore.

The disclosure of the Jemaah Islamiyah threat to Singapore came as a shock to Singaporeans because of a widespread popular perception that the city-state was a safe abode and that terrorism was alien to Singapore. It was for this reason that concern for the resilience of interreligious harmony—already a sensitive issue—grew more acute against the backdrop of the threat posed by terrorists and extremists who claimed to be acting in the name of religion. Needless to say, the threat was met with a slew of security countermeasures aimed at hardening targets, deeper surveillance, and closer operational cooperation with neighbouring countries. While hard security measures formed one prong of the counterterrorism effort, community engagement for the purpose of strengthening societal resilience formed the other. The growing threat of terrorism prompted a host of initiatives undertaken by the government in tandem with religious groups and civil society organizations to ensure the preservation of smooth communal relations even as security measures were advanced in the counterterrorism effort. It is notable that while many of these efforts have been spearheaded by the government, leaders of the various ethnic and religious groups have also adapted other independent strategies to complement government initiatives. These have included interreligious dialogue among the leaders of various religions.

Although interreligious dialogue has its merits, it is not sufficient to rely solely on those to foster greater understanding between communities. More often than not these dialogues are held between leaders of these religious groups but the reverberations of these events do not reach the lay person. At a deeper level, it should also be recognized that a central principle of interreligious dialogue has to be to "agree to disagree". This is because most religions would doubtless have a set of non-negotiable beliefs or norms, and it would be a fool's errand to expect these to be surrendered for the noble (yet naïve) search for universal values and perspectives. Ten Chin Liew warns of the risks of precisely such a search:

> It can be dangerous if sustained attempts to secure rational agreement fail, and continued disagreement is then attributed to perversity and a stubborn refusal to acknowledge what one must know to be the single truth. The suppression of those who know that they are in error may then be seen as justified.[19]

Religious and ethnic communities have coexisted in Singapore but more often than not run parallel to each other and in separate streams. In order to truly foster understanding about the religious "other" thence, the importance of everyday interaction must be emphasized. By getting to know the religious beliefs, traditions and customs of the "other", one humanizes them and is able to identify the similarities instead of highlighting perceived differences, preventing stereotyping.

LOOKING AHEAD

While Singapore has by and large managed to maintain harmony between religious groups, future challenges are likely to manifest in at least two forms. First, structural forces will doubtless bear heavily on interreligious relations in Singapore. Increasing instances of the politicization of religion is instructive in this regard. The region is already witnessing active efforts by political entrepreneurs to play on religious identities and differences, and religious faith and even personal piety is increasingly being mobilized in the service of politics. Yet, while these opportunists surely have taken to such tactics for reasons other than religious conviction, the arid reality is that these efforts have reaped dividends precisely because their followers do prioritize religion as a marker of identity, and in so doing are internalizing the religious narratives that they are being exposed to. To be sure, this dynamic is already recognized by the political leadership in Singapore:

> Singapore is a multi-religious society. The different religious groups have their own deeply held beliefs and precepts. While we accept and respect this diversity of religious teachings, we have seen many examples of other countries where religious differences have caused deep social divides and conflict. If one religion pushes hard to have its tenets and views

adopted by society at large beyond its own adherents, others will push back, sometimes even harder. This dynamic is accentuated if a religious group engages in politics, or if a political group uses religion to further its cause. Other religious groups will feel compelled to also enter the political arena to further their own causes or rival claims. Tensions will arise and social harmony can break down. Hence, we need to maintain a clear line between politics and religion in Singapore. Our politics and policies must serve all Singaporeans, regardless of race, language or religion. The Government must not take sides with any religious group when making policies. If politicians use the religion card for their own political purpose and agenda, and seek to sway voters through religious appeals, it will sow the seeds of division in our society, and undermine the inter-religious and social harmony we have painstakingly built.[20]

Yet, given the fact that the politicization of religion is taking place in Singapore's immediate geographical neighbourhood, and the fact that the strategic outlook of the island-state that has since independence been predicated on its vulnerability to external forces be they economic, political, or social, all this suggests an acute awareness of the potential damage that external influences may cause to the fabric of religious harmony.

This risk is amplified by a second challenge. With the advent of the digital age which has precipitated the proliferation of information and attendant growing concern for "fake news" today, it stands to reason that a country as connected to the outside world as Singapore via Internet and cyberspace will be rendered vulnerable. As it stands, religious activity in Singapore today already involves extensive use of online sermons and video conferencing. At one level, such exposure has indubitably enriched both doctrinal and theological understanding of religious traditions and faiths, and this should be welcomed. At the same time however, the same vehicles and medium provide for the transference of more controversial, less palatable ideas which, taken out of the cultural and historical context from which they derive, could serve to undermine interreligious harmony and pluralism in Singapore.

CONCLUSION

Religious pluralism is a core feature of Singapore's multicultural society. For the most part, Singaporeans of different religious faiths and persuasions have coexisted in harmony, and while history records a few incidences of religious tension, they have not yet posed an existential threat to society. At the same time however, there must be a clear-eyed realization that unmitigated expression and exercise of religious identity can be potentially divisive in how it may offend to the extent of causing conflict and even triggering violence if boundaries are transgressed. This is a reality that the state is only too acutely aware of. When considered against a national narrative predicated on the fragility of communal relations, a narrative that draws on historical experience of race riots, the conclusion that the political leadership has arrived at since independence is that relations between different faith and ethnic communities cannot—indeed, should not—be left to chance.

Some Singaporeans have argued that racial and religious harmony cannot be forced, and hence, these artificial mechanisms will not work. While there is certainly more than some measure of truth to this, and the best mechanisms are indeed those that arise organically rather than imposed on society, it also stands to reason that the road to that final destination of consummate interreligious understanding is paved with risks of exclusivism, misunderstanding, and overzealousness. It is for this reason that the role of the state to minimize those risks has been, and remains, instrumental.

Notes

1. Pew Research Center, "Global Religious Diversity", 4 April 2014, http://www.pewforum.org/2014/04/04/global-religious-diversity/
2. "The World's Richest Countries", *Forbes*, 22 February 2012, https://www.forbes.com/.../2012/02/22/the-worlds-richest-countries
3. "Singapore Is Second Safest Country in the World", www.asiaone.com, 12 August 2015, http://www.asiaone.com/singapore/singapore-2nd-safest-country-world
4. "Religious Conflict in Global Rise", *Reuters*, 14 January 2014.
5. "Religion, Terrorism and Threats to Singapore, the Region", *Straits Times*, 20 January 2016, https://www.straitstimes.com/opinion/religion-terrorism-and-threats-to-singapore-the-region
6. Mathew Mathews, Mohammad Khamsya bin Khidzer, and Teo Kay Key, "Religiosity and the Management of Religious Harmony: Responses from the IPS Survey on Race, Religion and Language", *IPS Working Paper*, no. 21, June 2014, p. 3.
7. Consider, for instance, Lai Ah Eng, ed., *Religious Diversity in Singapore* (Singapore: Institute of Southeast Asian Studies, 2008).
8. Mathews, Khamsya, and Teo, "Religiosity and the Management of Religious Harmony".
9. See, for example, Daniel P.S. Goh, Matilda Gabrielpillai, Philip Holden, and Gaik Cheng Khoo, eds., *Race and Multiculturalism in Malaysia and Singapore* (London: Routledge, 2012); Chan Heng Chee and Sharon Siddique, *Singapore's Multiculturalism: Evolving Diversity* (London: Routledge, 2019).

10. Robbie B. H. Goh, "Christian Identities in Singapore: Religion, Race, and Culture Between State Controls and Transnational Flows", *Journal of Cultural Geography* 26, no. 1 (2009): 1–23.
11. "In full: PM Lee on Race, Multiracialism and Singapore's Place in the World", *Today*, 29 September 2017.
12. S. Jayakumar, "Keynote Address by DPM Prof S Jayakumar at the IBA Rule of Law Symposium", 19 October 2007, https://www.mlaw.gov.sg/news/speeches/keynote-address-by-dpm-prof-s-jayakumar-at-the-iba-rule-of-law-symposium.html
13. Chan Sek Keong, "Multiculturalism in Singapore: The Way to a Harmonious Society", *Singapore Academy of Law Journal* (2013), pp. 88–89. http://journalsonline.academypublishing.org.sg/Journals/Singapore-Academy-of-Law-Journal/e-Archive/ctl/eFirstSALPDFJournalView/mid/495/ArticleId/500/Citation/JournalsOnlinePDF
14. Ibid.
15. K. Shanmugam, "Standing United Against the Terrorism Threat (Motion)", Singapore Parliamentary Reports (Hansard), 3 October 2017, http://sprs.parl.gov.sg
16. Kuah-Pearce Khun Eng, "Maintaining Ethno-religious Harmony in Singapore", *Journal of Contemporary Asia* 28, no. 1 (1998): 105.
17. "S'pore's Racial Harmony Is Not Natural and Needs Nurturing: PM Lee", *Today*, 29 September 2017.
18. K. Shanmugam, "Standing United Against the Terrorism Threat (Motion)".
19. Ten Chin Liew, "Religious Diversity, Toleration, and Interaction", in *Religious Diversity in Singapore*, edited by Lai Ah Eng (Singapore: Institute of Southeast Asian Studies, 2008), p. 557.
20. Teo Chee Hean, "Policy on Keeping Religion and Politics Separate", Singapore Parliamentary Reports (Hansard), 15 October 2012, http://sprs.parl.gov.sg

3

Christian Activism in Singapore

Terence Chong

Introduction

In 2009 a group of local Christian women mounted a challenge to the leadership of women's rights group, AWARE, and subsequently took control of it. They did so because they had felt that the non-governmental organization (NGO) had strayed from its original objective to champion gender equality in the workforce and, instead, actively promoted homosexuality and lesbianism amongst the young.[1] Not only did the takeover spark a national controversy, it also marked the coming of age of Christian activism in Singapore. The Christian takeover was neither by force nor underhanded means but transparently through institutional procedures. Armed with knowledge of the NGO's constitution and election process, the Christian women simply encouraged their supporters to sign up as members who then became eligible to vote in their preferred candidates to the top posts. The incident showed that, in addition to the usual reactive routines like online petitions or indignant letters to the press, the Singaporean Christian community had now accumulated the will and the know-how for concrete action when it came to advancing their moral values. This was a resolutely middle-class Christian feat.

The expansion of the Singapore middle class began in the 1980s. After decades of industrialization and strong economic growth, aided by favourable geopolitical conditions, this emerging middle class began to demonstrate typical characteristics such as mass consumption, the pursuit of intellectual and leisure activities, as well as greater purchasing power. Accompanying the growth of the Singapore middle class was that of the Christian community. This community grew from 14.6 per cent in 2000 to 18.8 per cent in 2015,[2] making it one of the fastest growing faiths in Singapore. In 2010, there were 350,000 Protestant and 219,000 Catholics, although these figures would have increased by now.[3] More pertinent to this chapter, studies have shown Singaporean Christians to be overrepresented in the middle class.[4] For example, Singaporean Christians are well educated with 32 per cent holding a university degree, more than any other religious community. Singaporean Christians are also more likely than any other religious community to live in private or landed property.[5]

This overrepresentation of Singaporean Christians in the middle class was generations in the making. High levels of proselytization on university campuses, active Christian networking amongst young upwardly mobile professionals, the use of English as primary medium of communication, and its associations with the West and modernity have, in varying degrees, contributed to it. As a result, Singaporean Christians are more likely than Singaporean Muslims, Buddhists, or Taoists to be professional, university-educated, and located in positions of leadership in different industries including business, politics and public service. This intersection of faith and affluence comes with profound socio-political ramifications. For example, how will conservative Christians tolerate a more morally diverse Singapore? How will they exert their influence and morality now that they are more deeply entrenched in the middle and upper-middle class? How will their increasing presence in public morality debates impact other religious communities in the country?

In addition, a more recent theological development has emerged to shape the public behaviour of local Christians, namely, the increasing popularity of the so-called "marketplace theology". Broadly speaking, this theology emphasizes the need to bring the Gospel beyond the walls of the Church into the real world where Christians engage actively as citizens and professionals. It encourages one's Christian identity and conduct to be a positive example of the faith to colleagues, friends and family members. Biblical passages used by marketplace theologians exalt Christians to be "the salt of the earth" and "the light of the world", but also for them to "Let your light so shine before men, that they may see your good works and glorify your Father in heaven" (Matthew 5:13–16). Consequentially, for the once stoic Christian who observed boundaries between the private practice of religion and public identity, the blurring of such boundaries is now perceived as necessary in order to bring souls to God and to be a light for the world. By extension, marketplace theology identifies the workplace as a realm for proselytization and conversion.

The middle-class status of Christianity and the popularity of marketplace theology will combine to magnify the presence of the Christian faith and its morality in the public sphere in the near future, if not already. This chapter looks at conservative Christian activism in Singapore and its possible consequences. At this point it is crucial to note that the local Christian community is a heterogeneous one with diverse theologies and attitudes towards society at large. Objectively speaking, the term "conservative Christian" should not necessarily denote intolerance or narrow-mindedness. After all, for the majority of local Christians, personal adherence to conservative moral values does not inevitably lead to the desire to impose them on others. Indeed, Christian activism is confined to a minority within the community. However, this minority may be argued to be disproportionately impactful in light of its socio-economic profile.

This chapter begins with a brief sojourn into our recent history to show that Christian activism was not rife during the country's developing years. Among the many reasons for this was the way the newly formed People's Action Party (PAP) government presented itself as a "moral state" that was both morally upright and morally conservative, thus reducing the impetus for any religious-based activism. This began to change in the 1990s when the demands of the global city and the chase for global capital prompted the government to accommodate more liberal lifestyles and attitudes. We thus see the conservative middle-class Christians begin to exert their influence and morality more noticeably from the mid-1990s onwards. This chapter proceeds to look at recent examples of Christian activism. It argues that these examples have resulted in a collective sense of wariness amongst non-Christians of different stripes. This chapter concludes with possible worst-case scenarios if this trend is exacerbated.

THE PAP "MORAL" STATE

It would be mistaken to assume that Christian activism has always been with us. Entirely forgivable in light of the increasingly frequent controversies over public morality sparked by conservative Christians. However, if we define Christian activism as the mobilization of the Christian community to resist or publicly express objections to events or public policy based on Christian morality and values, then it is a relatively new phenomenon. Of course there was the occasional moral objection to policies such as the abortion bill,[6] but on the whole Christian activism was generally unheard of. As demonstrated elsewhere, this was because of the way the new PAP government had proven itself to be a "moral" state.[7]

Public morality was one of the ways the PAP reached out to the majority working-class Chinese in the 1950s and 1960s. Made up of English-educated, bourgeois Chinese who were more comfortable with an Anglo worldview, the PAP leadership understood the need to reach out to the Chinese-educated masses who formed the base of the electorate. This gulf between the English- and Chinese-educated was more than economic in nature but also socio-cultural. The Straits Chinese, for example, many of whom were English-educated and more comfortable with Western cultural references, were economically and culturally distinct from the Chinese-educated who remained culturally oriented towards China. This distinction was keenly felt by both sets of Chinese communities. Indeed the Chinese-educated "held the English-educated in contempt for their lack of knowledge of Chinese culture and language, their 'commercial mindedness', and their receptiveness to 'yellow culture' such as juke-boxes, *Playboy* magazines, sex films and dancing".[8] This prompted the PAP to embark on an "anti-yellow culture" campaign in the 1960s to rid the consumer landscape of pornography, gambling saloons and vice. As former Prime Minister Lee Kuan Yew observed, such a move was useful for "outflanking the communists" which the PAP did with "puritanical zeal".[9]

In forming government, the PAP portrayed itself as "moral" in two distinct ways. Firstly, as a *morally upright* state that did not tolerate corruption, nepotism or patronage. To this end, the PAP state has always insisted on a high moral bar for those entering politics and public service. The ideals of integrity, lawfulness, honesty and impartiality were accorded high levels of political capital. Any erosion of its honesty and integrity would see a corresponding erosion of its political capital, resulting in a loss of legitimacy. This emphasis on moral uprightness extended to the PAP's insistence on its members donning white attire to symbolize purity and integrity. Secondly, the ruling party was perceived as a *morally conservative* state that guarded the populace against decadence and vice. It was seen as a protector of cultural conservatism, dominant heterosexual values, and traditional institutions like the nuclear family unit. The morally conservative state was trusted to keep liberal lifestyle values and practices from the West at bay while it embarked on mass industrialization.

Indeed, the PAP's concern with the morality of the nation heightened with increasing affluence and mass consumption. Fears that the ethnic Chinese population had become "Westernized" and vulnerable to "deculturalization",[10] led to the 1979 Moral Education Report that paved the way for the implementation of the Religious Knowledge Studies syllabus in the early 1980s, which not only raised religious consciousness amongst students in Singapore but also religious differences as well. The mainstream religions of Christianity, Islam, Buddhism, Hinduism, and Confucian ethics were taught to secondary school students. This education policy conflated religion with morality and made religious instruction central to moral education.

From the 1960s to the late 1980s, the PAP was extremely successful in demonstrating to the electorate its ability to reconcile economic pragmatism with a conservative brand of morality and lifestyle values. On one hand, it was open to multinational corporations and capital; on the other, it banned undesirable popular music like the Beatles' landmark album *Sgt Pepper's Lonely Hearts Club Band* and denying entry to musicians like Cliff Richards and Led Zeppelin because of their long hair. Even American comics like X-Men, Spiderman and the Avengers were banned in 1969 for perceived negative influence in light of their themes of violence and fantasy.[11] All this went a long way in reassuring many religious conservatives that regardless of the economic pressures (or temptations) faced by the city-state, it would always navigate its future with a reliable moral compass. This kept many of them firmly entrenched in their traditional spaces such as churches, temples or mosques, away from civil society or the political realm because they trusted the PAP state to make "morally right" decisions when it came to policy-making despite criticism and ridicule of the country's staid or boring image from liberal voices both domestic and abroad.

WHITHER THE "MORAL" STATE

All this began to change in the 1990s. Coming off the back of the 1985 recession, the PAP government was keen to identify sunrise industries to jumpstart the economy. One of the industries identified was arts and culture. The arts and culture industry was deemed to be important in two ways. Firstly, it was believed that the industry had the potential for job creation. Occupations such as arts administrators, curators, arts facilities managers, design and lighting technicians and so on would add greater diversity to the job market. Secondly, a more vibrant arts and cultural scene was deemed necessary to make the city a desirable place to work and live.[12] Arts and culture would attract global capital and foreign talent as well as to prevent highly skilled Singaporeans from migrating. In short, the government began to invest in hardware like theatres and performance facilities in order to inject greater artistic and entertainment buzz into the local scene in the hope of making the city more attractive to investors. And so began the Global City for the Arts campaign.

With the building of infrastructure came a softening of governmental attitudes towards moral conservatism. One high-profile example of this was the milestone 1992 Censorship Review Committee Report. Among its many recommendations was the introduction of the "Restricted (Artistic)" rating for the cinema. This allowed cinema-goers aged eighteen and above to watch films containing nudity and graphic sex scenes in local cinemas. The backlash from moral conservatives resulted in the raising of the minimum age to twenty-one and limiting such films to downtown cinemas, away from the presumably more conservative suburbs. Meanwhile themes like homosexuality, transgender challenges, AIDS, and other taboo issues were more readily explored in local theatre. This greater leeway enjoyed by theatre was down to the fact that it had a smaller, more educated audience, compared to the mass audience of local television. Nevertheless, such censorship relaxations had a positive impact on the arts and cultural scene. International observers began to take notice. *Time* magazine could barely contain its surprise:

> Culturally, Singapore is permitting artists to stage a range of socially and politically controversial performances. The club scene is wild and getting wilder. And Singapore is allowing the Internet to function with relatively few controls, prompting an explosion of online debate on formerly taboo topics. Progress has been uneven, but there is no mistaking today's trend toward greater freedom.[13]

Perhaps more alarming in the eyes of moral conservatives was the 2004 decision to build not one but two casinos, euphemistically known as "integrated resorts". Numerous public petitions were made, with the National Council of Churches of Singapore making clear that it opposed the casinos.[14] Closely following the casino announcement was the decision to set up the now-defunct topless Parisian cabaret show, *Crazy Horse*. Naturally there was resistance from conservatives. According to then Senior Minister Lee Kuan Yew, several ministers were against the decision as well. In an interview with the press, Lee was reported to have told his cabinet colleagues, "Let the show in. It does not make sense to keep things out in this globalized age".[15] The *Straits Times* went on to quote him as saying: "Look, once upon a time, Singaporeans watched peep shows. You know, you pay 10 cents and you turn an old film in a box at Chinese wayangs. Today, they are going to Paris, they go to the Folies Bergere. I mean it doesn't make sense anymore," he said, referring to the renowned topless cabaret show. "I said, 'Let it go.' So they said, 'No, we must stop this, stop that.' I said, 'You either go with the world and be part of the world, or you will find that we become a quaint, a quixotic, esoteric appendage of the world.'"[16]

This was of course a real turnaround from the "anti-yellow culture" campaign of the 1960s. What used to be non-negotiable moral values were now described as "quaint" and "quixotic". Nevertheless, heteronormative vice did not arouse conservative Christians as much as the spectre of homosexuality and "gay lifestyles". Although homosexual sex remains a criminal offence, there has been tolerance for homosexual narratives on the local theatre stage since the 1990s as long as such narratives were judged by the authorities not to portray homosexual lifestyle as glamorous or desirable. Indeed, the desire to be a global city made state tolerance for alternative lifestyles necessary. Popular quasi-policy literature like Richard Florida's 2002 book *The Rise of the Creative Class* that argued that cities with high concentrations of technology workers, artists, musicians, and LGBT (lesbian, gay, bisexual, transgender) communities possessed the "creative class", which, in turn, attracted more businesses and capital, were devoured by policy planners and government officials alike. Almost on cue, then Prime Minister Goh Chok Tong revealed that his government allowed homosexual employees into its ranks, many of whom occupied sensitive positions.[17] For many moral conservatives, this trend confirmed what they had begun to suspect, namely, conservative values and morals were sacrificed on the altar of economic growth and global city ambitions. More fundamentally, the PAP moral state that they had come to rely on to uphold conservative values was changing into something they no longer recognized.

The 2007 parliamentary debate over section 377A of the Penal Code which criminalizes sex between men was particularly instructive. This debate came about when then nominated member of parliament (NMP) Siew Kum Hong presented a petition to parliament concerning the unconstitutionality of section 377A. The feisty parliamentary debate effectively pitted moral conservatives against progressives, and cut across party lines with several PAP MPs speaking in support of the petition.[18] This led Prime Minister Lee Hsien Loong to conclude that, "When it comes to issues like the economy, technology, education, we [the government] better stay ahead of the game, watch where people are moving and adapt faster than others, ahead of the curve, leading the pack," but on issues concerning moral values, "we will let others take the lead, we will stay one step behind the front line of change; watch how things work out elsewhere before we make any irrevocable moves".[19] Arguably, this was interpreted by conservatives and liberals as an invitation to shape cultural norms and mindsets, with the understanding that if they did not take up this invitation to stand on the "front line of change", others would do so. Two years later, the first "Pink Dot" event was held.[20] Now an annual event, Pink Dot comprises songs, talks and festivities to celebrate diversity and the LGBT community in Singapore. The event has garnered international attention and has been a lightning rod for criticisms from moral conservatives.[21]

Two recent examples of Christian activism in 2014 have been instructive for different reasons. The first happened in February that year when Christian conservatives objected to the Health Promotion Board's (HPB) "normalization" of homosexuality in its frequently asked questions (FAQs) on sexuality. HPB's FAQs stated that, "A same-sex relationship is not too different from a heterosexual relationship. Both take the commitment of two people. It's also a connection of two families, cultures and sometimes racial backgrounds and values" and that, "Yes, homosexuals can certainly have long-lasting relationships. A homosexual relationship, like any other relationship, is based on values like trust, love, commitment and support."[22] Although the FAQs were published in November 2013, they only went viral in February 2014 and drew praise from the LGBT community and beyond for its factual and neutral approach to sexuality.[23] This, in turn, attracted the ire of Christian conservatives. Pastor Lawrence Khong of Faith Community Baptist Church criticized the FAQs in his capacity as chairman of church network LoveSingapore for its "pro-LGBT view".[24] Ruling-party MP, Lim Biow Chuan, also criticized HPB and filed a parliamentary question on the FAQs.[25] HPB responded by noting that its FAQs on sexuality were put together with the help of professional counsellors. The FAQs were part of HPB's programme to educate youth on sexually transmitted diseases and was meant as "a one-stop resource to provide factual information on sexuality and sexually transmitted infections (STIs)/HIV prevention from a public health perspective".[26] What was interesting about this case was the way Christian activism had again ventured into the realms of health education. This followed the AWARE takeover which was partly driven by concerns that the NGO, as a vendor for sex education classes, would normalize homosexuality.

The other was the controversial withdrawal of three children's books from the National Library after complaints from the public in July 2014. A member of the public had complained that three books found in the children's section were inappropriate for children. The three titles were *And Tango Makes Three* (a true story of two male penguins who raised a chick together), *The White Swan Express* (about adoption and features a lesbian couple) and *Who's in My Family* (which celebrates different family structures, including same-sex parents). The National Library's decision to withdraw the books in response to a single complaint sparked a backlash from the public, many of whom wondered why this was necessary as the titles had already been reviewed by its own librarians and found suitable. There were petitions to the library to reinstate the books; a public reading event was organized for parents to read the three titles to their children, while local writers also pulled out of events related to the National Library in protest.[27] In the end, all copies of *Who's in My Family* were pulped, while the other two titles were relocated to the adult section. The pulping of books by the National Library and its denial of useful information to the young was an abdication of its primary role as promoter of knowledge. It was a clear instance of a public institution bowing to conservative pressure.

The Singapore Christian community was, of course, not immune to events elsewhere in the world. America's "culture war" in the 1980s was instructive as an increasing number of so-called "hot-button" issues such as abortion, homosexuality, and censorship were polarizing American society according to ideological worldviews.[28] The spheres of education, law, arts and culture and, of course, politics became ideological and moral battlegrounds in which the struggle between conservatism and progressivism played out. As such, the increasing levels of Christian activism in Singapore should be understood in this broader context. Within the local landscape, however, I argue that many religious and moral conservatives believed that the erstwhile PAP moral state had abandoned the conservative values it had started out with for moral liberalization in order to attract global capital and talent. It signalled to them that this moral state was no longer willing to take the lead on public morality issues. PM Lee's announcement that the government "will let others take the lead" on public morality was interpreted as the clarion call to make themselves heard.

PUBLIC EXPRESSIONS OF CHRISTIAN IDENTITY AND CALLING FOR A CHRISTIAN NATION

As debates over public morality grew, the character of the local Christian community changed in two observable ways. The first was the *increased public expression of Christian identities*. Christian identities were no longer confined to the private sphere but expressed more confidently and with greater frequency in public. As mentioned above, marketplace theology encourages Christians to blur the lines between their professional and religious identities in order to be a good example of Christ in the workplace. This has applied not just to ordinary citizens but politicians as well. For example, it is not uncommon for younger politicians to publicly express their Christian faith on social media.[29] Senior civil servants have been known to cite biblical stories as sources of inspiration.[30] Local celebrities and personalities are open with regards to their Christian faith.[31] While the Constitution protects the rights of Singaporeans to publicly express and practise their religious beliefs, this suggests that the traditional boundaries between private and public identities are increasingly blurred. Such public expressions are signs of growing assuredness of Christian professionals at the top of their fields and in society, thus creating a virtuous cycle, where more people are willing to be identified as Christians because of the successful Christians before them. The religious impetus cannot be ignored either. For many Christians, public proclamations of their religious identity are interpreted as bold and personal acts of obedience to God. They see themselves as taking the step of faith to be God's witness by being positive examples of Christ and to willingly open their actions and behaviour to judgement, sometimes unduly harshly, from the outside world.

But not all religions are viewed equally in Singapore. Christianity's relatively higher socio-economic status means that the community is perceived differently from other religions. The more frequently public expressions of Christian identity are made by public figures, the greater the amplification of Christian presence in the public sphere. This amplification belies demographic reality with Christians making only 20 per cent of the population. Nevertheless it gives the perception of a shrinking neutral space among non-Christians which will, in turn, induce greater anxiety over the Christian influence in Singapore. This anxiety is not unwarranted. The Christian community has a track-record of proselytizing in local schools in the 1980s.[32] There are occasional reports of Christian volunteers attempting to convert non-believers as they lie in hospitals.[33] Local pastors have publicly expressed desires for Singapore to become a Christian nation despite the country's multireligious context, with some describing the country as the "Antioch of Asia".[34] Pastors have been hauled up by the authorities from time to time for insulting or denigrating other faiths like Buddhism and Taoism from the pulpit,[35] while members of the community have been charged with distributing anti-Islam pamphlets.[36]

It is thus not surprising that the increased public expressions of Christian identities by ordinary citizens, politicians and celebrities alike have resulted in a corresponding increase in anxiety amongst other religious groups. This may trigger non-Christians into similarly expressing their religious identities as Muslims, Buddhists, Taoists or Hindus in the course of their everyday life in order to restore some semblance of symmetry. This, in turn, would see religion becoming a more significant marker of identity than ethnicity or citizenship. We may be edging towards a situation where it would be regarded as good form to disclose one's religion before participating in public and policy debates as declaration of one's moral orientation. Such a situation would be a clear regression for Singapore.

Secondly, local Christians have routinely expressed the desire for Singapore to be a Christian nation with a Christian moral framework. For the most part, the backlash to events like the Pink Dot and censorship relaxation have come mainly from fringe groups in the Anglican, Methodist and independent Pentecostal folds. And though these fringe groups do not speak for the entire Christian community, they are the vanguard of moral activism. Unlike Malaysia and Indonesia where religious-moral activists are synonymous with conservative Islamic groups such as the political party Parti Islam SeMalaysia (PAS) or Islamic Defenders Front (FPI), respectively, faith-based moral conservatism in Singapore is undeniably Christian-led. Singaporean Muslims, the other major monotheistic religion in the country, have been contented to let Singaporean Christians do the moral championing because the latter's crusades against homosexuality, liberal sexual attitudes and other "vices", have largely aligned with their own values. Muslim activists, such as the Wear White campaigners protesting against Pink Dot, may occasionally join their Christian counterparts in publicly expressing their displeasure at so-called "alternative lifestyles". Nevertheless, this convenient alignment has allowed Singaporeans Muslims to take a backseat while their Christian counterparts do the heavy-lifting, so to speak. Perhaps less represented in the middle and higher-middle classes, and thus possessing less cultural and economic capital, Singaporean Muslims lack the political and economic confidence to champion their brand of morality as confidently as conservative Christians are wont to do. Not least, associations of Islam with issues of security, terrorism and fundamentalism may have made local Muslims more keenly sensitive to public scrutiny and may have reduced the community's appetite for championing Islamic morality in Singapore.

But will the penny drop for Singaporean Muslims when conservative Christians advance their calls for a Christian nation? The call for Singapore to be the "Antioch for Asia" dates back to 1978 when the late American evangelist Billy Graham preached to 337,000 people over five nights at the old National Stadium.[37] He prophesized that the city-state would not only become a Christian nation but also a regional node from which a Christian network would spread through missionary work. Since then the theme of Singapore as a Christian nation has been a recurring one. Over the years some pastors have called Singapore a "spiritual beachhead" from which Christianity would advance,[38] while others have prophesized that

Singapura (Sanskrit for "lion city") would be "returned from the demonic lion of Sang Nila Utama (the Malay prince who founded the pre-colonial settlement) to the Lion of the Tribe of Judah (representing Christ) in the fiftieth year of its independence in 2015".[39] Pentecostal pastors have also expressed their desire to see "cell groups" (or smaller prayer groups) in every block of Housing and Development Board flats and for Christian presence to be felt in the daily life of Singaporeans.[40] The desire to see the city-state as a Christian nation has inspired the LoveSingapore movement. It was formed in the mid-1990s as a loose coalition of different denominations seeking to raise Christian consciousness and to reimagine the nation as site of spiritual warfare. In 2001, LoveSingapore spent S$2 million on a media campaign to create "God consciousness" and rebrand God from a "dictatorial rule-maker" and "distant and unapproachable killjoy schoolmaster" to "the sort of person you'd like to get to know more about".[41] LoveSingapore was forced to redirect its campaign when the government banned the print and television versions of the advertisements.

THREE POSSIBLE REACTIONS

There will inevitably be reactions to these public expressions of Christian identity and calls to become a Christian nation in a multicultural society. There are three possible reactions from non-Christians and moderate Christians alike, and they are certainly not mutually exclusive. The first possible reaction to growing religiosity from the conservative Christian community is to *defer to authority*. To defer to authority is to trust that the state will not only protect the rights of other faith communities but to ensure that space for secular and civic discourse does not shrink. This reaction demands little effort from the individual and puts the onus squarely on the state to tackle the thorny matter of religious sensitivity. In light of the delicate nature of religious matters in a multicultural society as well as the government's constant reminders of the need to maintain religious harmony, many Singaporeans would prefer to leave such matters to the government.

This reaction may draw assurance from the panoply of laws and regulations over religious practices. At the entry level, the Societies Act makes it mandatory for any society that seeks to represent or discuss religious matters to be registered. The Societies Act allows the government to effectively ban religious groups if they are deemed to be "prejudicial to public peace, welfare or good order in Singapore".[42] The Penal Code and the Sedition Act serve as another mechanism for regulating religious accord.

The Penal Code makes it a criminal offence to defile a place of worship, disturb a religious assembly, utter words to insult religious sensitivities, and to arouse ill-will between religious groups.[43] The Sedition Act makes it an offence to "produce feelings of ill-will and enmity between different races or classes of the population of Singapore".[44] The Internal Security Act, part of the country's colonial legacy, allows the government to detain individuals without trial. The Act was originally against on communists in Malaya after the Second World War. It was enacted in 1987 against Catholic activists and more recently in 2001 against Jemaah Islamiyah members who were suspected of planning terrorist activities. Finally, and most specifically, the Maintenance of Religious Harmony Act, passed in 1990, addresses the use of religion to further other causes. The Act allows the government to issue a restraining order on any religious leader whom the Home Affairs Minister believes to be causing hostility between different religious groups, or promoting a political cause or that of any political party, or carrying out subversive activities under the guise of religious programmes.

However, deferring the issue to authorities does not mean that anxieties will subside. In fact they will only increase if non-Christians believe that conservative Christian activism will grow despite existing laws and regulations. Furthermore, and more crucially, the constant deferment of religious issues to the state will come with a longer term societal cost, namely, an underdeveloped ability amongst fellow citizens to engage with each other over religious differences in a civil and intelligent manner. The habit of making police reports over every perceived religious infringement or encroachment is the most obvious way of deferring issues to authorities. Police reports have become a convenient way for offended citizens to express their objection without having to engage sensitively and wisely with the other party. Over time, in the absence of civic discourse amongst citizens, resilience and tolerance will only decrease, leaving society more vulnerable and susceptible to indignation and outrage. This inability to engage in civic debate, in which both sides can lay out common ground and isolate areas of disagreement, may also result in the repression of these anxieties and finding release as gross overreactions to perceived religious encroachments further down the road.

The second possible reaction is *hypersensitivity* to any perceived religious encroachment or supposedly offensive remarks made by Christians. This happens when any faith-based activity may be automatically imputed with negative intentions. For example, social welfare efforts such as charities, food distribution events, or the provision of tuition organized by churches or para-church institutions may be interpreted by some as avenues for covert proselytizing. Church members, volunteers and pastors may be viewed by the non-Christian community to be engaging in social welfare with the intention of spreading the Gospel. A hypersensitive member of the public may take issue with routine expressions from church volunteers such as "Bless you" or "I'll pray for you" in the course of their charity work and confrontations may occur. Another example is how declarations of faith and religious values may be erroneously interpreted as politically charged or a clarion call for activism.

For instance, a pastor may stand at his pulpit on Sunday and exhort his congregation to pray for political leaders and the government. This pastor may announce that that God has installed secular leaders for His purpose and may even articulate bible passages such as: "I urge, then, first of all, that petitions, prayers, intercession and thanksgiving be made for all people; for kings and all those in authority, that we may live peaceful and quiet lives in all godliness and holiness" (I Timothy 2:1–2). In today's climate, it is not beyond the realm of possibility that a non-Christian in the audience, not understanding the biblical context, may capture this on his or her phone camera and circulate this online, resulting in interpretations by the non-Christian community as the desire to convert or influence political leaders. Misinformed or malicious interpretations may lead to the vilification of the church. Christians may, in turn, become more defensive and nurture a siege mentality with regards to the rest of the community. This siege mentality may easily lead to a persecution complex within the Christian community.

The third possible reaction is for other religious groups to, rather predictably, respond with a *reaffirmation of their own religious identity*. The affirmation of religious identity is not necessarily a negative development, even if prompted by competition. It may inject a renewed sense of mission and purpose into the community, as well as encourage a closer theological relationship between the believer and the divine. However, when this reaffirmation is driven by the fear that religious spaces may be shrinking or that believers may be lost to another faith then this affirmation is driven by anxiety and insecurity, and thus tinged with a passive-aggressive character. This reaffirmation can manifest in two ways. The first is the reaffirmation of form whereby religious dressing, rituals, and practices are insisted upon in public spaces. In the case of Islam this can be seen in the popularity of the tudung for Muslim women in Singapore. Studies have found that the donning of the tudung is purposeful signal to the rest of society of a Muslim woman's religiosity as well as her membership to the collective Malay Muslim identity.[45] The tudung is especially potent because it represents the conflation of "race" and "religion", thus deepening its significance in the public sphere. Such markers of distinction serve as everyday visual reminders to a Chinese-majority society of the presence of other minorities. The other is the reaffirmation of rights whereby the individual's religious rights or sensitivities must be championed or protected. For example, Muslims may insist that alcohol not be drunk or pork products not consumed in their presence by appealing to religious sensitivity. Others may insist on more local eateries and snack bars applying for halal certification even though such certifications are voluntary.[46] Unlike the tudung which marks out the individual's body and impacts no one else, the insistence that eateries go halal or that alcohol not be served at public events will impact the wider community, thus causing greater friction. Collectively, these actions suggest that any affirmation of religious identity prompted by anxieties over shrinking public spaces will only contribute to, not ease, these anxieties.

CONCLUSION

The moral activism that arose in response to the cultural liberalization of the 1990s will only grow as Singapore continues to deepen its networks into the global economy. Moving forward, Singapore will face two distinctive challenges. The first is to ensure that conservative Christian activism over public morality issues does not lead to greater tensions within society. While such Christian activism certainly has its place in the public sphere given that religious values cannot be divorced from morality issues, much of its focus in recent times seems to be on LGBT issues, particularly over the retention of section 377A. This has been symptomatic of larger concerns from conservative circles such as the perceived erosion of the traditional family unit and the general decline of morality in contemporary society. As bulwarks of morality, conservative Christian activists believe themselves to be the last line of defence against liberal lifestyles and cultural values that have now woven themselves into the fabric of global city culture. There is little the state or secularists can do to dissuade these Christian activists in light of the latter's deep convictions, and there are signals that conservative Christians are just getting started. For example, the recent establishment of the Alliance of Pentecostal-Charismatic Churches of Singapore (APCCS) is a clear sign that the Pentecostal community does not believe that the National Council of Churches Singapore (NCCS), comprising mainly of Protestant churches, speaks on its behalf.[47] This alliance of independent churches may be interpreted as an attempt to mobilize and distil scattered conservative voices into a single and coherent one. APCCS has made clear that it intends to work with government agencies to be "a blessing to the society".[48] In light of the different shades of conservatism, it would be constructive to encourage the moderate Christian majority to make their positions known over a variety of public morality issues. By speaking out more frequently, moderate Christians will demonstrate to other religious communities—and indeed their own—that the Christian community is a diverse one with many perspectives, and that the more attention-grabbing activism of conservative Christians is not representative of the broader community. This may go some way in easing the anxieties of other faiths.

The second challenge, related to the first, is the need to constantly reassure other faith communities of their place in Singapore society. This is easier said than done because of the different insecurities inherent in the Muslim and Buddhist communities. For one, the Malay-Muslim community differs in socio-economic profile from the local Christian community. The former community is more likely than other ethnic communities to be represented in lower-income strata.[49] And because of the associated social patterns of the lower income, there is a "significant overrepresentation" of the local Malay-Muslim community in crime, drug and prison statistics.[50] This socio-economic disparity between the Malay-Muslim and Christian communities will contribute to the anxiety of the former over any of the latter's perceived growth in influence over public morality issues. The Buddhist community, on the other hand, may feel vulnerable as its members are open to conversion by Christians. While it may be the largest religious community, its predominantly Chinese members make them more receptive to proselytization than Malay-Muslims. Adding to the anxiety is the corresponding decrease in Buddhists and increase in Christians between 2010 and 2015. In 2010 Buddhists comprised 44.2 per cent of the population and dropped slightly to 43.2 per cent in 2015.[51] Meanwhile the Christian community showed some gain from 18.3 per cent in 2010 to 18.8 per cent in 2015.[52] In response, Buddhist leaders have established youth groups and wings to roll out programmes to reach out to young Buddhists. Such programmes and mission trips are meant to make Buddhism more relevant to the lives of younger people and to energize them.[53] It is unlikely that such initiatives will cease as they are driven largely by the deep-seated anxiety of numerical erosion. These two challenges, along with others, will continue to dominate the religious landscape in Singapore. And though they have emerged from a variety of dynamic trends such as increased global fundamentalism and extremism, increased religiosity and the desire to express personal religious identities publicly, these challenges are also responsive to local conditions. In short, they may be exacerbated or moderated according to the developments from within the local Christian community.

Notes

1. Zakir Hussain, "Dr Thio Upset about Sexuality Programme", *Straits Times*, 24 April 2009.
2. Department of Statistics Singapore, *General Household Survey 2015*.
3. Department of Statistics Singapore, *Census of Population 2010: Statistical Release 1 on Demographical Statistics, Education, Language and Religion*.
4. Tong Chee Kiong, Eddie Kuo, and Jon S.T. Quah, *Religion and Religious Revivalism in Singapore* (Singapore: Ministry of Community Development, 1988); Terence Chong and Hui Yew-Foong, *Different Under God: A Survey of Church-Going Protestants in Singapore* (Singapore: Institute of Southeast Asian Studies, 2013).
5. Department of Statistics Singapore, *Census of Population 2010: Statistical Release 1*.
6. "Abortion Tantamount to Murder, Says a Woman MP", *Straits Times*, 30 December 1969, http://eresources.nlb.gov.sg/newspapers/Digitised/Article/straitstimes 19691230-1.2.77 (accessed 10 May 2018).
7. Terence Chong, "Filling the Moral Void: The Christian Right in Singapore", *Journal of Contemporary Asia* 41, no. 4 (2011): 566–83.
8. Yeo Kim Wah, *Political Development in Singapore 1945–55* (Singapore: Singapore University Press, 1973), pp. 177–78.
9. Lee Kuan Yew, *The Singapore Story* (Singapore: Times Edition, 1998), p. 326.
10. Goh Keng Swee, *Report on the Ministry of Education* (Singapore: Ministry of Education, 1978).
11. "Last Comic Shops Standing in S'pore?", *New Paper*, 21 July 2014, https://www.asiaone.com/singapore/last-comic-shops-standing-spore (accessed 10 May 2018).
12. See T.C. Chang, "Renaissance Revisited: Singapore as a 'Global City for the Arts'", *International Journal of Urban and Regional Research* 24, no. 4 (2000): 818–31; Lily Kong, "Ambitions of a Global City: Arts, Culture and Creative Economy in 'Post-Crisis' Singapore", *International Journal of Cultural Policy* 18, no. 3 (2012): 279–94.
13. Terry McCarthy and Eric Ellis, "Singapore Lightens Up", *Time*, 19 July 1999, http://content.time.com/time/world/article/0,8599,2054247,00.html (accessed 12 May 2018).
14. Kevin Wong and Glendys Sim, "Views Split Over Proposed Safeguards", *Straits Times*, 30 December 2004.
15. Pei Shing Huei, "Adjusting to the Realities of a Globalising World", *Straits Times*, 23 April 2007.

16. Ibid.
17. M. Nirmala, "Govt More Open to Employing Gays Now", *Straits Times*, 4 July 2003.
18. Shawna Tang, *Postcolonial Lesbian Identities in Singapore: Rethinking Global Sexualities* (London and New York: Routledge, 2016).
19. Lee Hsien Loong, "Parliamentary Speech on Section 377A", Singapore Parliamentary Reports (Hansard), 23 October 2007, http://sprs.parl.gov.sg
20. "Pink Dot" is a nod to Singapore's moniker "red dot" as well as the colour of the Singaporean identity card.
21. Regina Marie Lee, "'Traditional Values' Wear White Campaign Returning on Pink Dot Weekend", *Today*, 23 May 2016, https://www.todayonline.com/singapore/network-churches-revives-campaign-wear-white-pink-dot-weekend (accessed 14 May 2018).
22. Health Promotion Board, "FAQs on Sexuality", https://www.hpb.gov.sg/article/faqs-on-sexuality (accessed 16 May 2018).
23. Siau Ming En, "Health Promotion Board's FAQ on Sexuality Draws Positive Response Online", *Today*, 5 February 2014, https://www.todayonline.com/singapore/health-promotion-boards-faq-sexuality-draws-positive-response-online (accessed 16 May 2018).
24. Siau Ming En, "'Disappointed' MP Criticises HPB for Its FAQ on Sexuality", *Today*, 7 February 2014, https://www.todayonline.com/singapore/disappointed-mp-criticises-hpb-its-faq-sexuality (accessed 16 May 2018).
25. Ibid.
26. Hoe Pei Shan, "Health Board Tackles Gay Issues in FAQs", *Straits Times*, 5 February 2014, https://www.straitstimes.com/singapore/health-board-tackles-gay-issues-in-faqs (accessed 16 May 2018).
27. Tan Dawn Wei, "NLB Saga: Two Removed Children's Books Will Go into Adult Section at Library", *Straits Times*, 18 July 2014, https://www.straitstimes.com/singapore/nlb-saga-two-removed-childrens-books-will-go-into-adult-section-at-library (accessed 16 May 2018).
28. James Davison Hunter, *Culture Wars: The Struggle to Define America* (New York: Basic Books, 1991).
29. "No Need to Read Too Much into 'Inadequate' Facebook Post, Says Tan Chuan-Jin", *Today*, 7 September 2017, https://www.todayonline.com/singapore/no-need-read-too-much-inadequate-facebook-post-says-tan-chuan-jin (accessed 16 May 2018).
30. See, for example, an interview with then Commissioner of the Singapore Prison Service Soh Wai Wah, in Denyse Yeo, "We Are the First Drop of Water ...", *Challenge Online*, 26 November 2014, https://www.psd.gov.sg/challenge/people/cuppa/we-are-the-first-drop-of-water-soh-wai-wah-on-why-the-little-things-matter (accessed 16 May 2018).
31. See the list of stories featured on local website *Singapore Christian*, https://singaporechristian.com/category/singapore-celebrities/ (accessed 16 May 2018).

32. Tong, Kuo, and Quah, *Religion and Religious Revivalism in Singapore*.
33. Yen Feng, "SGH Warns Against Evangelizing", *Straits Times*, 26 May 2011.
34. Rick Seaward, "Singapore, an Antioch of Antiochs", *Salt&Light*, 8 February 2018, http://saltandlight.sg/news/singapore-an-antioch-of-antiochs/ (accessed 16 May 2018).
35. Yen Feng, "ISD Calls Up Pastor for Insensitive Comments", *AsiaOne*, 8 February 2010, http://news.asiaone.com/News/the+Straits+Times/Story/A1Story20100209-197516.html (accessed 16 May 2018).
36. Carolyn Quek, "Seditious Tract Duo Jailed 8 Weeks", *AsiaOne*, 11 June 2009, http://news.asiaone.com/News/the+Straits+Times/Story/A1Story20090611-147630.html (accessed 16 May 2018).
37. Melody Zaccheus, "Christians in Singapore Pay Tribute to Billy Graham", *Straits Times*, 23 February 2018, https://www.straitstimes.com/singapore/christians-in-spore-pay-tribute-to-billy-graham (accessed 10 June 2018).
38. Jean DeBernardi, "Global Christian Culture and the Antioch of Asia", in *Religious Diversity in Singapore*, edited by Lai Ah Eng (Singapore: Institute of Southeast Asian Studies, 2008).
39. Daniel P.S. Goh, "State and Social Christianity in Post-Colonial Singapore", *SOJOURN: Journal of Social Issues in Southeast Asia* 25, no. 1 (2010), p. 81.
40. Ibid., p. 78.
41. Mark Blair, Richard Armstrong, and Mike Murphy, *The 360 Degree Brand in Asia: Creating More Effective Marketing Communications* (Singapore: John Wiley, 2003), pp. 32–33, as cited in Daniel P.S. Goh, "State and Social Christianity in Post-Colonial Singapore".
42. Societies Act (Cap. 311), para. 4.2b.
43. Penal Code (Cap. 15), paras. 295, 296, and 298.
44. Sedition Act (Cap. 290), para. 3.2d.
45. Suriani Suratman, "Tudung Girls: Unveiling Muslim Women's Identity in Singapore", in *Melayu: The Politics, Poetics and Paradoxes of Malayness*, edited by Maznah Mohamad and Syed Muhd Khairudin Aljunied (Singapore: NUS Press, 2011).
46. Nur Syahindah Ishak and David Sun, "Food Sold in Cinemas not Halal-Certified: Muis", *Straits Times*, 17 September 2018, https://www.straitstimes.com/lifestyle/food/food-sold-in-cinemas-not-halal-certified-muis (accessed 20 September 2018).
47. Melody Zaccheus, "Some 50 Churches Set Up New Alliance to Serve as 'Additional Christian Voice'", *Straits Times*, 29 April 2018, https://www.straitstimes.com/singapore/some-50-churches-set-up-new-alliance-to-serve-as-additional-christian-voice (accessed 20 September 2018).
48. "Church Alliance Does Not Pursue Political Agenda", *Straits Times*, 7 May 2018, https://www.straitstimes.com/forum/letters-in-print/church-alliance-does-not-pursue-political-agenda (accessed 20 September 2018).
49. Walter Sim, "Many Poor Malays 'Do Not Seek Social Aid'", *AsiaOne*, 26 April 2015,

http://www.asiaone.com/singapore/many-poor-malays-do-not-seek-social-aid (accessed 25 September 2018).

50. Toh Yong Chuan, "Malay-Muslim Groups Urged to Tackle Challenges", *Straits Times*, 2 April 2017, https://www.straitstimes.com/singapore/malay-muslim-groups-urged-to-tackle-challenges (accessed 25 September 2018).

51. Department of Statistics Singapore, *General Household Survey 2015*.

52. Ibid.

53. Author's discussion with a Buddhist youth leader, 21 July 2018.

4

Rising Conservatism in the Singapore Malay-Muslim Community
Worrying Times Ahead?

Norshahril Saat

INTRODUCTION

In 2011, the late Minister Mentor Mr Lee Kuan Yew shared some critical reflections on the condition of the Malay-Muslim community in Singapore. In his book *Hard Truths to Keep Singapore Going*, Mr Lee opined, "I think we were progressing very nicely until the surge of Islam came and if you asked me for my observation, the other communities have easier integration—friends, intermarriages and so on, Indians with Chinese, Chinese with Indians—than Muslims. That's the result of the surge from the Arab states."[1] Mr Lee's assessment of the Muslim community's difficulty in integrating might have been shaped by demands from segments of the community over the years from the 1980s. The group is influenced by the Islamic resurgence movement, calling Muslims to be more committed to what they consider to be "Islamic", though in real terms, it actually refers to the conservative, ritualistic and puritan interpretations of religion.[2] Such requests include urging the People's Action Party (PAP) government to safeguard the madrasahs (full-time Islamic schools) surrounding the proposal by the government to implement Compulsory Education (CE) for all students up to primary six (for the Primary School Leaving Examinations, or PSLE) in the late 1990s and early 2000s. While the government had never intended to close down the madrasahs, and the CE proposal applies to all students notwithstanding to whether they are in the national schools or the madrasahs, a segment within the community felt the move was threatening the Islamic religious schools. In another example, Muslim resurgent groups also adopted the theological position that the donning of headscarves (tudung) for Muslim women is compulsory, including all female students in national schools. In 2002, four female students were turned away from school for putting on headscarves, because they did not comply with the Ministry of Education's no-headscarf rule for public schools. The tudung issue re-emerged in 2014 when some netizens openly raised it again online. Online campaigns have been the resurgent's modus operandi lately, as active participants on Facebook groups such as *Suara Melayu Singapura* (Voice of Singaporean Malays); *Singapore Muslims for Independent MUIS*[3] and *Singapore Muslims Against Liberal Islam*. These groups have attracted a large following within the Malay-Muslim community. In addition to this, the community has come under public scrutiny in light of the arrest of several Malay-Muslim Singaporeans for sympathizing with, if not already participating in, the transnational terrorist group ISIS (Islamic State of Iraq and Syria).

This chapter highlights some of the tensions between the Malay-Muslim community and the state in post-independent Singapore. It examines how the government, through Malay-Muslim members of parliament (MPs), and the other community leaders such as the Muslim religious and cultural elites, have responded to these issues. Since the September 11 attack on the World Trade Center in New York, the Singapore government has focused its efforts on combating violent extremism through the use of hard power (through the application of the Internal Security Act (ISA) which allows for detention without trial; regulation of ulamas who may speak publicly on Islam; and the denial of entry for undesired foreign preachers), as well as soft power through the encouragement of interfaith dialogues and cultural exchanges. It is hoped that this combination of hard and soft power can address the challenges of violent extremism. Nevertheless, the jury is out on whether the government and society as a whole have paid enough attention to non-violent extremism which could potentially also result in discord between different ethnic and religious groups, and thus undermine national integration.

While violent extremism, which refers to terrorism and radical acts that may result in loss of life or property, attracts more media attention, non-violent extremism is less eye-catching because it may not lead directly to any loss of life or property. However, it is no less dangerous because it may promote ideas which may fan the flames of discord and anger that may provide fodder for violence in the name of religion down the road. Sociologist Syed Farid Alatas distinguishes violent and non-violent extremism, and how the latter may lead to the former. He explains: "An ustaz [religious teacher] may engage in hate speech against Sufis without believing that they should be physically harmed. This may still encourage others who hate Sufis to perpetrate violent acts against them."[4]

Non-violent extremist Muslims adopt exclusivist stance both in community issues as well as those affecting non-Muslims. In Singapore, non-violent extremist Muslims have engaged in the following acts: they have belittled Islamic minorities such as the Shias and Ahmadiyahs; publicly vilified sexual minorities such as the LGBT (lesbian, gay, bisexual, transgender) community; cast doubts on alternative interpretations of religious traditions and label these interpreters as hermeneutics and liberals; rejected the merits of secularism while promoting Islamic exceptionalism; and expressed reservations towards interfaith dialogues and efforts. Should Singaporeans be concerned about growing non-violent extremism?

I argue that the focus on Islamic terrorism and national security has eclipsed other creeping forms of non-violent extremism within the local Malay-Muslim community. The Malay-Muslim community, rightfully, condemns terrorism and all forms of religion-inspired violence. However, such condemnation should not be the only indicator of the community's moderate character or ability to integrate with the rest of society. Other indicators such as the ability to jointly participate in communal and social activities or share the same perspectives on key issues are just as important. I contend that such indicators, at this point, are not obvious. The chapter begins with a discussion of increasing Islamic conservatism in Singapore that began with the Islamic resurgence movement in the 1980s, resulting in the growth of anti-secularist discourses. I proceed to discuss some recent issues that have impacted state-Muslim relations. To underline the growing exclusivism expressed by some in the Malay-Muslim community, the chapter will discuss the arrest of ISIS sympathizers between 2016 and 2017; the "Wear White Campaign" against LGBT in 2014; the controversy surrounding Imam Nalla Mohamed Abdul Jameel's sermon which included a prayer for protection against Jews and Christians in 2017. This section demonstrates how both violent and non-violent extremism can threaten social harmony in Singapore. Lastly, and by way of conclusion, the chapter assesses the state-Muslim relations in the years to come. Is there a future for moderate, reformist, and progressive voices in the community?

RISING ISLAMIC CONSERVATISM IN SINGAPORE

Historically speaking, Muslim communities across Southeast Asia have generally been characterized as inclusive in their religious outlook and tolerant of communities of different faiths and beliefs. Indeed, Muslims in the region are known as the "smiling face of Islam",[5] in contrast to the perceived hardline, firebrand, and exclusivist Islam practised in the Middle East, which is associated with Wahhabism. Such perceptions of the community changed with the Islamic resurgence movement in the 1980s. Describing the situation in Malaysia, Chandra Muzaffar defines the global Islamic resurgence movement as "the endeavour to re-establish Islamic values, Islamic practices, Islamic institutions, Islamic laws, indeed Islam in its entirety, in the lives of Muslims everywhere."[6] He adds that the Muslim resurgence strived to "re-create an Islamic ethos, an Islamic social order, at the vortex of which is the Islamic human being, guided by the Quran and the Sunnah."[7] The explanations for the resurgence are multifold and they include the fall of the Ottoman Empire in 1922, geopolitical events in the Middle East, the formation of the state of Israel in 1948, Israel's defeat of the Arab states in 1967, and the Soviet invasion of Afghanistan in 1979. While these episodes left the Muslim world feeling defeated and oppressed by the West, the rise of oil exports from Saudi Arabia in the 1970s and the Iranian revolution in 1979 gave the Muslim world a sense of hope. This hope was based on the belief that by returning to Islamic tenets enshrined in the Quran and Sunnah (sayings of the Prophet Muhammad) the Muslim world would be able to rise to be on par with the West, if not surpass it.

In Malaysia, the resurgence movement began in urban centres such as Kuala Lumpur and Bangi, while university campuses became popular for reading circles (*usrah*) led by student leaders. These Muslim student leaders also interacted with their regional counterparts including those from Singapore and Indonesia, thus explaining how these resurgence ideas also reached Singapore. For example, members of the then University of Singapore (later National University of Singapore) Muslim Society were active in promoting resurgence ideas in the city-state (discussed below).

This global resurgence saw Muslims in Southeast Asia becoming more puritan and fanatical with their faith. The issue is not about piety, but problems arose when this piety is conditioned or characterized by exclusivist interpretations of Islam and intolerance of alternative views. Ideas promoted by the Muslim resurgence during the 1980s were generally utopian in character. That is to mean many were not based on addressing concrete problems and contemporary issues but the desire to install archaic legal, political, and educational systems deemed Islamic to frame and confront modern reality.[8] Advocates insist on modes of punishments such as stoning and amputation, *shura* as opposed to parliamentary democracy, and beliefs couched in Islamic labels opposed to modern institutions and scientific knowledge. These resurgence groups refer to the Quranic verse

"Islam as *ad-deen*" (a way of life) as their guiding principle. They interpret the verse to mean the Islamization of the economy, state, knowledge, and culture, and make rhetorical pronouncements on how this Islamization process replace what they consider secular, Western, and colonial ways of life. Some observable changes the resurgence movement has had on Singapore society over the years include greater numbers of Muslim women donning the tudung; demand for halal eateries that clearly display the halal logo; clear expressions of religiosity in the display of decals on car windscreens with messages such as "Islam Is the Answer" or "Allah Is Great"; Muslims becoming less comfortable with aspects of Malay culture now deemed to be polytheistic; and fewer men and women intermingling with the opposite sex in public. Some have even become uncomfortable interacting with non-Muslims, or dining with people of other faiths, or wishing their friends "Merry Christmas" or other faith-based greetings.

Although the resurgence movement in Singapore has one main goal—to increase Islamic presence in the public and private domain—it is, in fact, made up of different and competing groups. For example, some local Muslim groups have adopted puritan versions of Islamic orientation and expect the local Malay-Muslim community to cease any cultural practice not in line with the traditions and practices of Prophet Muhammad. Conversely, there are local Sufi-inclined groups that emphasize the spiritual and mystical manifestations of the faith which purists consider innovations in Islam. Other groups believe in bringing the religion to society through *dakwah*; and are committed to spreading the teachings of Islam to non-Muslims and reaffirming it with less pious Muslims. The origins of these orientations originate from different countries and continents such as Arabia, India and Southeast Asia. When lobbying for local Islamic interests, these groups do not agree on which aspects of the faith to champion and which aspects to put on hold given the Singapore government's careful management of competing religious interests. Azhar Ibrahim argues that some of these groups align themselves with the state, either by working with or in state institutions, in order to enjoy the state's endorsement when speaking for the Muslim community.[9] There are others who refuse to be part of any government-linked institutions. They express their concerns via social media and letters to the press, and may include academics who are critical of the state's management of Islam in their publications, who express them as conforming to the Islamic perspective.[10]

In sum, the Islamic resurgence movement of the 1980s is key to understanding the psyche and religiosity of Singapore Muslims today because it marked a significant shift in their attitudes towards their personal faith and the role of Islam in public life. It also shaped the way certain groups, particularly tertiary-educated groups, view the Malay-Muslim community's relationship with the state and other non-Muslim communities. They demand that the state accommodate their right to live their lives as good Muslims even though what they truly desire is for a conservative brand of Islam to be the norm in Singapore. To them, respecting Muslim rights not only means recognizing Islamic schools, prayer spaces, ways of dressing, and diets, but also accommodating them.[11] The groups that champion this revivalist discourse include students from local universities and Islamic organizations, some of which have links to Malaysian revivalist organizations. This change in the Muslim community's behaviour and practices is most stark when contrasted against the community's depiction in popular culture in the past, such as P. Ramlee movies at the peak of the Malay film industry in Singapore during the 1950s and 1960s. Such movies depicted Malay women without the tudung in public interacting freely with the opposite gender. In fact, pictures of female teachers and students in madrasahs not donning the tudung, or having less stricter versions of the headscarves (exposing parts of the hair) can also be found in their school magazines. It could be argued that Malays then were more secular in their outlook, and though they were committed to the Islamic faith, their religious beliefs remained firmly restricted to the private domain.

Activists and university undergraduates who had championed the Islamic way of life during the 1980s are today occupying leadership positions in the civil service and religious organizations. Some are freelance religious teachers with significant followings in local mosques and on social media. Although some have changed their views over the years, others may still believe in the resurgence ideals that they struggled for during the 1980s, and this is reflected in some of the issues discussed below.

Violent and Non-Violent Extremism

The relationship between the Singapore government and the Muslim community has had its fair share of ups and downs since 1965, and can be characterized as occasionally tense but generally peaceful. Thus far, the Ministry of Home Affairs (MHA) has been able to nip any plans for violent extremism, such as terror attacks, in the bud. Nevertheless, scholars have highlighted other forms of tensions between the community and the government including, among others, the question of Malay loyalty to the state in times of war; their religiously inspired calls to lead separate lifestyles instead of integrating with the mainstream Chinese-majority; and the independence, or lack thereof, of Malay PAP MPs when articulating the community's interests.[12]

During the Goh Chok Tong administration between 1990 and 2004 three issues soured ties between the government and the Malay-Muslim community, namely, the move to make PSLE compulsory for all madrasah students (under the Compulsory Education Act 2000); the government's refusal to allow Muslim girls to don the tudung in primary schools; and the ISA arrest of fifteen Jemaah Islamiyah (JI) members. In 2001, in the context of the debate on compulsory education, the Goh government openly discussed the underperformance of the Islamic religious schools. It highlighted the high levels—close to 60 per cent—of dropout rates in madrasahs during the mid-1990s. Prime Minister Goh, in his 2000 National Day Rally speech, observed,

> The Malay MPs and I are most concerned that many Malay Singaporeans still do not fully realize the impact of the Knowledge Revolution on their children's future. They do not fully appreciate the need for their children to have some form of post-secondary education in the KBE. Not as many Malay students as we would wish are proceeding to post-secondary education. This is most unfortunate because the higher their educational level, the brighter their future.[13]

The government announced plans to introduce compulsory primary education for all Singaporeans. But some segments in the community felt threatened by this and linked it with the government's attempt to close the madrasahs.[14] Critiques to the move argue that this would eventually alter the madrasah curriculum at the primary levels by giving more weightage to secular subjects such as English, mathematics, and science. Many Muslim organizations responded to this announcement.[15] Religious teachers rallied Muslims against the government's moves fearing it would lead to the closure of the six full-time madrasahs in Singapore. The fact that the government continuously suggested that a madrasah education could not fulfil the requirements of the knowledge-based economy (KBE) only fanned the anxieties of the local Malay-Muslim community. Government leaders constantly reached out to students of Islamic studies and urged them to upgrade themselves by taking up vocational and market-related courses to supplement their Islamic knowledge, warning that it was unlikely that there would be enough jobs such as religious teachers and mosque administrators for all of them.[16]

Coming close at the heels of the madrasah issue was the tudung controversy. In 2001, four Malay-Muslim parents insisted that their young daughters be allowed to don the headscarves in their government primary school.[17] According to the Ministry of Education, students must be attired in the school's uniform and the tudung is not part of it, even though some schools allowed girls to wear long pants during physical education if they so wished. The four parents were warned to heed the school's policy and the mufti also stepped in to say that the parents should prioritize the education of their children over their dressing. The tudung issue re-emerged again in 2014,[18] this time the issue did not get much attention from the public unlike the previous one. The issue faded after government leaders and religious leaders sat down together in a closed-door dialogue session.

On a broader level, the Singapore government is perennially concerned with social trends and practices within the Malay-Muslim community that suggest they may not be integrating themselves with the mainstream by asserting their religious identity and needs. In 2001, addressing 150 Muslim leaders in a dialogue, Mr Lee Kuan Yew called on the community to be more integrated with the masses.[19] PM Goh echoed the sentiments the following year while speaking to 350 Malay Muslims,[20] reiterating that, "If more and more Muslims demand to see halal certificates of the caterers and restaurants before they agree to join non-Muslims for *makan*,[21] you send the signal of a community that wants to be exclusive. When that happens, the other communities will keep their distance."[22] State leaders also urged the local Muslim community not to overreact to issues affecting Muslims elsewhere in the world. For example in 2006, when caricatures demeaning the Prophet Muhammad were published in Danish newspapers, several Singaporean Muslim leaders issued a statement exhorting the local Malay-Muslim community not to react violently,[23] while the local Malay newspapers carried limited condemnation by Muslim leaders on the matter.

The perception of the Malay-Muslim community not integrating well with others only gathered steam with the arrest of fifteen members of terrorist group JI in December 2001. Government concerns over the vulnerability of the community to radicalism and the negative reaction to these arrests eventually led to several state-sponsored initiatives to engage the local Malay-Muslim community. Islamic Religious Council of Singapore (MUIS) devised a forward-looking and aspirational slogan "Masyarakat Melayu-Islam Cemerlang" (Malay-Muslim Community of Excellence) in 2004. MUIS also formulated a campaign to redefine the outlook and identity of local Malay-Muslims, appropriately named "Singapore Muslim Identity" (SMI).[24] SMI highlighted ten values that would define the Malay-Muslim identity. According to SMI, an ideal Singaporean Malay-Muslim: (a) holds strongly to Islamic principles while adapting itself to changing context; (b) is morally and spiritually strong to be on top of the challenges of modern society; (c) is progressive and practises Islam beyond forms or rituals and rides the modernization wave; (d) appreciates Islamic civilization and history, and has good understanding of contemporary issues; (e) appreciates other civilizations and is self-confident to interact and learn from other communities; (f) believes that good Muslims are also good citizens; (g) is well adjusted as a contributing member of a multireligious society and secular state; (h) is a blessing to all and promotes universal principles and values; (i) is inclusive and practises pluralism, without contradicting Islam; (j) and is a model and inspiration to all. These ten values have been repeated at every Friday sermon since its launch.

Likewise, the Singapore Islamic Scholars and Religious Teachers Association (Pergas) also responded in 2004 with a commissioned book entitled *Moderation in Islam: In the Context of Muslim Community in Singapore* that reinstated the community's disassociation from terrorism. If read in passing, the book can indeed be accepted as promoting a progressive and rational brand of Islamic values, in line with the tenets of Singapore's multiculturalism and multireligious society. For instance, it acknowledges that the concepts of *jihad* (struggle) and *baiáh* (pledge of loyalty) have been misinterpreted by the extremists to support terrorism.

However, the Pergas book makes several claims that are at odds with the realities of modern life. It states, for example, "whatever the form of secularism ... it is, in principle, conflicting with our understanding of religion" and "a Muslim cannot separate Islam from politics and politics from Islam."[25] Implicit in the book is the belief that Islam is in constant *conflict* with secularism, as opposed to accepting that Islam is *neutral* on secular principles of governance as long as they promote values such as justice, equality, and freedom of religion. The authors suggest that given the community's status as an ethnic and religious minority, Malay-Muslims can suspend needs for "Islamic" systems and institutions, and accept Singapore's Constitution and international conventions, as long as the state guarantees freedom of religion. Which begs the question, if given political power, would they consider implementing them?

ISA ARRESTS OF ISIS SYMPATHIZERS

During the 2000s Singapore was rocked by a series of arrests of JI supporters and militants who had planned to launch attacks on key installations including crashing a plane into Changi International Airport and bombing Mass Rapid Transit (MRT) stations.[26] The arrests continue to demonstrate that the Malay-Muslim community remains susceptible to radical ideologies that leverage on violence. The arrests also cast the spotlight on the community, and resurrected doubts on whether it can integrate with mainstream Singaporeans. In light of simmering questions over the community's loyalty to Singapore after it separated from Malaysia in 1965 and to the extent that the government made the decision to exclude the Malays-Muslims from sensitive positions in the armed forces because of doubts over their allegiance, the JI arrests only served to deepen such doubts in the minds of non-Malays.

JI's influence in the region has since declined significantly. The present terrorist threat to Singapore and its neighbouring countries comes primarily from sympathizers and returnees of ISIS, a terror group which seeks to establish an Islamic caliphate based in the Middle East. These sympathizers include Singaporean Muslims who not only promote ISIS messages via social media but also plan to travel to Syria to join ISIS. In January 2016, twenty-seven male Bangladeshi workers were arrested in Singapore for supporting Al-Qaeda and the ISIS struggle.[27] Later in May the same year, the government announced that eight Bangladeshi workers had planned to join the terror group and launch attacks in their home countries.[28] In July 2016, the authorities arrested Zulfikar Mohamad Shariff who was believed to be openly promoting ISIS ideas on social media.[29] In June 2017, the authorities detained Syaikhah Izzah Zahrah Al Ansari, an infant care assistant, for planning to travel to the Middle East to join ISIS, making her the first Singaporean female to be arrested.[30] In the following week after the announcement of Izzah's detention, two auxiliary police officers were arrested for openly sympathizing with ISIS's mission.

These ISA arrests once again placed the Malay-Muslim community under the spotlight. In response, the government launched a national security awareness campaign—SGSecure—in order to prepare Singaporeans psychologically in the event of a terror attack. The government also urged Singaporeans to remain calm, to help restore order, and appeal to non-Muslims not to target the Malay-Muslim community if such an attack were to occur, drawing lessons from similar attacks in Europe which have triggered Islamophobia. Similarly, the Malay-Muslim community has come out to strongly condemn terror attacks which have taken place elsewhere, and insist that the Islam practised in Singapore is of the moderate strain. Nevertheless, Islam's links to terrorism has prompted religious authorities to conduct proper screening of its religious teachers,

including establishing a directory of religious teachers called the Asatizah
Recognition Scheme (ARS).

Denouncing the LGBT Community

Condemning terrorism alone, however, is a necessary but insufficient
indicator of whether a community is moderate or not. A key indicator
of whether a faith-based community, regardless of its status as minority
or majority, is integrated into society is its attitude towards Singapore's
multicultural and secular way of life. Such faith-based communities
invariably face greater challenges in reconciling their values and norms
in global cities where new or alternative lifestyle values and practices are
more prevalent.

Islam emphasizes the importance of family values and the sanctity
of marriage between a man and a woman. The Prophet Muhammad also
highlighted the benefits of heterosexual marriage such as the joy children
bring to their parents. By the same token, Islam also respects the rights of
individuals not to get married. There is no conception of forced marriages
in Islam. Islam also ensures the right to "moral privacy", whereby a person
is accountable to God and not his or her peers. Furthermore, a Muslim
must not cause disharmony among citizens, bring about psychological
uneasiness in others, or insult those who are different.

Nevertheless, the local Malay-Muslim community is divided over
its response to the LGBT community. It has to be pointed out from the
outset that resistance to the LGBT community is not only a Malay-Muslim
issue as many in the local Christian community and other conservative
Singaporeans, too, do not approve of LGBT lifestyles. Every year, members
of the Malay-Muslim community would routinely denounce the annual
Pink Dot event. The Pink Dot began in 2009 as an open-air public festival
of music and speeches at Hong Lim Park, in celebration of diversity and
continues to this day. In 2014, a young Islamic religious teacher started the
"Wear White" campaign to counter Pink Dot by promoting the sanctity
of family and Islamic values. The Islamic teacher had planned to call on
Muslims at a local mosque to wear white clothes in order to show their
collective displeasure with the LGBT community. Interestingly, at least one
local church took up the call to wear white in support of the Wear White
initiative.[31] The then Mufti of Singapore, Dr Mohamed Fatris Bakaram,
issued a statement instructing mosques not to get in the crossfire between
the Pink Dot and the Wear White initiative.[32] While the Wear White initiative
has been less vocal, segments in the Malay-Muslim community believe

that the LGBT community is a threat to the Muslim faith in Singapore. The issue is occasionally brought up in closed door discussions attended by Malay-Muslim political leaders and the Muslim religious elites. Yet for a community which claims to accept pluralism and human rights, it harbours deep resistance against the LGBT community.

Separately, MUIS issued an internal advisory stating that it does not agree or approve the pervasiveness of the LGBT, and does not accept the efforts to promote it. It prefers to "help" those who are inclined to that lifestyle.[33] The council however rejects any confrontational approaches to the group.

While it is legitimate for the community to assert that traditional nuclear family institutions are integral to its belief system, it must respect the right to privacy and the freedom of choice for other communities. Moreover, it must also engage those who consider themselves LGBT Muslims because religious beliefs must go beyond a person's sexual orientation. The community will have to adopt mechanisms to accommodate non-Muslims and Muslims who may not practice a conservative brand of Islam because Singapore society will only become more complex as increased labour and talent flow into the global city to work, live and play.

In addition, the Malay-Muslim community has generally failed to draw a clear line between not condoning LGBT lifestyles and the implicit, even explicit, endorsement of hate speech against the LGBT community. Religious leaders have the right to take a moral position on LGBT issues in a civil and civic engagement but it is altogether a different issue to promote, or even turn a blind eye to, the hatred and vitriol directed against the LGBT community. Many from the Malay-Muslim community preferred to remain silent as long as it served their moral conservatism. The irony, of course, is that the values of Islam such as doing good, not harming others, and embracing diversity, all of which are constantly taught in religious classes, were conveniently forgotten, leaving their appreciation of such values merely at the rhetorical level, without understanding how turning a blind eye to such exclusivism contradicts these values too.

IMAM NALLA MOHAMED ABDUL JAMEEL'S SERMON

The private space of the mosque and its teachings came under question in 2017. In March that year, a short video clip was uploaded on social media that seemed to show Nalla Mohamed Abdul Jameel, a religious teacher from India who had been teaching in Singapore a few years, read a sermon at the Jamae Chulia Mosque on 6 January with the prayer "Grant us help against the Jews and Christians."[34] The supplication, read in Arabic, was not based on the Quran, but the teacher's own. The clip created an uproar among Muslims and non-Muslims alike, many of whom felt that such prayers had no place in multiracial Singapore. Both supporters and critics of Imam Nalla took their arguments to social media where most of the condemnation from the Malay-Muslim community was, again, directed at the whistle-blower instead of the religious teacher. Imam Nalla eventually made an apology for his remarks in front of leaders of other faiths in a synagogue, and later met the Minister for Home Affairs at the Ba'alwie Mosque where he apologized again. The imam was fined S$4,000 and deported back to India.

This case underlines the local Malay-Muslim community's insensitivity to hate speech when their faith and belief system are involved. According to UNESCO, hate speech is defined as "expressions that advocate incitement to harm (particularly, discrimination, hostility or violence) based upon the target's being identified with a certain social or demographic group. It may include, but is not limited to, speech that advocates, threatens, or encourages violent acts."[35] This case suggests that there is a tendency in some parts of the Malay-Muslim community to carry historic and negative perceptions of Islam's age-old adversaries into the present day. The key question here is what would have happened if the video clip had not been made public? Would such supplications, which are clearly at odds with multicultural Singapore, go unchallenged in local mosques? How many of such supplications have already been articulated? Would they, over time, be accepted as a normal part of Islamic discourse in Singapore by impressionable young Muslims? What types of ideas and perceptions would follow from such supplications? Finally, the Malay-Muslim community's condemnation of the whistle-blower suggests that it prefers not to deal with such problems in the open.

Understanding the Consequences of Non-Violent Extremism

The three cases above are by no means an exhaustive list of challenges facing the Malay-Muslim community in Singapore. Unfortunately, the spectre of Islamic-inspired terrorism often eclipses these challenges. The sequence of events that follow from the arrests of terrorist sympathizers in Singapore is a predictable one. Once these arrests are made public, Islamic and Malay community leaders will respond with public announcements and statements that the Malay-Muslim community rejects terrorism and violence, and pledges to do more to promote moderate Islam. These leaders will also repeat the refrain that Islam is a religion of peace and that ISIS sympathizers are misguided when interpreting the concept of jihad to mean "holy war".

Such well-rehearsed responses by leaders of the Malay-Muslim community invites us to consider if the public act of condemning terrorism automatically qualifies a Muslim as a moderate one. After all, the moderation of faith cannot be determined by a single test. How about non-violent extremism? For example, a person of any faith may reject violence or terrorism but may be resistant to secularism because of his or her religious values. Some religious elites maintain that Islam has an alternative to the secular system of governance and that Islam has a better system than democracy called the *shura*. However, differences between the two systems are never explained clearly, not to mention the simplistic representation of democracy by religious teachers as a homogeneous ideology without variation across the world.

Another example that reflects the reluctance of some in the Malay-Muslim community to embrace intrafaith diversity would be the dominant attitude within the community towards other Islamic minorities such as the Shia and Ahmadiyah communities. While the majority of Muslims in Singapore are followers of the Sunni school of thought, the Shias and Ahmadiyah communities are sizeable. And though these two minority groups are not harassed or openly criticized for their faiths, their status in Singapore remains unclear. For example, in 2017, a letter from the public was published in the *Today* newspaper enquiring of MUIS's position on the status of Shias in Singapore to which there was no clear response.[36] The religious elite's ambiguous position on Shias in Islam contradicts the Amman Message—an international declaration agreed by international religious scholars which indicates Sunnis and Shias as acceptable schools of thought in Islam—of which the former Minister-in-Charge of Muslim Affairs, Dr Yaacob Ibrahim, is a signatory.[37] For Ahmadiyah, the group is declared deviant by MUIS, based on a fatwa issued in 1969.[38]

CONCLUSION: WORRYING TIMES AHEAD?

The Islamic resurgence in the 1980s led to rising conservatism among Muslims in the region. In Singapore this increased conservatism has resulted in greater conservatism, and has gradually altered how the Malay-Muslim community observes its faith and the way it engages with a multireligious, secular and modern environment. This can be seen in the way the community dresses, its relationship with and private perceptions of other communities, its dietary patterns, as well as the values it prioritizes.

There is reason for concern over the Malay-Muslim community's ability to integrate into broader society. The examples above demonstrate that the impulse to express their religious beliefs remain strong and may lead to further differentiation in terms of consumption patterns, identity markers, moral systems, and ideals from the rest of society. The underlying issue in these examples is the deep-rooted belief that Islam and Islamic living are fundamentally incompatible with the modern world and all its trappings, which includes a secular government. As such, this secular government has to be tolerated and, at times, resisted, leading to occasional attempts from individuals within the Malay-Muslim community who take it upon themselves to manifest and actualize a more Islamic, more morally and theologically acceptable way of living which, more often than not, is at odds with contemporary realities. Nevertheless, there are Singaporean Malay-Muslims who see no contradiction between Islamic life and a secular environment. Some of these include Habib Syed Hassan Al-Attas, the imam of Ba'alwie Mosque. As an active member of the Inter-Religious Organization (IRO), he enjoys significant standing in the community. Syed Hassan works tirelessly for solutions to the controversies such as those above. For instance, in the case of Imam Nalla, he hosted breakfast for the imam and the Home Affairs Minister to soothe tensions. During the fasting month in 2017, Syed Hassan organized a dialogue between the local Sunnis and Shias in order to bridge the gap between followers of the two sects.

Syed Hassan is candid with his views on the Malay-Muslim community in Singapore. He worries that the community is becoming more extreme in its beliefs partly because it is importing religious and theological ideas from the Middle East. Concerned about religious teachers in Singapore who have been trained in Middle Eastern universities, he opined, "If they cannot answer them [theological queries], they [Singaporean religious teachers] will ask their mentors and teachers [from the Middle East]. And many, though not all their teachers, will interpret according to the situation in their country."[39] Besides Syed Hassan, Malay-Muslim academics and lawyers have also been articulating alternative discourses in the public domain to challenge exclusivist tendencies. For example, the Department of Malay Studies at the National University of Singapore (NUS) offers modules that expose students to progressive voices in other parts of the Muslim world.

Some of the modules touch on legal reforms and introduce them to the writings of progressive Muslim intellectuals and thinkers in the region. Students are also exposed to the impact of *fatwas* (religious rulings) on the community's quest for modernization.[40] Since its founding in 1968 by sociologist Professor Syed Hussein Alatas, the department has been countering dogmatic ideas, and equipped students with critical views on traditionalist and conservative discourses.

MUIS has responded positively to these alternative discourses. While most of its religious teachers are trained in traditional Islamic sciences at local madrasahs and Al-Azhar University in Egypt, MUIS is open to inviting progressive speakers from the West. These include Professor Ebrahim Moosa and Professor Khaled Abou Fadl, academics who have been championing a contextual approach to reading the Quran and traditions of the Prophet. Professor Quraish Shihab, a progressive Quran exegete from Indonesia, has also been invited to speak to religious teachers on reading the Quran with an emphasis on its values rather than its form.

What matters at the end of the day is how Singaporean Malay-Muslims, and indeed Singaporeans of other faiths, remain firmly rooted in the real world. This requires repeated calls for the community to face up to the challenges of globalization; and not to envisage a triumphant theological return to the glorious days of the Prophet Muhammad fourteen centuries ago. It is the duty of the state and community leaders to ensure that the progressive voices in the Malay-Muslim community remain strong and influential.

Notes

1. Mr Lee's views on the Malay/Muslim community did not represent the views of the government, and he was speaking in his personal capacity.
2. Azhar Ibrahim, *Contemporary Islamic Discourse in the Malay-Indonesian World: Critical Perspectives* (Petaling Jaya: Strategic Information and Research Development Centre, 2014), pp. 35–36.
3. MUIS is the Islamic Religious Council of Singapore. It is a statutory board that is partly funded by the government and supported by the community. It is a religious bureaucracy that oversees the administration of Islam in Singapore.
4. Syed Farid Alatas, "Against the Grain: Extremism, Terrorism and What We Must Do", *The Edge Malaysia Weekly*, 25–31 July 2016, http://www.theedgemarkets.com/article/against-grain-extremism-terrorism-and-what-we-must-do
5. Martin van Bruinessen, "What Happened to the Smiling Face of Indonesian Islam? Muslim Intellectualism and the Conservative Turn in Post-Suharto Indonesia", *RSIS Working Paper*, No. 222 (Singapore: S. Rajaratnam School of International Studies, 2011).

6. Chandra Muzaffar, *Islamic Resurgence in Malaysia* (Petaling Jaya: Fajar Bakti, 1987), p. 2.

7. Ibid.

8. Shaharuddin Maaruf, "Religion and Utopian Thinking Among the Muslims in Southeast Asia", in *Local and Global Social Transformation in Southeast Asia*, edited by Riaz Hassan (Kuala Lumpur: Dewan Bahasa dan Pustaka, 2005), pp. 315–31.

9. Azhar Ibrahim, *Contemporary Islamic Discourses in the Malay-Indonesian World*, pp. 91–94.

10. See Hussin Mutalib, *Singapore Malays: Being Ethnic Minority and Muslims in a Global City-State* (London and New York: Routledge, 2012).

11. Noor Aisha Abdul Rahman, "Shariah Revivalism in Singapore", in *Islam in Southeast Asia: Negotiating Modernity*, edited by Norshahril Saat (Singapore: ISEAS – Yusof Ishak Institute, 2018), pp. 196–203.

12. Lily Zubaidah Rahim, *The Singapore Malay Dilemma: The Political and Educational Marginality of the Malay Community* (Kuala Lumpur: Oxford University Press, 1998), pp. 82–109.

13. Cited in Norshahril Saat, "National Day Rallies: Tracing the Development of the Malay Community (1990–2015)", in *Majulah! 50 Years of Malay/Muslim Community in Singapore*, edited by Zainul Abidin Rasheed and Norshahril Saat (Singapore: World Scientific Press, 2016), p. 72.

14. Hussin Mutalib, *Singapore Malays*, pp. 63–77.

15. Among the players that engaged in the debates besides the Malay MPs and MUIS include Majlis Pusat, AMP, Pergas and Perdaus. See "Schooling for All 'Threaten' Madrasahs", *Straits Times*, 1 April 2000; Ahmad Osman, "Accept Govt's Word on Madrasah", *Straits Times*, 9 April 2000; Liang Hwee Ting, "Wanted—Pledge on Madrasahs", *Straits Times*, 15 April 2000; Ahmad Osman, "Let Islamic Schools Go National", *Straits Times*, 29 April 2000.

16. Lydia Lim, "Devout Muslims, Loyal Singaporeans", *Straits Times*, 2 March 2004.

17. Jaime Koh, "Tudung", http://eresources.nlb.gov.sg/infopedia/articles/SIP_2013-09-30_123324.html (Singapore Infomedia).

18. Amir Hussain, "Govt's Stance on Tudung Issue Evolving, Says PM Lee", *Today*, 24 January 2014, https://www.todayonline.com/singapore/govts-stance-tudung-issue-evolving-says-pm-lee.

19. Irene Ng, "Integrate or Separate—Malay's Pick", *Straits Times*, 4 March 2001.

20. Susan Long, "S'pore at Risk if Races Assert Separate Identities", *Straits Times*, 3 February 2002.

21. Halal means permissible in Islam. *Makan* is a Malay word for eat.

22. Susan Long, "S'pore at Risk if Races Assert Separate Identities".

23. See "Singapore Muslim Groups Oppose Violent Response to Cartoons", *Dow Jones International News*, 9 February 2006.

24. MUIS, *Risalah for Building a Community of Excellence* (Singapore: Majlis Ugama Islam Singapura, 2006), https://www.muis.gov.sg/-/media/Files/OOM/Resources/Risalah-eng-lr.pdf

25. Quotes from the book in Mafoot Simon's article, who reviewed the book. See Mafoot Simon, "Soul-Searching Continues for Muslims in S'pore", *Straits Times*, 2 October 2004.

26. Valerie Chew, "Jemaah Islamiyah's Bomb Plot", http://eresources.nlb.gov.sg/infopedia/articles/SIP_1411_2009-01-20.html (Singapore Infomedia).

27. Shea Driscoll, "27 Radicalised Bangladeshis Arrested Under ISA: What You Need to Know in 8 Points", *Straits Times*, 20 January 2016.

28. Kelly Ng, "8 Bangladeshis Who Plotted Terror Detained", *Today*, 3 May 2016.

29. "ISA Arrest: How Singaporean Zulfikar Mohamad Shariff Spread Radical Ideology on Facebook", *Straits Times*, 29 July 2016.

30. Danson Cheong, "Radicalised Female Infant Care Assistant from PCF Sparkletots Detained Under ISA for Pro-ISIS Activities", *Straits Times*, 12 June 2017.

31. Nur Asyikin Mohamad Salleh, "Mosques Told Not to Get Caught in LGBT Crossfire", *Straits Times*, 21 June 2014.

32. Ibid.

33. Laura Elizabeth Philomin, "MUIS Urges Mosques Not to Take Confrontational Stand on LGBT Lifestyles", *Today*, 21 June 2014.

34. Toh Yong Chuan, "Shanmugam Appreciates Imam's Sincere Apology", *Straits Times*, 6 April 2017.

35. Iginio Gagliardone et al., *Countering Online Hate Speech*, UNESCO Series on Internet Freedom 2015, p. 10, http://unesdoc.unesco.org/images/0023/002332/233231e.pdf

36. Shafie Halim, "MUIS Should Debunk Sunni-Shia fallacies", *Today*, 26 June 2017.

37. Dr Yaacob Ibrahim stepped down as Minister on 1 May 2018.

38. https://www.muis.gov.sg/-/media/Files/OOM/Fatwa/Ahmadiyah-Malay.pdf

39. Zainul Abidin Rasheed and Norshahril Saat, "Moderate Islam in Singapore: In Conversation with Habib Syed Hassan Al-Attas", in *Majulah! 50 years of Malay/ Muslim Community in Singapore*, pp. 239–42.

40. Noor Aisha Abdul Rahman, "Muslim Personal Law Within the Singapore Legal System: History, Prospects and Challenges", *Journal of Muslim Minority Affairs* 29, no. 1 (2009): 109–26.

Part II

NATIONAL AND ETHNIC COMMUNITIES

5

"New" Chinese Immigrants in Singapore
Localization, Transnational Ties and Integration

Elaine Lynn-Ee Ho and Fang Yu Foo

Introduction

In September 2015 the China Cultural Centre (CCC) was established in Singapore by the Chinese Ministry of Culture in China, representing one of at least fifty such global centres envisioned by 2020. According to a news report in Singapore, such centres are meant to "promote [China's] culture and further bolster its soft power abroad".[1] Separately, the planned opening of the Singapore Chinese Cultural Centre (SCC) was also underway. Helmed by the Singapore Federation of Chinese Clan Associations, the SCC would showcase "Singaporean-Chinese" culture. When asked about the potential overlap between the CCC and SCC, the chief executive of SCC replied, "There is no duplication because we will be promoting our uniquely Singapore Chinese culture while theirs will be all about those from the mainland."[2]

When the SCC was opened in May 2017, Singapore Prime Minister Lee Hsien Loong noted that the "Chineseness" in Singapore is distinct from those of the Chinese populations in Mainland China, Hong Kong, Indonesia, Malaysia and Taiwan. He highlighted three traits distinguishing Singapore's variant of Chineseness: "the inculcation of positive traditional values, the embrace of multiculturalism, and bilingualism".[3] While it is arguable whether those traits are distinctly Singaporean, what emerges from the above exchange are the contested ways in which Chinese identity is represented and experienced in Singapore among co-ethnics from different nationality backgrounds.

Since the 1990s, the Singaporean state has used managed migration to meet skills shortages and boost declining fertility rates. China serves as a key source country of new immigration to Singapore. New cohorts of Mainland Chinese immigrants (henceforth PRC immigrants) have converged in Singapore in response to demands for investor, skilled and unskilled migrants. China's rise as a global power presents new business opportunities for Singapore, but also renewed anxieties towards immigrant integration. The targets of Singapore's integration project today are the new Chinese migrants who left China after 1979 (i.e., 新移民 *xinyimin*). Since they share the same ethnicity as the majority Chinese population in Singapore, policymakers had thought such co-ethnics would integrate easily. However, the Singaporean-Chinese invoke a "localized" Singaporean identity, using their regional affiliations in the ancestral land—predominantly the coastal provinces of China—to differentiate themselves from the more recent PRC immigrants who come from a wider range of Chinese provinces. Even if the recent immigrants have the same regional roots as the Singaporean-Chinese, the former's later period of migration to Singaporeans is framed as another indicator that further sets them apart from the latter.

This chapter examines how similarity amongst co-ethnics from different nationality backgrounds generates tensions over national identity and belonging, thus calling into question presumed expectations of integration. The chapter also examines the contested aspects of integration given the countervailing pressures of localization and transnationalism, and probes what integration means for a multicultural society like Singapore. The chapter is informed by twenty-eight interviews that were conducted with twenty PRC immigrants in Singapore from 2014 to 2015; the authors also conducted follow-up interviews with a selection of interviewees. The interviewees comprised twelve males and eight female immigrants aged 35 to 65 years old. The interviewees had immigrated through the employment pass scheme or as entrepreneurs and investors, but subsequently transitioned to become Singaporean permanent residents or citizens by the time of the interviews. They were recruited through personal contacts and through snowballing contacts. Both authors are Singaporean-Chinese who were born and bred in Singapore, but have forged strong personal or professional networks in Mainland China. The interviews were conducted in Mandarin and lasted for forty-five minutes to two hours. The first author has also conducted research on Chinese migration since 2008, including studying the re-migration of diasporic descendants, such as the Singaporean-Chinese, to the ancestral land. This wider knowledge base on Chinese migration informs the analysis of the co-ethnic tensions discussed in this chapter. All respondent names used in this chapter are pseudonyms.

Section 2 provides an overview of how multiculturalism manifests as policy in Singapore and the way that past and present Chinese migration is contextualized within it. Section 3 then examines the tension between expectations of localization and the reality of sustained transnational ties experienced by PRC immigrants in Singapore. Sections 4 and 5 focus on challenges to integration given widely held perceptions that Singapore is a "Chinese" nation (due to its population composition) as compared to the multicultural ethos that the Singaporean state and society maintains. The chapter concludes by reflecting on the implications of these research findings for Singapore.

CHINESE MIGRATION IN MULTICULTURAL SINGAPORE

Singapore is a multicultural society but a majority of the population are of Chinese ethnicity, comprising 74.3 per cent of the population.[4] In popular parlance, those known as "local Singaporean-Chinese" (or Chinese-Singaporean) were born in Singapore and are descendants of earlier waves of Chinese immigrants who arrived during the nineteenth and early twentieth centuries. The "pioneer immigrants" were mainly young and poorly educated male peasants from five major dialect groups (Cantonese, Hokkien, Hakka, Hainanese and Teochew) and they came from provinces in coastal China such as Guangdong, Fujian and Hainan Island.

Multiculturalism (or multiracialism as it is known officially) is considered one of the founding tenets in Singapore's nation-building and statehood. In 1965 the newly independent government saw that maintaining racial harmony was essential for Singapore's social stability and for the new city-state to thrive economically. The government had inherited a plural mix of immigrant populations (primarily from China and India) that lived alongside the indigenous Malay and mixed-race Eurasians. To formalize the government's belief in racial equality, policies on constitutional recognition for the main racial groups, an ethnic quota in public housing allocation and bilingual education were enforced. But such policies categorize complex and fluid ethnic identifications into overarching racial groupings. The classification of ethnic groups in Singapore is known in popular parlance as the "CMIO" model, referring to the Chinese, Malay, Indian and Others respectively.

Contemporary immigration has introduced greater complexity to the ethnic plurality of Singapore in two ways. First, the spectrum of cultural diversity represented in Singapore today is greater than those captured in the rigid CMIO model. Such cultural difference cuts across different types of ethnic groups, nationalities, socio-economic profiles, and religion. If the variety of ethnic groups represented are all compressed within the "Others" category, it could make that classification too general to be meaningful for policymaking purposes. To be effective, integration policies have to be tailored to the changing demographics of the population, including recognizing the "superdiversity" contained within Singapore.[5]

Second, there are new cohorts of immigrants that share the same ethnicity (i.e., co-ethnics) as the Chinese or Indian populations who were born and bred in Singapore. Such immigrant co-ethnics are categorized under the same ethnic group as the locally born Singaporean-Chinese or Singaporean-Indians under the CMIO model, but they embody cultural traits that are perceived to be distinct from those who consider Singapore their birthplace. Locally born Singaporeans identify with Singapore as their natal land and associate this with their national identity, thereby conflating birthplace with national belonging. The social divisions arising from co-ethnic differentiation has implications for integration, which assumes that new immigrants would adapt to a model of multiculturalism premised on stable inter- and co-ethnic relations.

Under Singapore's managed migration policy, PRC immigrants enter through a range of visa categories differentiated by their qualifications, past work experience, the type of work they undertake in Singapore, and income levels. The period of migration also matters as the immigration criteria changed over time, requiring higher salary levels in order to qualify for the employment pass (for professionals in skilled occupations) and the right to bring in dependants who would be sponsored by the lead migrant's visa. Dependant passes have become increasingly difficult for migrants on the lower skilled "S" pass to secure. Changes to immigration criteria can impact a migrant's experience and perception of integration, not only individually but also collectively as a cohort (i.e., a group of people who were required to fulfil the immigration criteria of a particular time period in order to migrate to Singapore).[6]

Concerns over integration and social cohesion are related to questions over whether the PRC immigrants who have naturalized or are potential citizens would understand Singapore's political standpoint and maintain its national interest in the event of a disagreement between the smaller city-state and China. China's disputed claim over the Spratly Islands resulted in tension points between Singapore and China during 2016–17 when the former maintained it supported using international law to decide on the competing territorial claims between China, Brunei, Malaysia, the Philippines, and

Vietnam. News reports and commentaries in both Singapore and China debated the implications of China's claims for national sovereignty and the expectations it may have of Singapore as a "co-ethnic" nation, which should support its position on international affairs.[7]

LOCALIZATION AND TRANSNATIONALISM

In the politics of everyday life, contested aspects of Chinese identity are evinced in a variety of ways. At an organizational level, the PRC immigrants have established new associations that are separate from the ones associated with earlier waves of Chinese immigrants (i.e., the pioneer immigrants in Singapore). For example, Montsion[8] has conducted research on the new clan associations established by PRC immigrants in Singapore. These new clan associations are closely associated with emigration from Mainland China after 1979 and affiliated with a diverse range of provinces in Mainland China. The leadership of the new clan associations partner the pioneer Chinese clan associations and other Singaporean organizations or institutions for joint activities, but the former reflects a distinctly mainland Chinese membership base and culture.

Although not all PRC immigrants or Singaporean-Chinese are members of clan associations, the two groups encounter one another in their daily lives in Singapore, such as in the workplace, residential spaces or public space. Such encounters at times deepen a sense of social difference between the two groups of Chinese in Singapore.[9] Yang[10] discusses, for example, the case of a ferocious quarrel between an older Singaporean lady and a younger female migrant from China who were on the same public bus. The vitriol was recorded by a member of the public and uploaded to YouTube, garnering approximately 150,000 views and 450 comments. Even though not all encounters in daily life between the two groups are sensationalized in this way, ordinary and fleeting exchanges can still accentuate the social differences between co-ethnics. The Singaporean-Chinese demarcate their identities from the PRC immigrants by prioritizing what they perceive as an overarching Singaporean identity that expresses national solidarity with ethnic minority groups that have natal ties to Singapore (i.e., Malays, Indians and Eurasians). An example of this was the event, "Cook a Pot of Curry Day", which galvanized Singaporeans islandwide to cook curry, considered Singaporean's "national dish", on the same day, in response to a widely publicized controversy generated when a Mainland Chinese family complained about the smell of curry cooked by their Indian neighbours.[11]

The PRC immigrants themselves are prone to develop endogenous social networks in Singapore. Several of the PRC immigrants interviewed in our study said the nature of their work orientates them towards specializing in their business or cultural knowledge of China. Resultantly, this means they have fewer opportunities to use English and to interact with "local" Singaporeans. Sharing her experience, an interviewee (Heather, female, immigrated in 1997) said "my work mainly targets Chinese clients, which means most of the time I still use Chinese to communicate ... Many friends say that, although I have been to Singapore for so many years, my English language proficiency has not increased." Another interviewee (Zhong, male, immigrated in 1998) observed that many PRC immigrants spend their leisure time with one another. He said, "Many new immigrants go to Chinatown, visit China-style restaurants to make up for their emotional loss [of being away from home]; afterwards they go to the cinema to catch a [Chinese] blockbuster movie then head home to chat with their friends back in China.... how much of these activities have elements of the Singaporean culture?"

Nonetheless, it is important to distinguish between the different cohorts of PRC immigrants found in Singapore, and with it their experiences and perceptions of integration.[12] Almost half of those in the study sample came to Singapore during the 1990s, and the interviewees drew a distinction between the "老新移民 lao xinyimin" (an earlier cohort of PRC immigrants) and the "新新移民 xin xinyimin" (a newer cohort of PRC immigrants, that is, those who came from the mid-2000s onwards). In the quote above, Zhong identified as a 老新移民 lao xinyimin and he was reflecting on the leisure habits of the newer cohorts. The cohort who came to Singapore during an earlier period felt that they had to work harder to integrate both in the workplace and during their leisure time. They explained that this was because there were fewer PRC immigrants living in Singapore at that time which meant they could not socialize only with fellow nationals from China. Moreover, they lived in the public housing estates which was more affordable for their income range and they worked in jobs that required them to interact with local Singaporeans, both of these conditions meant they learned about local mores and sought to become a part of, rather than seek comfort in being separate, from Singaporean society.

Several of the PRC immigrants we interviewed who belong to the newer cohort concurred that the 老新移民 lao xinyimin had worked harder to integrate than the efforts or intentions demonstrated by the newer cohort of PRC immigrants. For example, Rachel (female, immigrated in 2012) said, "Recently I got to know more [老新移民 lao xinyimin]. I think they have lost touch with China … a lot has changed for them in terms of their living environment and their mindset … They know [they have to] expand their social circle [in Singapore] … and as a result it expands their horizon … [Sometimes] they will bring us along. New immigrants like myself may still see Singapore through the eyes of a tourist and not think about these [matters]."

Commenting on the 新新移民 xin xinyimin, one of the 老新移民 lao xinyimin added that the recent cohort tend to identify more strongly with China as a rising economic power which might affect their willingness to integrate in Singapore, whereas the older cohort had left China when it was still a low-income developing country and aspired towards building a new life in Singapore. When asked about their ties to Singapore as compared to China, the 老新移民 lao xinyimin expressed their commitment to remain in Singapore. One of them (Lucas, male, immigrated in 1991) expressed, "I think that [those of] us who have been here for more than twenty years, there is no intention to leave Singapore for other countries. [We] have a stable life and for people who can stay in Singapore for twenty plus years, it means you are doing quite well." The views expressed above trouble popular perceptions that the PRC immigrants do not want to or are unable to integrate. Rather, the discussion highlights the need to distinguish how different cohorts of immigrants experience Singapore and their integration intentions.

Nonetheless, the PRC immigrants who felt they have gradually become incorporated into Singaporean society also recognized that their transnational ties to China would remain regardless. Amongst them, Ma Ning (female, immigrated in 1991) reflected, "If you ask me, deep in my heart I am willing to become a Singaporean. But no matter what passport I am holding, I [was born] a Chinese national [and] it is where my cultural roots lie … I was not born in Singapore nor did I grow up here. Yet what I learned in society, the place that offered all the good things to me, it is Singapore." Another interviewee, Betty (female, immigrated in 2002), expressed similar sentiments and described China as "where your roots lie in your heart [but] Singapore [has] become a second home". Others noted that their children, the second-generation who were born in Singapore, have different attachments from the first-generation migrants. For instance, Lucas (male, immigrated in 1991) reflected on the attitudes of his children who were born and had grown up in Singapore: "My children are the younger generation [and they feel] different. When I ask my children to return to China, they do not like it … They feel that China is very weird because they seldom go to China."

The PRC immigrants we studied understood the importance of integrating but questioned the narrative of what it means to integrate. For example, Zhong (male, immigrated in 1998) said, "I think the new immigrant has to take the initiative to integrate into Singapore. However, it does not mean that integrating into Singapore translates to a loss of self. Integration is understanding how the society functions [but] everyone has his/her own characteristics. You cannot demand the society to be a uniformed one; every individual definitely has his/her own traits." Another interviewee, An Ni (female, immigrated in 2008) shared, "Personally I do not like the term 'new immigrant' (新移民 *xinyimin*). Even for those of us who have been here for twenty plus years, [Singaporeans still] call us 'new immigrants' ... What is considered 'new', where is the boundary drawn? ... I think many instances of integration happen naturally and silently, they are not publicized." As these interview quotations show, cognitive borders that are drawn to demarcate "new immigrants" can have the opposite effect of undermining the spontaneous aspects of integration.

Integrating into Singapore's Heterogeneous Chinese Cultural Fabric

In considering integration, policymakers assume that a stable societal fabric of co-ethnic and interethnic relations exist. This section troubles such perceptions by discussing the heterogeneity contained within co-ethnicity, while the next section will consider the limited interaction that the PRC immigrants have with non-Chinese ethnic groups in Singapore (i.e., on interethnic relations).

The PRC immigrants pointed out that getting to know local Singaporean-Chinese culture presents complications when one considers the heterogeneous Chinese dialect groups contained within this category. Use of Chinese dialects was once discouraged by the Singaporean state which introduced Mandarin as part of the bilingual policy in 1959, making it the common medium of communication amongst Singaporeans of Chinese ethnicity. However, dialects have persisted in vernacular use and there is today a growing movement amongst younger Singaporeans to preserve such languages as part of their cultural heritage. When PRC immigrants first arrived in Singapore, they expected to be able to get by with speaking mainly Mandarin. However they soon realized otherwise. For example, Li Li (female, immigrated in 2010), attended a course at the neighbourhood community centre to get to know "local" Singaporeans.

She found that the majority of her course mates were older Singaporeans who spoke Chinese dialects fluently but struggled with Mandarin; that generation had grown up speaking vernacular dialects rather than learned Mandarin as a taught language in schools. Li Li noted, "I think when they speak Mandarin to me, they are accommodating me and even so it requires effort [on their part]." Acquiring even basic knowledge of the range of Chinese dialects in Singapore (e.g., Hokkien, Cantonese, Teochew and Hakka) can prove challenging to the PRC immigrants. An Ni (female, immigrated in 2008) noted that younger Singaporeans "can use Chinese to communicate [and] they can speak different dialects such as Cantonese, Hokkien, etc.". She added, "When [I am] with a group of [Singaporeans], we can communicate in English but once they switch to dialect there is no way we can still communicate."

The PRC immigrants also shared that there were few opportunities for them to practise and gain confidence in using English if they interacted with Singaporean-Chinese who are conversant in Mandarin. Heather (female, immigrated in 1997) observed that "as long as [the PRC immigrants] are interacting with Singaporean-Chinese, it is unlikely that they will speak to us in English". She continued, "Just like you know I am not good in English, naturally you would not speak to me in English. Furthermore using Chinese, we can still communicate. Over time as long as they see me they would speak Chinese, unless of course they cannot speak the language." Li Li (female, immigrated in 2010) further observed that integration "involves two groups of people: locals and new immigrants" but "there is no push factor for 'locals' to make friends with new immigrants". While the focus of public debate has been on the *unwillingness* or *inability* of the new immigrants to integrate into Singaporean society, equal emphasis must be placed on whether Singaporeans are adapting to an evolving social fabric that comes with demographic change. Integration is a two-way street. As Singapore had developed a national identity through immigration in the past, it is continuing to do so today through the convergence of new ethnic and nationality groups on its shores.

INTEGRATING INTO MULTICULTURAL SINGAPORE

Integration into multicultural Singapore can be meaningful only if it extends to interactions with the non-Chinese ethnic minorities too. However, almost all of the PRC immigrants in the study expressed that they have very limited interactions with such persons (the exception was a person whose job required him to interact with a wide range of "locals"). For example,

Peter (male, immigrated in 2008) explained, "There are many people whom you get to meet, but in terms of forging friendships with the other races … I am very unfamiliar with their cultures, so our interaction is not so in depth [*sic*] to form a friendship." Another PRC immigrant, Betty (female, immigrated in 2002) expressed that "the chances [of meeting other races] are very low". She added, "One look outside, you still see that the Chinese are the majority and now there are a lot of PRC immigrants … after all the country has a bilingual environment and this is attractive to the immigrants since they still get to speak Chinese." The ethnic minorities whom they met were described as neighbours whom they interacted with only superficially or, as Peter described, the "security officers and [low-skilled] workers who are Malays and Indians".

The views presented above pose two troubling concerns: first, the limited exposure that the PRC immigrants have with non-Chinese Singaporeans; and second, their perception that the ethnic minorities are primarily from a lower socio-economic stratum than them. Unlike locally born Singaporeans from different ethnic backgrounds who went to the same schools or, for the men, experienced national service together, the PRC immigrants who arrive at a later life-stage have few such opportunities to develop a range of social interactions with Singapore's ethnic minorities in a variety of spatial settings.

A survey of Singapore Citizens and Singapore Permanent Residents (n=2000) conducted by the Institute of Policy Studies (IPS) in 2016 found that most respondents signalled they interacted with those of other races in a variety of settings. However, a greater proportion of respondents from ethnic minority backgrounds expressed that being from the Chinese majority race is an advantage in Singapore (i.e., 63 per cent of Malay, 62 per cent of Indian and 72 per cent of Others). The same study found that new immigrants were often judged to be more racist than Singaporeans. Those from China were viewed to be at least "mildly racist" by 65 per cent of all respondents (i.e., Chinese, Malays and Indians). More specifically, 40 per cent of Malays and 42 per cent of Indian respondents found the new immigrants from China to be "very racist/moderately racist"; comparatively, 23 per cent of Malays and 24 per cent of Indian respondents expressed the same of the Singaporean-Chinese.[13]

The IPS survey finding on how Malay and Indian ethnic minority groups strongly perceive that PRC immigrants are racist towards them, alongside the qualitative findings presented in this chapter of how the PRC immigrants themselves expressed having limited interactions with the ethnic minorities in Singapore, signal the likelihood of deepening cultural segmentation in society. More research on the qualitative views of the ethnic minorities towards new immigration remains to be done in order to fully comprehend the implications of perceived racism amongst Singapore's ethnic minorities and new immigrants, and ways of bridging cultural divisions. Such bridging needs to take place on two levels: first, towards perceptions that belonging to the majority Chinese race is an advantage in Singapore society, and second, towards perceptions that the PRC immigrants are more racist towards them than the Singaporean-Chinese.

For now, it is only possible to postulate the outcomes of such deepening cultural segmentation on the relations between ethnic minorities and the PRC immigrants. One possibility is it could deepen the social alienation amongst non-Chinese Singaporeans who feel disconnected from the Mainland Chinese cultural identity that is embodied by the PRC immigrants in Singapore. The distinctive cultural identity of the PRC immigrants has become increasingly manifest in the urban landscape, such as the manifold restaurants featuring Mainland Chinese regional cuisine in Geylang or Chinatown, as well as within food courts and coffeeshops.[14] Another possibility is new convivial relations may be forged within neighbourhoods and the common spaces in which Singaporeans and the new immigrants converge. Existing ethnographic research[15] has focused attention on the microinteractions between Singaporeans from different walks of life, and with new immigrants, pointing out not merely aspects of cultural segmentation, but more importantly the windows of opportunity in which such barriers can be demolished in fleeting or sustained ways.

LOOKING AHEAD

The challenges to integration are real and should not be downplayed. Two further insights can be derived from the examples of countries that are similarly facing integration challenges to do with new immigration. Migration research in countries such as Australia, Canada, the United Kingdom and the United States has shown that the first generation typically finds it more difficult to integrate since their language skills, cultural norms and mindsets are deeply intertwined with their countries of origin. It is the second and future generations that will develop more resilient ties with their parents'"host country", which has in turn become the birthplace of the next generations. Singapore's experience with earlier waves of immigration, including from China, has proven the case. Integration takes time and should be regarded as an aspiration to work towards, rather than an outcome desired in the here and now.

That is not to say that present-day integration policies are in vain. Integration policies instil awareness that Singapore has been changing and will continue to change through immigration, but the policy approaches may be modulated in the directions below. First, policies can remind Singaporeans that the onus of integration does not lie solely on the shoulders of the new immigrants, but it is also the responsibility of Singaporeans to simultaneously adapt to a changing Singapore. In this regard, schools, workplace and housing are key crucibles for fostering meaningful interactions between different ethnic and nationality groups in Singapore. Second, inasmuch as a sense of national identity is important to Singapore, integration approaches also need to enable Singaporeans to recognize that identity formations are always under negotiation and in-the-making, rather than a finished product. Such an approach towards integration might gradually lend to a less defensive "us versus them" posture, and one that is more open towards the manifold reasons and social ties that bring Singaporeans, new Singaporeans and other types of immigrants together in the same space, at the same time.

Third, while Singaporeans tend to see "immigrants" as a homogeneous category differentiated only by the axes of ethnicity, religion or nationality, as this chapter has shown, even within these subcategories there exist significant diversity. The heterogeneity of the Chinese or Indian new immigrant populations mean that, on one level, policymakers must identify a variety of ways to reach out to those different groups and bridge the differences they have with the Singapore-born local population. On another level, Singaporeans must learn to disassociate negative experiences with certain immigrants from the possibility of positive experiences that can be gained with other types of immigrants, and remain willing to reach out to new immigrants in the different spaces where they co-mingle, such as in schools, workplaces, the communal spaces of housing estates and more.

Fourth, some Singaporeans retain the view that the new immigrants treat Singapore as a stopover or a stepping stone to get to other more attractive living or work destinations. Not all new immigrants will remain in Singapore for the long haul, but this can be turned into an advantage for globalizing Singapore. Other nations consider remigration an opportunity to develop an "affinity diaspora". Affinity refers to connections borne out of biographical ties, such as through residency in a country over a period of time, which allows for cultivating emotional attachments to the place and people there.[16] Decentring perceived qualities of blood relations, ancestry and birth place can lead to greater appreciation for our affinity with the immigrants living amongst us, fostering social respect and inclusion.

Immigrants who have remigrated can be considered a potential resource pool for Singapore in the longer term, by paving economic opportunities for Singapore abroad and bridging cultural differences.

Lastly, to identify recommendations for how integration policies can be effective for a heterogeneous immigrant population, researchers and the public need more data on the changing demographic characteristics of Singapore. Currently, information on the number of immigrants by ethnicity, nationality, visa (indicative of socio-economic status), religion or residency concentration is not publicly available whereas such data for other major immigrant receiving countries can be obtained either through government websites accessible to members of the public or released to academic researchers who request for such information to inform policies and wider public discussion. Alongside this, more qualitative research on the views and experiences of both ethnic minorities and the new immigrant groups in Singapore needs to be done in order to more fully comprehend the nuances of how immigration is changing multicultural Singapore. Integration can be more successful only if it is approached as collaborative project undertaken by the government and partners in society.

Notes

1. Leong Weng Kam, "Completed China Cultural Centre to Boost Arts Exchange", *Straits Times*, 1 September 2015.
2. Ibid.
3. Mayo Martin, "New Arts Centre Will Promote Chinese Culture That Is Singaporean-Centric: PM Lee", *Channel NewsAsia*, 19 May 2017, https://www.channelnewsasia.com/news/lifestyle/new-arts-centre-will-promote-chinese-culture-that-is-singaporean-8864144 (accessed 23 April 2018).
4. Department of Statistics Singapore, *Population Trends 2017*, p. 5, https://www.singstat.gov.sg/-/media/files/publications/population/population2017.pdf (accessed 16 April 2018).
5. Superdiversity refers to deepening diversification within societies, such as along the axes of ethnicity, socio-economic status and more; Fran Meissner, "Mainstreaming and Superdiversity: Beyond More Integration", in *Mainstreaming Integration Governance: New Trends in Migrant Integration Policies in Europe*, edited by Peter Scholten and Ilona van Breugel (Cham: Palgrave Macmillan, 2018), pp. 215–33.
6. Elaine Lynn-Ee Ho and Fang Yu Foo, "Debating Integration in Singapore, Deepening the Variegations of the Chinese Diaspora", in *Contemporary Chinese Diasporas*, edited by Min Zhou (Singapore: Palgrave Macmillan, 2017), pp. 105–25.
7. Chong Zi Liang, "National Day Rally 2016: Singapore Must Stand by Its Principles on South China Sea", *Straits Times*, 22 August 2016, https://www.straitstimes.com/politics/spore-must-stand-by-its-principles-on-south-china-sea (accessed 24 April

2018); Zhu Feng, "China's Mindset on the South China Sea Needs to Withstand the 'Singapore Test'" [中國的南中國海心態需經得起"新加坡考驗" *Zhongguo de nanzhongguohai xintai xu jingdeqi 'xinjiapo kaoyan'*] *Lianhe Zaobao*, 5 May 2016, https://www.zaobao.com.sg/forum/views/world/story20161005-674287 (accessed 24 April 2018).

8. Jean Michel Montsion, "Chinese Ethnicities in Neoliberal Singapore? State Designs and Dialect(ical) Struggles of Community Associations", *Ethnic and Racial Studies* 37, no. 9 (2014): 1486–504.

9. Elaine Lynn-Ee Ho, *Citizens in Motion: Emigration, Immigration and Re-Migration Across China's Borders* (Stanford, CA: Stanford University Press, 2019).

10. Peidong Yang, "Psychoanalyzing Fleeting Emotive Migrant Encounters: A Case from Singapore", *Emotion, Space and Society* 31 (2019): 133–39.

11. Ho, *Citizens in Motion*.

12. The cultural distinctions that exist between Chinese co-ethnics have been studied in other country contexts, such as Canada, Philippines and Myanmar; respectively Miu Chung Yan, Karen Lok Yi Wong and Daniel Lai, "Subethnic Interpersonal Dynamic in Diasporic Community: A Study on Chinese Immigrants in Vancouver", *Asian Ethnicity* 20, no. 4 (2019): 451–68; Teresita Ang, "Influx of New Chinese Immigrants to the Philippines: Problems and Challenges", in *Beyond Chinatown: New Chinese Migration and the Global Expansion of China*, edited by Metta Thuno (Copenhagen: NIAS Press, 2007), pp. 137–65; Elaine Lynn-Ee Ho and Lynette J. Chua, "Law and 'Race' in the Citizenship Spaces of Myanmar: Spatial Strategies and the Political Subjectivity of the Burmese Chinese", *Ethnic and Racial Studies* 39 (2016): 896–916.

13. Mathew Mathews, "Channel NewsAsia-Institute of Policy Studies (CNA-IPS) Survey on Race Relations", 19 August 2016, https://lkyspp.nus.edu.sg/docs/default-source/ips/CNA-IPS-survey-on-race-relations_190816.pdf (accessed 21 May 2018).

14. Sylvia Ang, "The 'New Chinatown': The Racialization of Newly Arrived Chinese Migrants in Singapore", *Journal of Ethnic and Migration Studies* 44, no. 7 (2018): 1177–94.

15. See, for example, Lai Ah Eng, "The Kopitiam in Singapore: An Evolving Story about Migration and Cultural Diversity", *Asia Research Institute Working Paper*, No. 132 (Singapore: Asia Research Institute, 2010) on *kopitiams*; Amanda Wise and Selvaraj Velayutham, "Conviviality in Everyday Multiculturalism: Some Brief Comparisons between Singapore and Sydney", *European Journal of Cultural Studies* 17, no. 4 (2014): 406–30 on the neighbourhood of Taman Jurong.

16. Elaine Lynn-Ee Ho, "Cosmopolitanism Disposition: Cultivating Affinity Ties", in *Living with Myths in Singapore*, edited by Loh Kah Seng, Thum Ping Tjin, and Jack Meng-Tat Chia (Singapore: Ethos Books, 2017), pp. 191–98.

6

Singapore Malays
State-Community Relations, Complexities and Possibilities

Walid Jumblatt Abdullah

Introduction

"Every citizen, Chinese, Malay, Indian or some other race, should know that someone of his community can become President, and in fact from time to time, does become President," asserted Prime Minister (PM) Lee Hsien Loong in explaining the People's Action Party (PAP) government's decision to reserve the 2017 Presidential Elections (PE) for Malay candidates.[1] The decision, unsurprisingly, garnered a mixed reception from Singaporeans. While some were pleased with the prospect of the first Malay president in more than forty-six years, others lamented the move to be, at best, unwise, and, at worst, politically motivated. After all, the previous PE in 2011 was a hard-fought four-way contest with the PAP-preferred candidate, Dr Tony Tan, former Deputy Prime Minister, winning just 35.2 per cent of the votes, with his closest challenger Dr Tan Cheng Bock, a former PAP member of parliament (MP), attaining 34.9 per cent of the vote share. There was speculation in some quarters that the decision to reserve the 2017 PE for Malay candidates was to, in fact, prevent Dr Tan Cheng Bock, who had become a vocal critic of the party he had since left, from putting himself up as candidate again and to pave the way for a PAP-preferred candidate.[2] Eventually, former PAP stalwart and Speaker of Parliament, Halimah Yacob, became President after the two other Malay candidates who had expressed interest in contesting were deemed to be ineligible by the Elections Department.[3] To be fair, not all reservations over the 2017 PE were cynical grumblings. Some expressed the genuine concern that making exceptions for a particular ethnic group for an office as important as the

Presidency was a contradiction of the principle of meritocracy that many Singaporeans hold sacrosanct. The government, while acknowledging that many held this concern, disagreed that meritocracy had been ignored. Then Minister-in-Charge of Muslim Affairs, Dr Yaacob Ibrahim, noted that the move was opposed by some Singaporeans who felt that it was "against the strain of meritocracy as they believe in", yet in the same speech, averred that Singaporeans "do not want, and cannot accept, tokenism".[4]

The 2017 reserved PE is an important episode for the Malay community as it encapsulates much of the long-held concerns of Singaporean Malays living in a Chinese majority nation. From ideological tensions between the principle of meritocracy and the need for minority representation in the highest office of the land; trust in the Malay political leadership; and the position of the Malays vis-à-vis the government, these issues go to the heart of Malay integration into the wider Singapore community. This chapter is not about the rights and wrongs of the reserved PE per se; but rather, it uses the episode as a springboard to illustrate the issues of integration that the Malay community faces. I postulate the following arguments in this chapter. Firstly, the Malay community's issues with regard to integration are different from those of the other main ethnic minority group, namely, the Indians; and indeed, are taken to be dissimilar by the PAP government. Secondly, certain state policies that directly impact the Malay community, however well intentioned, could inadvertently result in a greater detachment between the state and the Malays on one hand, and the Malays and the other ethnic communities on the other. Finally, I propose the following to tackle the matter. Firstly, contrary to what many local academics have argued, I contend that the existing racial classifications—Chinese, Malay, Indian and Others (CMIO)—used by the state must be retained in order to allay anxieties that Malays may have about their minority position in Singapore. Secondly, it is imperative that members of the Malay political leadership—both from the PAP and opposition parties—are given more space to discuss and champion issues that are important to the community, in order to instil and strengthen trust between the Malay community and the state.

THE "MALAY PROBLEM": "INTEGRATION" AND BEYOND

The so-called "Malay problem" has been discussed by both academics and political elites alike since Singapore's independence in 1965. For one, the Malay community is behind the other ethnic communities by way of education and income. In 2010, the proportion of Malays who had attained university education was 5.1 per cent; compared to 22.6 per cent and 35 per cent for the Chinese and Indians, respectively.[5] The percentage of households with income levels of more than $10,000 was at 23.1 per cent for the Chinese, 22.6 per cent for the Indians, and 7.2 per cent for the Malays.[6] While the Malay community has made noticeable improvements over the years, it remains behind the other ethnic groups. This is in addition to other social challenges which are said to disproportionately afflict Malays such as drug consumption, high divorce rates, and teenage delinquency. Lily Zubaidah Rahim argues that the government's responsibility for the socio-economic problems of the community should be discussed, asserting that structural factors and the perpetuation the cultural deficit hypothesis—where Malays are depicted and believed to be lazy or a people who shun worldly achievements due to culture and religion—have impeded the community's progress. For her, the cultural deficit hypothesis hurts Malays in two ways. First, access to important positions may be restricted for Malays if PAP leaders, and the Singapore community in general, have negative perceptions about Malays. If Malays are deemed to be less hardworking and less competitive than other ethnic groups, they are less likely to be entrusted with important positions. Second, Malays themselves may internalize these perceptions, and they may eventually become self-fulfilling prophecies.[7] On the other hand, others have argued that the community must shoulder a portion of the blame for its own shortcomings.[8] The situation is made more complicated by the fact that Singapore is a Chinese-majority country in a Malay-Muslim-majority region, or as Huxley describes it, a "Chinese nut in a Malay nutcracker",[9] and that Malays are constitutionally recognized as indigenous to Singapore such that it is the "responsibility of the Government to protect, safeguard, support, foster, and promote their political, educational, religious, economic, social and cultural interests and the Malay language".[10] These factors not only mean that the government has to carefully navigate Malay issues because of the complex politics which arise from their minority status in the country, but also consider the majority status of the community in the region, as well as their indigenous status.

A note on integration is due. It has been maintained by many quarters, especially state elites, that Malays—who are almost always Muslims, such that the terms "Malay" and "Muslim" are often conflated in Singapore[11]— have to do more to integrate with other ethnic communities. In the past, PAP leaders have justified the lack of access of Malays to senior positions in the military with the assertion that, in case of war with a Malay-Muslim neighbour, Singapore Malays could have divided loyalties. Founding Prime Minister Lee Kuan Yew himself observed that it would be "tricky business for the SAF [Singapore Armed Forces] to put a Malay officer who was very religious and had family ties in Malaysia, in charge of a machine-gun unit."[12] Later in 2010, Lee would cause disquiet amongst the Malay community when he claimed that it was difficult to integrate Malay-Muslims due to the latter's increasing adherence to what he perceived to be strict Islamic principles and norms.[13] In recent years, the rise in Muslim extremism has led to repeated calls by the PAP government for Malay Singaporeans to "stand alongside" the state in efforts to counter the menace of terrorism which, in turn, obliges Malay-Muslims to continually reassert their loyalty and moderation.[14] However, although the PAP government continues to exhort Malay Singaporeans to make the effort to integrate with the rest of Singaporeans, there are clear suggestions of obstacles to integration. For example, local surveys indicate that Malay Singaporeans perceive themselves to be at the receiving end of racial discrimination the most, vis-à-vis other races.[15] This is despite observations elsewhere that the Malay community is more likely to vote for the ruling party, and surveys which indicate that Malays are more "committed" to Singapore than other ethnic groups.[16] There are strong suggestions that the Malay community rallied behind the PAP in the 2015 General Elections when the ruling party won 69.8 per cent of the popular vote.[17]

All this suggests that "integration" is a complex term which means different things to different stakeholders. It is thus salient to clearly delineate what it means. At times it is used so loosely that it could even denote assimilation.[18] In this chapter, I argue that for the term "integration" to have any utility in the Singapore context, it must be understood as how one community relates to the others. To be integrated does not entail giving up one's uniqueness or character in favour of a broader, more encompassing national identity. Neither would it mean that one has to surrender one's personal or religious beliefs or values to dovetail into a multicultural society. Rather, it would mean that each community is given the private and physical space to practise its faith and culture, while at the same time, recognizing other communities' right to such spaces. This is important especially for the Malay community for whom race and religion matter more in defining their identity than the other ethnic communities.[19] To be integrated would neither, for instance, require a Malay Singaporean to stop believing in Islam, nor necessitate that Malays accept all religions to be true; rather, just as Malays believe Islam to be true, they should be comfortable with others believing that their own faiths are the true paths to God. Furthermore, to be integrated socially would mean that Malays are treated as equal citizens by their fellow Singaporeans. It would thus be a challenge to achieve integration if Malay Singaporeans are persistently portrayed and perceived as the "problematic" community always in need of state assistance or token representation. This does not mean that the problems currently facing the Malay community should be swept under the carpet or shunned in the pursuit of political correctness. Indeed, integration would demand that each community is confident enough to honestly identify its challenges, and work with others for solutions.[20] These solutions require forthright discussions that interrogate structural and cultural factors such as the immutability of meritocracy as the bedrock of Singapore society. Such discussions must be conducted in good faith and take place amongst mature citizens who see each other as equals. In the meantime, the government adopts an ultra-cautious approach toward managing race and religion. This point will be further developed later.

As noted above, the Malay community is perceived differently from the other main minority group, the Indians. Generally speaking, not only are Malays less well-off than Indians in socio-economic terms, the spectre of a Muslim-majority region and the threat of Muslim extremism add different political and existential challenges for the community. The state's different treatment of the Malay community, vis-à-vis the Indian minority, is evident in the provision of a cabinet position for a "Minister-in-Charge of Muslim Affairs" as well as an Islamic Religious Council of Singapore (MUIS) under the direct purview of the state.[21] Meanwhile community leaders are often called for a closed-door dialogue when "sensitive" issues emerge (and details of such meetings are often not revealed to the public);[22] every National Day Rally speech will include an address in Malay by the sitting Prime Minister; special concessions are made for the Malays in terms of education;[23] *inter alia*. Yet, other differences exist in the state's treatment of the two communities. Ethnic Indian ministers have helmed the more prestigious and important ministries such as Finance, Home Affairs and Foreign Affairs whereas ethnic Malay ministers are given seemingly lower key positions;[24] there have only been five Malay ministers since independence whereas there are five ministers of Indian descent in the current cabinet;[25] Indians are not met with the same apprehension when it comes to occupying key positions in the military, to name a few. It is this chapter's contention therefore that when one speaks of "minority" issues in the context of Singapore, a clear distinction must be made between the Malays and Indians. While there are issues that impact both communities (such as racial discrimination), there are many areas where the issues associated with each community differ markedly. Geopolitical and socio-economic realities described earlier contribute to the different situations facing the Malay and Indian communities.

UNINTENDED CONSEQUENCES OF STATE POLICIES

The reserved 2017 PE is used to demonstrate a broader point in this section, namely, state policies at times, even if well intentioned, could negatively impact the Malay community. The government's rationale for reserving the 2017 PE for a Malay candidate was the need for minority representation. It was asserted that many Singaporeans still voted along ethnic lines and, by extension, minority candidates would find it difficult to win should there be an open contest.[26] However, this is a strange assertion as Singapore had an Indian president, S.R. Nathan, who served from 1999 to 2011. Though he was elected unopposed twice, President Nathan was reported to have been popular with and respected by many Singaporeans.[27] Furthermore, some Singaporeans have expressed their wish for Tharman Shanmugaratnam, the current Senior Minister and ethnic Indian, to be the next Prime Minister,[28] thus challenging the government's assertion that Singaporeans were not yet ready for a non-Chinese Prime Minister,[29] or that Singaporeans voted along ethnic lines.

Perhaps what was actually meant was that it would be difficult for a *Malay* minority to be voted in through an open election. This would be more plausible since existing associations of Malays with negative traits like laziness and incompetence[30] may very well influence voting decisions. Whatever the reality may be, reserving the PE for an ethnic group while maintaining that the election would be based on meritocracy is an apparent contradiction. Unsurprisingly, the government's attempt to argue that there was no contradiction between meritocracy and the reserved PE did not convince many sections of the public. Singaporeans expressed their discontent mostly online. The subsequent walkover victory for Halimah Yacob saw the trending of the hashtag #notmypresident.[31] It must be said that Halimah was a genuinely popular figure amongst some Singaporeans; and that the displeasure displayed by numerous Singaporeans was not directed at her, but at the reserved PE or the fact that they could not exercise their vote because of the walkover.

There was some resemblance between the reserved 2017 PE and the Group Representation Constituency (GRC) that was implemented in the 1980s. The GRC is a form of Party Block Vote system, whereby instead of competing in single-member districts, political parties would have to field a team of four to six candidates, one of whom had to be a non-Chinese candidate. The winning party would then take all seats. Naturally, this arrangement disproportionately favoured large political parties which were able to mobilize more resources and candidates.[32] Former Prime Ministers Lee Kuan Yew and Goh Chok Tong both expressed concerns over "racial voting trends", and posited that Malay candidates could lose their seats in the future if only single-member districts remained.[33] What is pertinent to this chapter is the fact that the Malay community was also apprehensive of the GRC system at that time, and expressed unease over the possibility that elected Malay MPs would face a credibility problem if they were seen to be riding on the coat-tails of their Chinese counterparts to get into Parliament.[34] Nevertheless, on both occasions, in spite of discontent from segments of the public, and in keeping with its overall paternalistic approach to politics and governance, the government pushed its electoral reforms through. However, there seemed to be more vociferous opposition to the changes to the reserved 2017 PE, partly because social media had opened up new avenues to articulate dissent.

In both cases, the sequence of events were as follows: the government proposes a new, controversial amendment to existing electoral laws; there is resistance from some Singaporeans; the government justifies the changes by invoking its responsibility to safeguard minority representation, especially the Malays; and the changes are eventually implemented. Whether the changes were well intentioned or to entrench the power of the ruling party, or perhaps a combination of both, is irrelevant to this chapter. What is germane though is that the Malay community was used, in both cases, as justification for those changes. This may have unintended implications such as a greater disconnect between the Malays and the other ethnic communities. For instance, it reinforces the perception that Malay community continues to require special concessions and, in this case, one which is perceived to undermine the principle of meritocracy. Jeraldine Phneah, a young blogger who writes on socio-political issues, cautioned that a possible consequence of the election is that "it may end up unintentionally reinforcing stereotypes instead".[35] Indeed, the rhetoric online was, at times, viscerally chauvinistic against the Malay community over the electoral changes.[36] It was not uncommon to see criticism directed not just at the electoral reform, but also at Halimah personally, and even more disconcertingly, at the Malay community in general. No doubt, these sentiments may not be reflective of the general populace, but it is nonetheless alarming that such comments were articulated at all.[37] In sum, the reserved PE which was intended—ostensibly—to elect a President who would unite the nation via minority representation ended up straining the multiracial fabric of the country.

On its part, the government insisted that meritocracy had not been compromised. It was understandably difficult for PAP leaders to assert otherwise as meritocracy is one of Singapore's founding principles, one which had been explicitly cited as the main reason for Singapore's separation from Malaysia in 1965.[38] Instead, what should have happened—once the PAP decided the reserved PE was the way to go—was the initiation of an honest, open conversation about the inherent contradictions between meritocracy and minority representation, and why the latter may be needed at the expense of the former on occasion. While there was no guarantee that such a conversation would have assuaged the unhappiness of *all* Singaporeans, it would have been a good opportunity to further explain a controversial policy decision. Both the GRC system and reserved PE are, in essence, affirmative action policies. This is not to say that they should not be implemented but that greater endeavours by the state were needed for deeper discussions on the trade-offs between democracy, minority representation, and meritocracy in Singapore.

In sum, the 2017 reserved PE was symptomatic of how policies which are intended to benefit local Malays may, paradoxically, have negative consequences, especially if the sentiments of both the community and other Singaporeans are not taken into account. Such consequences may include apprehension from both the Malay community and other ethnic communities towards the former; resulting in a deeper divide between ethnic groups, as well as the opportunity to resurface and reaffirm old stereotypes and prejudices around the Malay community. It would be prudent to explore the worst-case scenarios associated with each of these problems.

1. The Trust Deficit

It must be stated from the outset that there is no reason to presume that the trust between the Malay community and the state is low. Malays in general, have tended to vote for the PAP, suggesting a level of trust between the government and community. At the same time, it cannot be denied that there are areas for improvement. A perennial source of grumbling among Malays is the lack of representation in the cabinet, which is taken by some in the community to be indicative of the government's trust in the Malay community's ability to deliver at the highest level. Another source of unhappiness is the exclusion of Malays from key positions in the military. More undesirable outcomes may ensue if such concerns fester. For one, the community will perpetually be on the defensive and thus instinctively suspicious of any government policy—however well intentioned—that involves the Malays. Thus, even when government programmes that benefit the community are implemented, the first reaction from Malays would be to look for underlying political motives, with the reserved PE a case in point.

This trust deficit may result in more profound consequences. If Malays do not trust their government leaders, including Malay ministers and MPs, they would presumably look to alternative authority figures. The situation may be ripe for political entrepreneurs to exploit this trust vacuum. Sections of the Malay community would be more susceptible to the rhetoric of identity politics and equality which appeal to perceptions of marginality and disadvantaged status. In the absence of trust between the community and the government, it is not at all inconceivable that there would be personalities who would capitalize on the discontentment of Malays to portray the state or the ruling party as an entity which has side-lined the Malays. Such rhetoric has already been demonstrated in recent events around the world. The rise of Donald Trump to the White House, far-right parties in Western Europe campaigning to put an end to immigration, cultural diversity and racial mixing, and Britain's decision to leave the European Union have shown that no population is immune from the divisive rhetoric of identity politics. Such rhetoric become particularly combustible when coupled with economic concerns. As such the lack of trust between the Malays and the PAP government should not be dismissed lightly even if it is not yet at a critical stage.

2. Problematic Use of "Meritocracy"

As public unhappiness over the reserved 2017 PE has shown, Singaporeans see the principle of meritocracy as the bedrock of Singapore society. Yet, what is meant by "meritocracy" is often muddled in public discussions. Singaporeans are largely accepting of the GRC system even though it problematizes our common definition of meritocracy. As already argued, the PAP's unwillingness to admit that the spirit of meritocracy may have to be, from time to time, compromised for other equally noble and worthy reasons such as ethnic representation was unhelpful for the political maturity of the country. It was a missed opportunity to explore philosophical, political, and practical implications of a trade-off between meritocracy and representation.[39] Such trade-offs are part and parcel of managing a multicultural society with diverse needs and interests; and open discussions over the need for such trade-offs would have contributed to the political maturity of the country. Such discussions are especially important for minority groups like the Malay community. If Malays begin to doubt the robustness of meritocracy, they could end up becoming less trusting of the state, as have been argued by Lily Zubaidah and Hussin Mutalib. For instance, the relative lack of Malay ministers vis-à-vis Indian ministers in cabinet may raise questions as to why the government was eager to install a Malay President but yet comfortable with having only one minister (Masagos Zulkifli is currently the only full minister in cabinet). Indeed, one could extend the argument to permanent secretaries or the position of the Chief Justice, where the Indians are far better represented than the Malays.

It must be said that lately, there have been serious discussions taking place within Singapore society on the utility and weaknesses of meritocracy, as it pertains to inequality.[40] Such discourses need to be explored further, and extended to include the racial dimensions expounded above.

3. Tokenism

One unfortunate consequence of the reserved 2017 PE is the perception of President Halimah as a token President because she did not "earn" the victory in an open contest. The same criticism has been directed at minority MPs who are elected in the GRCs. As explained above, tokenism could pose challenges down the road. Firstly, Malay leaders in politics or public service may be viewed by the wider Singaporean community as less capable than their ethnic counterparts because they require specific regulations and measures—or crutches—to reach where they are. In addition, because of minority ethnic representation, Malay candidates do not compete against the best Chinese or Indian candidates but against the best among themselves. As such, the intensity of competition, whether for political positions or the Presidency, is very much lowered. This reinforces public perceptions that Malay leaders have an easier route to their positions. Secondly, this cycle of public perceptions go on to further entrench the negative stereotypes of Malays being incapable, lazy, incompetent, and in need of concessions to get ahead. Worse still, these concessions have to be made for the Malays at the expense of meritocracy. Not only do these perceptions impede the development of bonds between Singapore Malays and non-Malays, they raise the spectre of ethnic tokenism. Such a spectre is a burden borne by Malay leaders and community.

MOVING FORWARD: ENSURING STURDY STATE-COMMUNITY RELATIONS

All this is not to suggest that the state's relationship with the Malay community is in dire straits. I have already recognized above that the Malay community has displayed strong electoral support for the PAP. At the same time, in light of the above discussion, there can be several measures taken to further improve relations between the two. I propose the following. Firstly, contrary to what has been argued by many intellectuals and academics, I contend that the existing ethnic classifications in Singapore must be kept. The CMIO model, I argue, is actually necessary to allay any fears Malays may have about their minority status in the country. The model is predicated upon acknowledging each ethnic group's distinctiveness, and allowing space for each group to exercise that uniqueness, provided it does not encroach upon the overriding needs of the country. Instead of behaving as if ethnic differences do not exist or are entirely constructed, the CMIO model takes them as a given and attempts to work around those differences. Each person's ethnic identity is stated in the identification cards, and many policies are centred on these identifications. For instance, there is an ethnic quota for public housing. Each ethnic group is allocated a percentage of the houses in a neighbourhood, roughly commensurate with the national proportion, in order to promote intermingling between the different ethnicities. The GRC system requires members of a minority race to be part of a team contesting for parliamentary seats. Schools celebrate the different holidays of each major ethnic group.

Naturally, the CMIO model is not without its flaws. It is possible that organizing society around parochial ethnicities may further entrench these very identities. The CMIO model has been critiqued, rightly so, by many observers. Nur Diyanah Anwar argues that "assimilating into a comprehensive Singaporean identity may not be impossible, but it is difficult because of the priority placed on one's race".[41] Another academic, Elaine Ho, called for the classifications to be "dissolved even more".[42] Even though the CMIO model has already been tweaked to permit double-barrelled identification for children with parents of different ethnicities, thus allowing for some flexibility in ethnic classification, the ethnic origins of Singaporeans continue to be a key factor in the administration of the local population.[43]

While these calls are well intentioned, it would be a risk and overly optimistic to assume ethnic distinctions and prejudices would dissipate with the abolishment of the CMIO categories. The current data suggests that many Singaporeans are still racial in outlook—which is distinct from being racist—in many spheres of their life. In this case, being "racial" means that the concept of "race" or ethnicity is integral to the daily lives of Singaporeans. For example, over 70 per cent of Singaporeans find that race is a "very important/important" part of their identity.[44] Additionally, stories of quotidian racism are abound, some more benign than others, many of which have little to do with the state's imposition of CMIO categories or ethnic-based policies. Most Malays and Indians say that they have encountered racism from other Singaporeans.[45] In view of the racial nature of Singaporeans and the racist sentiments present in any society, it would be unwise to remove current ethnic classifications because it would take away official recognition of different ethnic groups. In such a situation, it is invariably the minority ethnic communities that would be most adversely impacted. For example, Malays, or Indians for that matter, would be unable to request for representation of their community as they would no longer be recognized by the state. Hence, while retaining the CMIO classification has its shortcomings, it does appear to be the better option in view of the need to protect, or at least recognize, the status of ethnic minorities.

Secondly, I suggest more openness in the state's dealings with the Malay community. At the moment, the approach taken by the state can be best characterized as overly cautious, consistent with its overall handling of ethnic-religious matters. A recent Parliamentary exchange between Masagos Zulkifli, Minister for the Environment and current Minister-in-Charge of Muslim Affairs, and Faisal Manap, the only Malay opposition MP, illustrates this. This exchange was prompted by Faisal who raised the perennial issue of local female Muslim nurses and uniformed officers not being allowed to don the hijab under current rules. Masagos took issue with him for highlighting "potentially discordant" issues in the public domain. PM Lee subsequently demonstrated his support for Masagos' rebuke of Faisal via his Facebook page.[46] This exchange was noteworthy for a few reasons. One, as noted by Faisal himself, as an elected MP, it is his responsibility to communicate his constituents' concerns; and two, if Parliament was not the "appropriate" venue to debate these matters, where then would such discussions take place? Furthermore, Faisal was merely echoing the findings of the Suara Musyawarah Report—a report commissioned by the former Minister-in-Charge of Muslim Affairs— which stated that many Muslims found the donning of the hijab to be of importance to them.[47] To be sure, the PAP's reasons for such an approach are well documented and are not without basis: ethnic and religious issues have a peculiar emotive potential that could stir up unnecessary sentiments among citizens. Yet, there is a genuine worry that if Parliament is not viewed as an appropriate platform for elected Malay officials to enunciate the community's grievances, Malays in general may feel there is no available state platform for them to speak their mind. The local Malay community is essentially urged to trust government leaders and not ask questions on such sensitive issues in public. However, such an approach may not be practical in the era of free-flowing information in which where everyone has a platform to air their opinions, however trivial. In fact, having open discussions in Parliament where government leaders are able to confidently put across their justifications for policies, especially controversial ones, would not only boost the credibility of the ruling-party, but would also enhance the trust Malays have in the government as a whole. Not only should opposition MPs be allowed to champion Malay issues in an open manner, I argue that PAP Malay MPs too should be given the space to do so. Often, PAP Malay MPs have lamented the negative perceptions of them from the Malay community. In the eyes of some within the community, these PAP Malay MPs are more akin to tools of the state rather than representatives of the community. Hussin Mutalib documents successive Malay leaders who have admitted this. Othman Wok, the only Malay member of the first cabinet in post-independent Singapore, confesses to having been labelled as an "infidel" by his fellow Malays; Yatiman Yusof, who joined the PAP in 1987, said that his own close friends chastised him for joining the PAP; similar sentiments continue to be articulated by contemporary MPs.[48] A possible remedy to this negative perception would be to permit Malay MPs to express disagreements—from time to time—with government policies, especially when significant segments of the community have reservations with those policies. The reserved PE would be a case in point where some Malay MPs could have acted as conduits for the concerns and disapproval of many Malays. Instead, as in most other instances, the PAP Malay MPs stuck to relaying and justifying government policy to the community resulting a lost opportunity for the Malay parliamentarians to serve as voices for the community. No doubt, the reserved PE reform would have been implemented even if they had articulated these concerns publicly. In all likelihood there would still be Malays who would have questioned these parliamentarians for their inefficacy in changing the government's course of action. But at the very least, it would have assuaged the unease felt by some Malays that their Malay MPs were not representing their concerns.

The PAP's reluctance to allow for dissenting views from within the party to be publicly aired is understandable. The government desires to project a united front so as to not weaken public confidence in it and, consequentially, keeps internal disagreements behind closed-doors. Yet, I contend that it may be wise to allow these Malay MPs more opportunities to be raising pertinent issues in public with state elites in an amicable and sensitive manner. If integration is to be achieved then open discussions on the rights and responsibilities of the Malays should not be avoided, but rather, encouraged. Honest conversations do not necessarily entail finger-pointing and inflaming sentiments; rather, mature and level-headed deliberations can, and in fact, should take place amongst politicians, community leaders, activists, and the general populace. Singapore's parliamentarians have, after all, displayed the ability to engage in difficult conversations in a fruitful manner. The parliamentary session called by PM Lee in 2017 in the face of accusations of abuse of power by his siblings demonstrated that the MPs, from both parties, can ask tough questions, and that Parliament is a place for robust discussions.[49] Indeed, the PM's decision to put a private family matter under public scrutiny won plaudits from many.[50] A similar openness to Malay issues, coupled with maturity from parliamentarians, would no doubt receive similar appraisals.

On a similar note, it would be prudent for the government to engage with the Malay community on a broader level, and not just rely on leaders of community organizations such as Mendaki, MUIS, Religious Rehabilitation Group (RRG), Singapore Islamic Scholars and Religious Teachers Association (Pergas), for feedback.[51] Engaging with a more diverse audience, including critics, would not only make the process of consultation more inclusive, but would also augment its credibility. Consultation should go beyond engaging only with community elites who are assumed to represent the community; but also include individuals who may disagree with the government and its policies in the numerous dialogue and consultation exercises the government has with the community. The openness of the government towards diversity and dissent from within and without would bode well for its standing, and for state-community relations.

CONCLUSION

Singapore's success in managing a multiethnic and multireligious society is no mean feat. By most indicators, the country has performed exceptionally well in ensuring that the different ethnic groups live peacefully side-by-side. The absence of ethnic clashes or riots since independence is an achievement which goes a long way in justifying the PAP's government's approach towards ethnic management. At the same time, this chapter has suggested areas for improvement. While there are educational, social and familial issues confronting the Malay community, as is the case with the other ethnic groups, this chapter has chosen to focus on the political side of the equation. It is my contention that a stronger relationship between the state and the community, manifested in the trust the latter places in the Malay political leadership, would positively impact the other spheres of concern too. The sturdier the relationship between the political elites and the community, the easier it would be for Malays to support governmental policies on education and social issues. Sociologist Robert Putnam's argument is pertinent here. He postulates that having high levels of trust between different groups of citizens on one hand, and between the state and citizens on the other, positively impacts governance and democracy.[52] Similarly, this chapter does not call for an overhaul of the PAP's approach to managing ethnic groups. As imperfect as the CMIO model is, it remains, by my estimation, the best option in light of the prevailing circumstances. The model acts as a safety net for the Malays. The GRC system, constitutional acknowledgement of the indigeneity of the Malays, the existence of Mendaki and MUIS, *inter alia,* are all possible because of the CMIO model. If "Malay" as an ethnic category ceases to exist as a legal and/or political term, then these provisions would be moot as well. Much about Singapore's accomplishments can be admired. In celebrating the city-state's astonishing track record in maintaining social order, it is worthwhile to take a step back to assess what has worked in ensuring this, and what can be improved upon.

Notes

1. "Next Presidential Election to Be Reserved for Malay Candidates", *Channel NewsAsia*, 8 November 2016, https://www.channelnewsasia.com/news/singapore/next-presidential-election-to-be-reserved-for-malay-candidates-p-7719928 (accessed 4 January 2018).
2. Such sentiments were mostly articulated online, and at times, in visceral fashion.
3. The two aspirants are Salleh Marican and Farid Khan.
4. Lianne Chia, "Singapore Must 'Never Compromise' on Qualifying Criteria for Elected Presidency", *Channel NewsAsia*, 7 November 2016, https://www.channelnewsasia.com/news/singapore/singapore-must-never-compromise-on-qualifying-criteria-for-7695128 (accessed 3 January 2018).
5. Department of Statistics Singapore, *Census of Population 2010, Statistical Release 1,* "Demographic Characteristics, Education, Language and Religion", p. 8, https://www.singstat.gov.sg/-/media/files/publications/cop2010/census_2010_release1/cop2010sr1.pdf (accessed 4 January 2018).
6. Department of Statistics Singapore, *Census of Population 2010, Statistical Release 2,* "Households and Housing", p. 99, https://www.singstat.gov.sg/-/media/files/publications/cop2010/census_2010_release2/cop2010sr2.pdf (accessed 4 January 2018).
7. Lily Zubaidah Rahim, *The Singapore Malay Dilemma: The Political and Educational Marginality of the Malay Community* (Kuala Lumpur: Oxford University Press, 1998), pp. 52–53.

8. Nasir provides both perspectives, and argues for a middle ground approach—which sufficiently takes into account both the government's and community's failures—in understanding the "Malay problem". See Kamaludeen bin Mohamed Nasir, "Rethinking the 'Malay Problem' in Singapore: Image, Rhetoric and Social Realities", *Journal of Muslim Minority Affairs* 27, no. 2 (2007): 309–18.

9. Tim Huxley, "Singapore and Malaysia: A Precarious Balance?", *Pacific Review* 4, no. 3 (1991): 208.

10. Article 152, Constitution of the Republic of Singapore. Refer to https://sso.agc.gov.sg/Act/CONS1963 (accessed 4 January 2018).

11. Lily Zubaidah Rahim, "Governing Muslims in Singapore's Secular Authoritarian State", *Australian Journal of International Affairs* 66, no. 2 (2012), p. 171.

12. Chua Beng Huat, "The Cost of Membership in Ascribed Community", in *Multiculturalism in Asia*, edited by Will Kymlicka and He Baogang (New York: Oxford University Press, 2005), p. 191.

13. Han Fook Kwang, Zuraidah Ibrahim, Chua Mui Hoong, Lydia Lim, Ignatius Low, Rachel Lin, and Robin Chan, *Lee Kuan Yew: Hard Truths to Keep Singapore Going* (Singapore: Straits Times Press, 2011).

14. Neo Chai Chin, "PM Lee Urges Malay-Muslim Community to Stand with Government to Tackle Extremism", *Today*, 20 June 2017, http://www.todayonline.com/singapore/stand-govt-tackle-self-radicalism-pm-lee-urges-malay-muslim-community (accessed 9 January 2018).

15. According to a survey by the Institute of Policy Studies, 26.4 per cent of Malays have felt being racially discriminated against regarding a job or job promotion, as compared to 5.7 per cent and 24.2 per cent for the Chinese and Indians respectively. See Mathew Mathews, "Insights from the IPS Survey on Race, Religion and Language", http://lkyspp2.nus.edu.sg/ips/wp-content/uploads/sites/2/2013/04/Insights-from-the-IPS-Survey-on-Race-Religion-and-Language.pdf (accessed 8 January 2018).

16. Hussin Mutalib, *Singapore Malays: Being Ethnic Minority and Muslim in a Global City-State* (Abingdon and New York: Routledge, 2012), pp. 101–2.

17. Walid Jumblatt Abdullah, "The Malay Community: Voting Trends and Issues", *The Round Table: The Commonwealth Journal of International Affairs* 105, no. 2 (2016): 205–15.

18. Michael D. Barr and Jevon Low, "Assimilation as Multiracialism: The Case of Singapore's Malays", *Asian Ethnicity* 6, no. 3 (2005): 161–82.

19. Mathew Mathews, "Insights from the IPS Survey on Race, Religion and Language".

20. These solutions can either be community-based or introduced at the national level.

21. Walid Jumblatt Abdullah, "Of Co-optation and Resistance: State-Ulama Dynamics in Singapore", *Journal of Church and State* 58, no. 3 (2016): 462–82.

22. Amir Hussain, "Govt's Stance on Tudung Evolving, Says PM Lee", *Today*, 25 January 2014, http://www.todayonline.com/singapore/govts-stance-tudung-issue-evolving-says-pm-lee (accessed 9 January 2018).

23. Under the Tertiary Tuition Fee Subsidy (TTFS) scheme, Malays with a per capita household income of S$1,000 are entitled to free education: the scheme is a manifestation of the government's "constitutional commitment" with regard to article 152. TTFS is administered by Mendaki, a Malay self-help group supported by the government that is supposed to the community's development. See Mendaki, https://tfas.mendaki.org.sg/Home/GetFAQ (accessed 9 January 2018).

24. The most "prestigious" ministry that has been led by a Malay is the Ministry of Communications and Information, formerly helmed by Dr Yaacob Ibrahim, who, as mentioned earlier, was concurrently the Minister-in-Charge of Muslim Affairs.

25. The five Malay ministers since independence are Othman Wok, Ahmad Mattar, Abdullah Tarmugi, Yaacob Ibrahim and Masagos Zulkifli. The five ministers of Indian descent currently in the government are Tharman Shanmugaratnam (Senior Minister and Coordinating Minister for Social Policies), Vivian Balakrishnan (Foreign Affairs), K. Shanmugam (Home Affairs and Law), S. Iswaran (Communications and Information), and Indranee Rajah (Prime Minister's Office).

26. "In Full: PM Lee on Race, Multiracialism and Singapore's Place in the World", *Today*, 29 September 2017, http://www.todayonline.com/singapore/full-pm-lees-speech-race-multiracialism-and-singapores-place-world (accessed 9 January 2018).

27. Lim Yan Liang, "Singaporeans Pay Tribute to SR Nathan", *Straits Times*, 24 August 2016, http://www.straitstimes.com/singapore/sporeans-pay-tribute-to-s-r-nathan (accessed 9 January 2018).

28. Tharman had to address the matter, "categorically" stating that he did not wish to be Prime Minister. See Patrick John Lim, "DPM Tharman 'Categorically' Rules Himself Out from Becoming PM", *Channel NewsAsia*, 28 September 2016, https://www.channelnewsasia.com/news/singapore/dpm-tharman-categorically-rules-himself-out-from-becoming-pm-7821338.

29. "Race, Religion Still Matter When Voters Cast Ballots: PM Lee", *Today*, 1 March 2017, http://www.todayonline.com/singapore/ethnic-considerations-never-absent-when-singaporeans-choose-leader-says-pm-lee (accessed 9 January 2018).

30. For a discussion on the origins of such stereotypes, see Syed Hussein Alatas, *The Myth of the Lazy Native: A Study of the Image of the Malays, Filipinos and Javanese from the 16th to the 20th Century and its Function in the Ideology of Colonial Capitalism* (London and New York: Frank Cass, 1977).

31. Charissa Yong, "Social Media Abuzz over Halimah Yacob's Presidential Walkover", *Straits Times*, 12 September 2017, http://www.straitstimes.com/politics/social-media-abuzz-over-halimah-yacobs-presidential-walkover (accessed 10 January 2018).

32. Netina Tan, "Ethnic Quotas and Unintended Effects on Women's Political Representation in Singapore", *International Political Science Review* 35, no. 1 (2014): 27–40.

33. Hussin Mutalib, *Singapore Malays*, p. 89.

34. Ibid., pp. 89–90.

35. Jeraldine Phneah, "Why Are Singaporeans Upset about the Presidential Election

Walkover", 12 September 2017, http://www.jeraldinephneah.com/presidential-election-walkover/ (accessed 10 January 2018).

36. The Malay author in this piece communicates sentiments that were expressed him by his non-Malay friends. See Suhaile Md, "PE 2017: Unintended Consequences for the Malay Community", *Middle Ground*, 8 September 2017, http://themiddleground.sg/2017/09/08/pe2017-unintended-consequences-malay-community/ (accessed 10 January 2018).

37. See this commentary: Zarina Jaffar, "Support and Unhappiness over Elected Presidency Turns into a Racial Mud Sling Like No Other", *Online Citizen*, 21 September 2017, https://www.theonlinecitizen.com/2017/09/21/support-and-unhappiness-over-elected-presidency-turns-into-a-racial-mud-sling-like-no-other/ (accessed 10 January 2018). Zarina laments the vitriol abuse hurled at Malays online.

38. For a discussion on the separation episode, see Albert Lau, *A Moment of Anguish: Singapore in Malaysia and the Politics of Disengagement* (Singapore: Times Academic Press, 1998).

39. There have been many academic works detailing the tensions between meritocracy and multiracialism. See, for example, Terri-Anne Teo, "Perceptions of Meritocracy in Singapore: Inconsistencies, Contestations and Biases", *Asian Studies Review* 43, no. 2 (2019): 184–205.

40. Teo You Yenn, *This Is What Inequality Looks Like* (Singapore: Ethos Books, 2018). Professor Teo's book generated a national discussion on inequality and, to some extent, meritocracy.

41. Nur Diyanah Anwar, "Move Beyond Identifying Singaporeans Based on Ethnicity", *Today*, 6 November 2014, http://www.todayonline.com/singapore/move-beyond-identifying-sporeans-based-ethnicity (accessed 4 February 2018).

42. Rachel Au-Yong, "Debate on Whether Race Classification Is Still Relevant", *Straits Times*, 19 January 2016, http://www.straitstimes.com/singapore/debate-on-whether-race-classification-model-is-still-relevant (accessed 4 February 2018).

43. Ibid.

44. See Mathew Mathews, "Insights from the IPS Survey on Race, Religion and Language".

45. Ibid.

46. Charissa Yong, "Parliament: Masagos Questions Faisal Manap's Motives for Raising Divisive Issues", *Straits Times*, 4 April 2017, http://www.straitstimes.com/singapore/parliament-masagos-questions-faisal-manaps-motives-for-raising-divisive-issues (accessed 9 February 2018).

47. Leonard Lim and Andrea Ong, "Spotlight on Tudung Ban and Racial Harmony", *Straits Times*, 13 September 2013, http://www.asiaone.com/singapore/spotlight-tudung-ban-and-racial-harmony (accessed 9 February 2018).

48. Hussin Mutalib, *Singapore Malays*, pp. 82–83.

49. See Zakir Hussain, "Lee Hsien Loong Refutes Siblings' Charges of Abuse of Power over Oxley House", *Straits Times*, 4 July 2017, http://www.straitstimes.

com/singapore/pm-refutes-siblings-charges-of-abuse-of-power-over-oxley-house (accessed 8 February 2017).

50. For instance, see Robert Boxwell, "Singapore's Lee Hsien Loong Is Right to Choose Parliament to Respond to His Critics—It's What Lee Kuan Yew Would Have Done", *South China Morning Post*, 24 June 2017, http://www.scmp.com/comment/insight-opinion/article/2099577/singapores-lee-hsien-loong-right-choose-parliament-respond (accessed 8 February 2017).

51. In 2014, there was a push by some Malay/Muslims for the hijab to be allowed for nurses and frontline government positions. PM Lee Hsien Loong met up with about 100 representatives from the Malay/Muslim community, and these individuals were invited to the event. It was a closed-door session. Not only could the event have done with more transparency, it could have also benefited with more diversity in terms of the list of attendees. See Amir Hussain, "Govt's Stance on Tudung Evolving", *Today*, 25 January 2014, https://www.todayonline.com/singapore/govts-stance-tudung-issue-evolving-says-pm-lee (accessed 3 May 2018).

52. Robert D. Putnam, *Making Democracy Work: Civic Traditions in Modern Italy* (Princeton: Princeton University Press, 1993).

7

"What Kind of Indian Are You?"
Frictions and Fractures Between Singaporean Indians and Foreign-Born NRIs

Laavanya Kathiravelu

Introduction

In April 2016, a news blog post titled, "Singaporeans take back Mandarin Gardens from Indian expats",[1] was met with much more interest than is usually garnered by happenings in the community. Describing how migrant Indians asserted dominance over the management committee of a condominium in the eastern part of Singapore, the post claimed that as a result, they started using management funds for activities that unfairly represented the interests of expatriate Indians. The changes that they had attempted to make included instituting a cricket pitch for the children on condominium grounds,[2] replacing a Thai restaurant with an Indian one, and using communal funds for Deepavali celebrations. The post continued that Singaporeans clawed back control by showing up in force at the next Annual General Meeting of the condominium, which had even been dubbed "Mumbai Gardens" as a result of the overrepresentation of expatriate Indians in the estate.

Regardless of the veracity of the claims made, the above anecdote brings very starkly into relief the frictions and contestations between migrant and newly immigrant communities on the one hand, and Singaporeans on the other. By migrants, here I refer to temporary migrants on work or dependant visas, whose stay in Singapore is linked to their employment or family. This group is typically considered highly transient with little attachment to the country, and who will eventually leave. New immigrant communities here refer to migrants who have obtained either citizenship or permanent residency status in the last ten years, but who are still differentiated from locally born Singaporeans, and often not seen as "authentically" or culturally Singaporean.[3] What is more interesting here is that the immigrant community that has come under scrutiny is not an ethnic outsider. In fact, under the multiracial "CMIO" (Chinese, Malay, Indian, Others) framework, Indians occupy an important constitutive position in the Singaporean state.

Herein lies the puzzle. The fissures within the Indian community then are not indicative of deep-rooted racism against a differently racialized Other who cannot be incorporated within the nation. The Singaporean state, in its multiracial definition, already has a space for the inclusion of immigrant ethnic Indians. Instead, this points to cultural differences that the shared racial and ethnic tag of "Indian", subsumes. "Indian", in referring to both race and nationality, easily conflates significant cultural and nationality differences between Singaporean and immigrant groups with shared country of origin. The same can be said for the race label "Chinese" that assumes a coherent cultural unity despite the fact that recent Chinese migrants and diasporic Chinese have decades of politically and culturally divergent experiences. Despite the impression given by these unitary race/national/cultural labels that the integration of ethnically similar Others is automatic or unproblematic, the converse has been true. The conduct of both non-resident Indians (NRIs) and immigrants from the People's Republic of China (PRC) is often perceived as incompatible with what is seen as a Singaporean ethos of multiracialism and cultural tolerance, which entails a give-and–take mentality when living together in diverse spaces.

This chapter seeks to interrogate the divergence in attitudes as well as social behaviour between expatriate Indians and Singaporean Indians. It also takes demographic differences between these groups as a starting point. In doing so, I am not seeking to exaggerate or reify differences between the two communities, but instead caution against easy racial categorizations that may impede efforts at integration. In fact, there have always been divisions within the Indian community in Singapore, as Rajesh Rai's much-needed book on the Indian diaspora pre-1945 demonstrates through its interrogations of the colonial governance of religious diversity and the social divisions engendered by subregional differences within the South Asian diaspora.[4] Sinha's short monograph on the Indian community in Singapore also hints at how some of this is translated into contemporary complexity.[5] In extending these discussions, what this chapter aims to demonstrate is that the speed and scale at which the Indian community is now changing through immigration is generating unique consequences and challenges for a shared national identity and a cohesive sense of community in the Singaporean nation-state.

After a discussion of demographic shifts that have taken place over the past fifteen to twenty years in Singapore, particularly in relation to Indian migrants, a note about methodology is included, discussing how it informs the findings of this research. Then the chapter dives into three interrelated themes—civilizational discourse, north vs south, and authentic Singaporean vs imposter foreigner—in order to demonstrate the oppositional politics that characterizes issues of integration between local Indians and foreign NRIs. In the penultimate section, some suggestions are given for how a better integration can be achieved through addressing some of the key fractions brought up earlier in the chapter. Finally, reflections are offered on what a divided Singaporean Indian community entails for the nation and notions of a shared national identity.

DEMOGRAPHIC CHANGES IN THE
INDIAN POPULATION

The intensity and significance of the divides within the Indian community must be understood within the context of the rapid growth of Singapore's population and the concurrent rise in socio-economic inequality. Singapore's total population has increased by almost 85 per cent in the last twenty-five years (1990–2015). The percentage of citizens of the total Singaporean population has decreased by about 15 per cent in the same period.[6] In addition to this number, we must also take into account the numbers of newly naturalized citizens, which are difficult to estimate accurately, but which we can assume make up the bulk of the growth in the citizen population, given that Singapore's total fertility rate (TFR)[7] has been below replacement levels since 1990.

Despite this large increase in population, primarily through immigration, the Singapore state has managed to keep stable the ratios of the different ethnic communities. There have only been small shifts of less than 3 per cent across groups. This has been read as an effort to preserve social stability in the country by maintaining an ethnic Chinese majority (through immigration primarily from Malaysia as well as Hong Kong and the PRC), and ensuring Malays and Indians stay as the largest minority groups.[8] Significant to note is that this policy of encouraging immigration of people of Chinese, Malay and Indian heritage is based on the assumption that co-ethnicity will result in easier integration. This assumption however, is problematic and erroneous as this chapter goes on to demonstrate. Here I want to suggest that while shared citizenship status and ethnicity do play a part in enabling integration, the example of Singapore demonstrates that culture, social networks and socio-economic status may emerge as more significant in creating social cohesion and an inclusive sense of national identity.

Within this context of ethnically driven immigration, the percentage growth of Indians was an enormous 964 per cent, giving an indication of the numbers of naturalizations and permanent residencies that were granted to this particular ethnic community between 1990 and 2015.[9] The most significant characteristics of the Indians who were granted citizenship during this period are their high levels of educational attainment and their concurrent employment in high-income jobs. This is evidenced by the fact that Singaporean Indians' average monthly household income was higher than the national average household income in 2010, as compared to 2000, where it was below the national average and before the influx of new citizen Indians.[10] This corresponds to the most significant period of growth in the Indian population, which was between 2000 and 2010. This growth can be seen as part of the big push towards naturalization and increased granting of PRs in the late 2000s, which inevitably favoured highly educated and qualified Indians. Similarly, in 2010, 35 per cent of Indians had a university degree, which was more than 12 per cent higher than the national average. In 2000, only 16.5 per cent of Indians had a university education, less than 5 per cent higher than the national average. Singaporean Indians did experience social mobility during this period of the country's rapid development, as did the rest of the citizen population, but the performance of Indians has outstripped the national average. This increase cannot only be explained by the social mobility of Indians but also by the demographic make-up of new citizens and PRs. This recruitment (through the Work and Employment Pass schemes) and eventual naturalization of highly qualified and educated individuals is part of the Singapore state's initiative, started in 1990, to bolster its declining population through the attraction and retaining of what the state deems are desirable individuals and families. This was articulated explicitly by then Deputy Prime Minister Lee Hsien Loong in 1992, who suggested that it was part of a strategy to deal with the brain drain of educated Indians out of Singapore.[11] The recruitment of "well-qualified and successful professionals" has led to the creation of a strata of Indians in Singapore who are quite different in social and economic practices to the local-born.[12] Differences in what sociologists term economic and social capital, are then one of the key differentiators between local-born

Singaporean Indians and naturalized or expatriate NRIs.[13] While there has been some work that explores the tensions between new immigrant Chinese and local-born Singaporean Chinese,[14] there has been virtually no parallel study done on Indians, although their increase in terms of absolute numbers has been far larger.

A Note on Methodology

This chapter is based on a series of twenty-five interviews with expatriate Indians of different immigration statuses undertaken in 2017. While some informants had lived in Singapore for more than fifteen years, and had taken up permanent residency or citizenship, others had only lived in the city-state for a couple of years and were on temporary Employment Passes. Interviewees were of both genders and ranged from their mid-twenties to their late fifties. The main criteria for recruitment was middle-class status,[15] as defined by income level, and other markers of status such as the ability to speak fluent English, a university education, or a white-collar, well-paying job. It is important here to emphasize that this chapter draws in particular from conversations and interviews with upper middle-class Indians—an elite amongst the larger group. A snowball sample was utilized, with initial interviewees referring their friends and family. Important to note is that a Singaporean Indian researcher, and a graduate student of Indian nationality undertook interviewees separately. The interviewer effect meant that Indian expatriates generally felt more comfortable expressing sentiments that could be regarded as xenophobic when the interviewer was a co-ethnic of Indian nationality, although interviewees could also have been naturalized Singaporeans. In addition to semi-structured interviews, material for this chapter also draws from publicly available census data and media reports. In the interest of reflexivity, it is also important to mention that the author's long-term research on diversity in Singapore as well as her own experiences as a Singaporean Indian inform the writing of this chapter.

The Civilizational Discourse

Within the Indian community, the narrative of civilization is one that is invoked to establish hierarchy and superiority over the Other. The language of being more civilized or developed can be seen as akin to the labelling of nations as "First World" or "Third World". Singaporeans are extremely familiar with this mode of speaking about themselves and their country, measured in terms of development indices. In fact, a book written by Singapore's longest-serving Prime Minister, Lee Kuan Yew, is titled *From Third World to First: The Singapore Story 1965–2000*. In much of these discussions, Singapore is compared favourably to its Southeast Asian neighbours—and most often, Malaysia. As part of the "Asian Tigers", including Taiwan, Hong Kong, and South Korea, Singapore saw rapid growth from the 1960s to the 1990s. This has invariably led to comparisons with other nations, including India, which had, at the time, not yet embarked on its liberalization policies, and was thus still acknowledged to be "underdeveloped". These comparisons between nations have found their way into thinking not just about the economic development of a country, but also of its people. Indians from India are, in this formulation, backward in values and attitudes. Caste consciousness and its prevalence amongst NRIs is often invoked by Singaporean Indians as an example of this backwardness, who, in large part, find any discussion of caste uncomfortable and irrelevant.

Inversely, NRIs and new Indian immigrants in Singapore also use similar civilizational discourses to describe how they are different (and often superior) to Singaporean Indians. In this case, they appeal to the idea that India is the older civilization and nation, with a far more developed and sophisticated heritage and culture. Many NRIs think of Singaporeans as not being in touch with their heritage or having lost any real Indian culture, with the Singaporeanized version seen as archaic or a poor imitation of the *authentic*. What is defined as "Indian culture", becomes a convenient demarcation of boundaries between who can be considered *really* Indian. The traditions and practices that have then evolved in the diaspora and that have been influenced by the surrounding culture of Southeast Asia, are seen as a perversion of *pure* or *true* Indian culture. This narrative is invoked particularly in relation to the practice of Hinduism, as elaborated on later in the chapter.

This discourse of civilization is a flexible one. It is used to invoke backwardness, a lack of culture and adherence to religious norms, but at the same time, is also cited when describing Singaporean Indians as conservative. Here, urban India is described as more progressive in terms of attitudes towards marriage, cohabitation, dress and cross-gender interactions. This narrative is a means to speak back to Singaporean South Asians who often have a stereotyped and homogeneous notion of India as old fashioned in values, particularly in relation to gender and women. Urban Indians who have migrated to Singapore may describe the difficulties of forming friendships or relationships with their Singaporean Indian counterparts because of different perceptions of what are appropriate social norms. Interestingly, it is predominantly Singaporean Indians who are seen as socially conservative, and friendships are often more easily struck with middle-class Singaporean Chinese, than Singaporean Indian counterparts, who are perceived as having more progressive attitudes that translate into shared social activities. This preference may be, in turn, shaped by the socio-economic class cleavage between NRIs and Singaporean Indians. Working-class Singaporean Indians are seen to be less educated and thus have less progressive attitudes that are shaped by a more religious and less secular and "modern" set of values and beliefs. For many upper middle-class Indian migrants from larger metropolitan areas in India or who have previously lived in the West, Singaporean Indians represent a more conservative and almost fossilized version of Indian culture, and one that they seek to disassociate themselves from. This devaluing of working-class Singaporean Indians can be seen as in part informed by the state's larger nation-building narrative of elitism that foregrounds the contributions of business leaders and political figures, but not the indentured migrant labour that built many key institutions in the city.[16] This means that working-class Indians are left out of key representations of nationalism and celebrations of the nation's development. This elitist orientation is also reflected in Singapore's immigration policy, where it is only the formally skilled and educated who have access to permanent residency and eventual citizenship, while the low-waged worker without much formal education is always kept temporary and precarious in their affiliation to the state. Within discourses of integration and change within the Singapore Indian community, there is then an inevitable but unarticulated comparison with NRIs, who do better in school, and get higher paying jobs, embodying the ideal citizen who needs little assistance from the state. In this juxtaposition, the local-born working-class Indian is always seen as lacking. These implicit classed comparisons generate resentments within the community, where each group makes claims on the nation on grounds of either indigeneity or merit. The claim of each group competes to be seen as more legitimate than that of the other.

THE NORTH-SOUTH INDIAN DIVIDE

A key way in which the trope of "local vs NRIs" is articulated within the Indian community in Singapore is by invoking the differences between North and South Indians. It is important to note that there are significant and complex historical and political differences between northern and southern states in India. However, in the Singaporean context much of this complexity is erased, with labels like "North Indian" and "South Indian" based primarily on embodied and visible markers such as skin colour and linguistic ability rather than an understanding of the geographical origins of the individual. Newcomers who have been naturalized or attained permanent residency in the last twenty to twenty-five years often fall within the category of North Indian and local-born are considered South Indian. This is a simplistic equation and overlooks the numbers of second-, third- and fourth-generation North Indians who live in Singapore. It also ignores the fact that many new immigrants are Tamil or from other parts of South India such as Andhra Pradesh. It is thus a largely imprecise and arbitrary divide with specific inbuilt prejudices and values.

In the "North-South Indian" trope, the South Indian becomes synonymous with the southern state of Tamil Nadu, being dark skinned and only being able to speak one South Asian language—Tamil. Part of this association comes from the fact that Tamils were the overwhelming majority of Indians who were initial migrants to Singapore, with the "I" in the CMIO tantamount to being Tamil. Tamil, for many years, was the only Indian language taught in Singapore state schools.[17] State radio and television channels also mainly broadcast programmes in Tamil. And while Tamils range in skin tone, the majority of Tamils are dark skinned. The trope of the dark-skinned, dirty and smelly Indian is not just one that is prevalent in wider Southeast Asia but also in India where colourism is still widespread; and to be darker skinned implies lower status and often lower caste positions as well. In Singapore, this translates to the perception that Singaporean Indians, particularly Tamils, are lower than lighter skinned Northern Indians in the social hierarchy. This further perpetuates the stereotype that Singaporean Indians who have been in Singapore for generations and may have descended from convicts that the British brought to the island for labour are less cultured and sophisticated. As one of the new migrant informants on this project described to our interviewer, "What do you expect? These people are descendants of convicts and prisoners." This drawing of lines between North and South then also becomes a way of establishing status and hierarchy.

Tamil Nadu stands out as the only state in India that has resisted the teaching of Hindi as one of the key languages in state schools.[18] Instead, in homage to its rich literary and cultural traditions, there is strong support among Tamils in Tamil Nadu for the teaching of Tamil and not Hindi, which is seen by many as a foreign language. The lack of knowledge of Hindi, which is taught in most other states in India and spoken by the vast majority of middle-class Indians,[19] is then seen as indicative of a lack of "Indianness". And because Tamils, and by association Singaporean Indians, are unable to access Hindi literature, film or humour because they do not speak the language, which is seen as a key marker of Indian identity, they are not accepted by NRIs as authentically Indian. Furthermore the global dominance of Hindi as the premier Indian language has accelerated through popular culture, and in particular the popularity of Bollywood films. This has added to the feeling of dislocation for Tamil-speaking Singaporean Indians not just within the local Indian community but also within the larger global Indian diaspora.

We should however be careful not to overstate the significance of language or the "North Indian" status in creating the divides between local-born Indians and NRIs. For instance, NRIs are still perceived as *foreign* by Singaporean Indians who happen to be North Indian such as the local Punjabi community despite being ethnically similar for reasons that will be elaborated on in the next section.

The creeping significance of Hindi amongst the Singaporean Indian population can be seen from the shift in languages spoken within the community. Tamil speakers have seen a decline from 58.2 per cent to 54.2 per cent. Almost all other South Asian languages have also seen a decline, except Hindi speakers who have grown from 1.5 per cent to 3.8 per cent, an increase of more than 100 per cent in the space of ten years.[20] This has, predictably, led to demands for the teaching of other South Asian languages, including Hindi, in government schools. However as Jain and Wee demonstrate,[21] there is an inverse correlation between proportion of citizens and total enrolment in Hindi. The demand for Hindi to be taught in local schools is, in fact, coming from new immigrants and Indians on Employment Passes in Singapore. This increased attention and resources dedicated to the teaching of Hindi is seen by Singapore Indians as a threat to the dominance of a Singaporean Tamil identity.

More ground-up changes within the community include the increased dominance of new immigrant Indians in temples, particularly in leadership and management roles.[22] This has also changed the nature of worship in shifting towards India for scriptural and theistic authenticity, while delegitimizing the everyday rituals that have marked the practices of Southeast Asian Hinduism. Instead, practices that are common in temples in India or Sri Lanka are increasingly transported to Singaporean Hindu spaces of worship, resulting in the devaluing of a Southeast Asian brand of Hinduism and the belief that the people who practise it are doing so incorrectly. And example of this would be the inclusion of Bharat Mata, depicted as India's goddess of freedom waving the Indian flag during a local temple festival. Everyday superstitions and oral traditions that often have syncretic roots in their blending with local Malay heritage or Chinese customs have also particularly been devalued. The increased codification of Hindu forms of worship can also be attributed to the rise of Hindu nationalism in India, and the influx of immigrant South Asians has no doubt transferred some of these discourses to Singapore.

AUTHENTIC SINGAPOREAN VS IMPOSTER FOREIGNER

"Were you born here?" This was a question I was asked repeatedly when I first started conducting research on diversity in Singapore in 2011. Having lived in Singapore almost all my life, this query about my identity was unusual and alerted me to a crisis of identity that has manifested in Singapore. The frequency with which that question came up was revealing; and it was invariably followed by the query, "Are you Singaporean?" This attempt to "place" me within a hierarchy of immigration status and nationality is characteristic of the tensions and the everyday characterizations and divisions that individuals utilize to make sense of everyday life in a culturally and ethnically diverse city-state. While this attempt at characterization and placement is not restricted to the Singapore Indian community, I suggest that it is more difficult to differentiate between NRI or expatriate and newly immigrant Indians and locals—given that both groups could be seen as part of the larger middle class, composed of both upper and lower middle classes. Arguably, it may be more difficult for the majority ethnic Chinese population to differentiate between new immigrant and local-born Indians, both of whom exhibit subtle differentiations of dress, speech, comportment and mannerisms. This preoccupation with trying to determine what kind of "Indian" I am is also telling of the differentiations that non-Indian Singaporeans make of those with Indian ancestry. Even for these non-Indian Singaporeans, confrontation with conspicuous displays of wealth by NRIs is discomforting, and fuels growing general xenophobic sentiments directed at new migrants.

The Singaporean national identity may be constantly evolving but there are certain key markers that establish *authentic* belonging. Singlish, the creole that is predominantly made up of Malay, Chinese dialects and English, is one important component of Singaporeanness. Most middle-class Singaporeans possess the ability to effectively code-switch between Singlish and a more standard form of English. As such, the use of Singlish at appropriate moments can quickly establish if you are an insider or outsider. Many of the middle-class NRIs who were interviewed for this research, and who had lived in Singapore for more than a decade (some for almost two decades), did not speak Singlish with much ease. They did not generally consider Singlish important to their everyday interactions, which rarely took place in the "heartland" spaces of Singapore. They also often spoke Indian-accented English, which again was seen as a marker of their foreignness, in opposition to an assimilated identity marked by a mastery of Singlish. They tended to be in their fifties or sixties and had brought their children to Singapore at a young age, typically when their children were below the age of ten. Many had moved to Singapore from a location other than India, typically the United States or the United Kingdom, but also from places as unusual as Latin America. Sincere about their attachment to Singapore, many emphasized that they had now lived in Singapore longer than they had in any other city, and espoused the unique position of being in Asia while close to their country of origin, yet being able to enjoy a highly efficient and safe lifestyle which is seen as impossible almost anywhere else in the world. Singapore, in this sense was appreciated for being a space of opportunity and desired lifestyle, but also, significantly, for being welcoming of the diversity that they embodied and the skills that they possessed.

For this strata of NRIs, their children, in many ways, became the proxy of establishing their "Singaporeanness". In interviews, many speak proudly of their sons having done national service (NS) by going into compulsory military conscription for two years. NS is an important marker of belonging and for demonstrating allegiance to the nation, even among local-born Singaporeans, as a survey by the Institute of Policy Studies effectively demonstrated.[23] Exhortations such as "My son speaks in Singlish to the guys he met in NS," further attempt to establish that their children, having grown up in Singapore, are truly local. However, such narratives are often complicated by the fact that many of these children attended international schools and universities abroad, and are perhaps more a part of a global cosmopolitan elite than typically Singaporean in their experiences. While many of these second-generation Singaporeans choose to stay in the country and build their careers and families here, a significant proportion also remain in the United States or other parts of the West after their university education. These children may be following their parents' trajectories but retaining Singapore citizenship for an eventual return. In the middle-class Indian imaginary however, North America is still very much the space with the most social and cultural capital, although Singapore is fast catching up, particularly with recent political developments that have made the former less welcoming to non-white immigrants.

A Divided Singaporean Indian

Increasing inequality in the city-state is an issue that has gain prominence both in public policy spheres as well as among a disgruntled local populace.[24] Tensions are inevitable when income and socio-economic inequality manifests within a community that is perceived by the state in largely homogeneous terms. The first step in addressing these issues of NRI integration into the Singaporean Indian community is to acknowledge that "Indians" are not homogeneous in their needs and expectations as citizens. Indicators of social mobility that suggest that Singaporean Indians as an ethnic group are experiencing better outcomes in comparison to their ethnic counterparts must be contextualized with the high percentages of immigration and naturalization. Local-born Singaporean Indians from the lower middle class, in particular, are often neglected in the state's heralding of an ethnic minority community for its upward mobility. As one of my local-born respondents commented after an event where this social mobility was showcased and celebrated by the government, "It is not us who are earning $8,000 a month!". The statement, made in front of a group of local-born Singaporean Indians, did not need any further elaboration as it was clear that the speaker was articulating a collective sense of exasperation over misrepresentations of the community. Local-born Indians, problematically, view NRIs in rather homogeneous terms, as uniformly wealthy and socially mobile. This group is then also blamed for changing the identity of a well-established Singaporean Indian community, considered one of the key elements of Singapore's multicultural make-up.

Income inequality does not just entail different spending power or consumption patterns, but also vastly different everyday life experiences and standards, as the previous sections of this chapter have sought to show. One very visible example of this is residential segregation—with most NRIs living in condominiums, many in the expensive east coast area of Singapore, as the opening vignette showed. The larger disposable incomes of this group allow for some mode of self-segregation, rather than a dependence on the state's social housing scheme. On the other hand, most local-born Singaporean Indians live in Housing and Development Board (HDB) flats which discourage ethnic minority enclaves through the ethnic quota scheme.

There is a disconnect between lived reality and state rhetoric for many lower middle-class Singaporean Indians. This challenges the value of strict ethnic categories based solely on a person's country of origin or ancestry. Rather than addressing welfare, education and community needs of Singaporeans using the CMIO classifications, a more targeted approach may be a means-tested allocation of resources. I am not the first to point out the problems that a strict racial classification system entail,[25] but extending the system to immigration policies and integration has proven detrimental to efforts to build a united national identity.[26] As this chapter has sought to demonstrate, it is quickly becoming apparent that it is socio-economic class that is the key divisive factor within the Singapore Indian community, and notions of shared ancestry and racial similarity have done little to overcome it.

Creating a more equal society in terms of class would mean that divisive life experiences like private schooling and an overseas university education would not entail such varying life experiences that would, in turn, lead to different social networks and spheres of interaction. Policies put in place in the past few years that have restricted PRs' and foreigners' access to public education will exacerbate existing divides by pushing PRs and non-Singaporean residents into private international schools in increasing numbers. And while the institution of NS for PRs and children of PRs has been lauded as key to integration, such top-down initiatives are necessary but insufficient for overcoming class divisions. Integration is a process that is necessarily slow and which will evolve over time. Even in mature immigrant societies such as the United States, it is acknowledged that immigrants and children of immigrants are changing the nature of American cities in ways that are not completely predictable.

In addition to the more obvious economic inequalities that lead to different life trajectories, the everyday divides like living in different neighbourhoods, going to different schools and interacting with different social networks also make the local-born Singaporean Indian feel separate to their NRI counterpart, regardless of the fact that they may also be Singaporean citizens. Social networks and friendships based on ethnicity and class are the norm. However, within the context of fostering urban integration, more needs to be done to encourage interaction and understanding across ethnicity and class, so that anxieties and fears of status threat, where one group's position is taken over by another, are mitigated.

Contact theory[27] predicts that increased contact between people who are different to one another will lead to more positive interactions and attitudes towards diversity. One of the reasons for this is that personal contact allows people of different groups to be seen as individuals, and not through the lens of stereotypes and ethnic caricatures. While this claim has been contested over decades, a seminal study by the Max Planck Institute for Religious and Ethnic Diversity in 2013 across fifty urban neighbourhoods demonstrates that more frequent interaction goes along with more positive attitudes to immigration.[28] One way to better enable integration is to provide opportunities and spaces for local-born Singaporeans and new citizens to mingle and meet. The HDB policy of encouraging ethnic intermingling by instituting ethnic quotas has been largely successful, and this could be adapted to also promote interactions between old and new citizens. Rather than targeted events where members of communities are expected to mingle and meet within a specific time frame and environment, the encouragement of more organic and less scripted interactions in schools, workplaces and the semi-public spaces of void decks and neighbourhood playgrounds are where fleeting interactions can act as a basis for deeper intercultural understandings to develop. The institution of mixed neighbourhoods where people from different socio-economic backgrounds can meet and mingle on an everyday basis is key in this.

CONCLUSION

Far-right political parties have been gaining ground in Europe because of their anti-immigration agenda. Meanwhile US President Donald Trump was elected in 2016 by riding a wave of national anxieties, one of which was illegal immigration and its perceived social consequences such as job loss and rising crime. It is imperative that we in Singapore do not also stumble down the path of xenophobia where people deemed "foreign" are discriminated against and excluded from full participation in national and city life. It is important to remember that integration is a two-way street; both local-born citizens and new immigrants have to do their share to integrate into a polity and nation that will be altered by their presence. Nevertheless what must be acknowledged first and foremost is that high levels of immigration will necessarily change the face of a country.

In his speech in Singapore during a visit in May 2018, Prime Minister of India Narendra Modi invoked Singapore's multiracial population as a marker of its unique identity. Speaking to an audience composed mainly of NRIs, he then acknowledged that those who had made Singapore their home had also then become part of that multiracial complexion. And importantly, they were now the bridge that linked Singapore to India. He was speaking at an event that celebrated new business and innovation links between the two countries. However, in his narrative, as in that of many other political leaders, the historical migration, cultural and trading links between these two states is always invoked as the background to current close relations. Drawing on the idea of historical continuities is politically expedient, but this chapter has sought to show that current trajectories of migration and mobility are demographically different from older migration trends. In particular, this new wave of migration has instituted new class divisions within the Indian community which have, in large part, trumped cultural and historical affinities. The former also comes at a different stage in Singapore's national development, where older connections with an ancestral homeland are diminished. These new mobilities will surely result in new challenges and anxieties for the nation and its people.

Notes

1. "Singaporeans Take Back Mandarin Gardens from Indian Expats", *theindependent. sg*, 27 April 2016, http://theindependent.sg/singaporeans-take-back-mandarin-gardens-from-indian-expats/

2. In Singapore, it is only the expatriate South Asian (Indian and Sri Lankan), British and Australian communities who play cricket.

3. The year 2008 marks the height of immigration to Singapore. Since then, average annual numbers of newly naturalized citizens and PRs has fallen. Chua Beng Huat, *Liberalism Disavowed: Communitarianism and State Capitalism in Singapore* (Singapore: NUS Press, 2017), p. 93.

4. Rajesh Rai, *Indians in Singapore 1819–1945* (New Delhi: Oxford University Press, 2014).

5. Vineeta Sinha, *Singapore Chronicles: Indians* (Singapore: Straits Times Press, 2015).

6. Hui Yang, Peidong Yang, and Shaohua Zhan, "Immigration, Population, and Foreign Workforce in Singapore: An Overview of Trends, Policies, and Issues", *HSSE Online* 6, no. 1 (2017): 10–25.

7. The decline of Singapore's TFR has resulted in many policy changes and incentives to encourage Singaporeans to have more babies. However, after a slight increase in the 1980s, there has been a steady decline in new births.

8. Gavin W. Jones, "Population Policy in a Prosperous City-State: Dilemmas for Singapore", *Population and Development Review* 38, no. 2 (2012): 311–36; "Number of New Immigrants Let in Will Reflect Racial Ratio—Dr Tay", *Straits Times*, 1 August 1989, p. 20.

9. Yang, Yang and Zhan, "Immigration, Population, and Foreign Workforce in Singapore".

10. Department of Statistics Singapore, *Census of Population 2010, Statistical Release 2*, "Households and Housing", p. xi. https://www.singstat.gov.sg/-/media/files/publications/cop2010/census_2010_release2/cop2010sr2.pdf

11. Ritu Jain and Lionel Wee, "Cartographic Mismatches and Language Policy: The Case of Hindi in Singapore", *Language Policy* 17, no. 1 (2018): 99–118.

12. Sinha, *Singapore Chronicles: Indians*, p. 43.

13. The NRI has become an important economic and political category for the Indian state, with this group of affluent Indians remitting significant amounts of their

income back to India, as well as influencing national politics through support of leaders like Narendra Modi who enjoys massive popularity amongst NRIs in the United States, for example.

14. See, for example, Hong Liu, "Beyond Co-Ethnicity: The Politics of Differentiating and Integrating New Immigrants in Singapore", *Ethnic and Racial Studies* 37, no. 7 (2014): 1225–38.

15. This was defined by having an income of more than S$5,000 a month, which is over the median income (50th percentile) of Singaporeans in 2017. https://www. singstat.gov.sg/-/media/files/publications/reference/sif2018.pdf (accessed 11 June 2019).

16. For an example of this, visit the Indian Heritage Centre in Singapore.

17. Ritu Jain and Lionel Wee, "Multilingual Education in Singapore: Beyond Language Communities", in *Multilingualism and Language in Education: Sociolinguistic and Pedagogical Perspectives from Commonwealth Countries*, edited by Androula Yiakoumetti (Cambridge: Cambridge University Press, 2015), pp. 67–85.

18. Tamil is also recognized as an official language in the Indian union territory of the Andaman and Nicobar islands.

19. Many working-class Indians do not speak Hindi, but only their regional language.

20. Department of Statistics Singapore, *Census of Population 2000, Statistical Release 2*, "Education, Language and Religion", https://www.singstat.gov.sg/ publications/cop2000/cop2000r2; Department of Statistics Singapore, *Census of Population 2010, Statistical Release 1*, "Demographic Characteristics, Education, Language and Religion", https://www.singstat.gov.sg/-/media/files/publications/ cop2010/census_2010_release1/cop2010sr1.pdf

21. Ritu Jain and Lionel Wee, "Cartographic Mismatches and Language Policy".

22. Lee Wei Fen, *Exclusively Sacred: Community, Worship, and Voluntarism in Singapore Hindu Temples* (MA thesis, National University of Singapore, 2013).

23. Leong Chan-Hoong, "Social Markers of Integration: What Matters Most to Singaporeans?", in *Migration and Integration in Singapore*, edited by Yap Mui Teng, Gillian Koh, and Debbie Soon (New York: Routledge, 2013).

24. See, for example, Lin Suling, "Commentary: Tackling Inequality by Moving from Emotion to Action", *Channel NewsAsia*, 7 April 2018, https://www.channelnewsasia. com/news/commentary/esso-petrol-pump-attendant-tackling-inequality- singapore-10100032

25. See, for example, Michael Hill and Lian Kwen Fee, *The Politics of Nation Building and Citizenship in Singapore* (London: Routledge, 1995); Nirmala S. Purushotam, *Negotiating Language, Constructing Race: Disciplining Difference in Singapore* (Berlin and New York: Mouton de Gruyter, 1998).

26. See Walid Jumblatt Abdullah's chapter in this volume for a different perspective of the CMIO category.

27. Gordon Allport, *The Nature of Prejudice* (Reading: Addison-Wesley, 1954).

28. See "Diversity and Contact ('DivCon')", *Max Planck-Gesellschaft*, http://www.mmg. mpg.de/en/research/all-projects/diversity-and-contact-divcon/ for details.

Part III

POLITICAL DIVIDES AND
A DIVIDED POLITY

8

Protest and the Culture War in Singapore

Daniel P.S. Goh[1]

INTRODUCTION

In January 2001, artists and activists gathered at a forum organized by local theatre company, The Necessary Stage, to discuss cultural activism in Singapore. The artists and activists, fresh from their collaborative engagement to build an experimental civil society network called The Working Committee, discussed "Protest, Provocation, Process", as the title of the forum indicated. Alvin Tan, the founder and artistic director of The Necessary Stage, was a key organizer of The Working Committee. The discussion revolved around the state's approach to dissent and protest, from crackdowns in the early decades to censorious proscriptions in more recent years. Tan was no stranger to the latter, having been accused in 1994 by the local media of dabbling in "Marxist" forum theatre. One of the three speakers, the esteemed pioneer of bilingual plays in Singapore, the late Kuo Pao Kun, spoke from his personal experience of draconian extrajudicial detention in the 1970s.

The forum was a rare event. After a decade of social liberalization under then Prime Minister Goh Chok Tong, public forms of protest were still seen as anti-government provocations that were unacceptable in Singapore. Holding a forum on protest could itself be construed by the authorities as a provocation. Yet, there was little critical sting in the discussion. Instead, there was a sense of discomfort among the activists about the changing relationship between the illiberal state and protesters. At the forum, Kuo said,

Comparing the 1960s or the 1970s to the present, the kind of relationship between protesting artist or groups and the government is very different.

People really saw one another as enemies in the 1960s to the 1980s. And the government would actually kill these people. But, today the arguments between the art groups and the government are like disputes within a family.[2]

Seventeen years later, in March 2018, a family-like dispute about protest was aired in Parliament. Kok Heng Leun, Artistic Director of the Drama Box and who represented the arts sector as nominated member of parliament (NMP), raised objections to the last of the four examples used to illustrate a "serious incident" that would come under increased police powers in the new Public Order and Safety (Special Powers) Act. The hypothetical example used was a peaceful, sit-down protest in the Central Business District, which grew over a week to impede traffic flow and affect business. In characteristically deferent tone, Kok asked the Minister to "share ... why she thinks that the powers under the Criminal Procedure Code or the Public Order might be insufficient to cover" this hypothetical peaceful protest. Citing civil activists' criticism of the legislation as targeted at peaceful protests, the Second Minister for Home Affairs Josephine Teo defended the example as showing a "large-scale public disorder" disrupting the daily lives of ordinary Singaporeans, not a mere protest.

Kok persisted, arguing that the example should refer to "a protracted disruption" rather than merely "a disruption to daily businesses", and called for greater accountability, suggesting that an official report be submitted to Parliament in the event the powers are used. At this point, the debate turned testy. Teo pointed out that there was nothing to prevent members of parliament (MPs) from asking questions and debating the incidents. Kok pursued his point. After some exchanges, Minister Teo threw down the ultimate gauntlet, the ballot box,

> if a serious incident as envisioned in clause 3 has happened, do you not think that the public demands an explanation? Do you not think that the public would already expect a report to be tabled? And that even without a Parliamentary Question, any self-respecting Minister knows that he has to respond. I do not think you need to write it into a Bill. The Minister will have to stand for election.[3]

The evolution of the discomforting debates over protests in Singapore is illustrative of two trends that this chapter seeks to analyse. The first trend is the growing acceptance by the state of the need to provide spaces for protest, as can be seen in the Minister's assiduous effort to distinguish between a peaceful protest and a large-scale public disorder. It is also indicative of the liberalization of public sphere when artist-activists bristled with discomfort about protest in the isolated space of the Substation in 2001, while in 2018, their representative debated with a government minister on protest in Parliament. This acceptance is grounded in the developmental state embracing neoliberal capitalism and globalization in the late 1990s. As a result, the developmental state, which sees its primary role as the developer of economic and human resources through distinct policies and incentives, began to produce regulated spaces of protest that, as I shall argue, turned protest from moral acts into spectacular means for publicity.

The second trend is complex. As more peaceful protests are enacted in Singapore, protests have increasingly become a space for the culture war between Singaporeans who espouse socially conservative values and those who champion progressive values. The general features of this culture war are similar to the culture wars taking place in Western societies in terms of the value propositions, political orientations and issues of contentions. The main issues of contentions are over sexuality, immigration and multiculturalism. However, the culture war in Singapore takes on a distinct political shade due to the cultural contradictions in the developmental state's formation.

The cultural contradiction originated in the politics of the 1980s and early 1990s when the state pitted conservative "Asian values" (generally interpreted to be hard work, deference for authority, and privileging community interests over those of the individual) against liberal "Western" values (generally interpreted to be liberalism, decadence and individualism) to stem the wave of democratization in Asia. This period also saw the rise of fundamentalist religious movements, with the conservative state conditioning their political orientation. However, the developmental state moderated its conservatism and liberalized the public sphere in the late 1990s to 2010s, as it embraced globalization and sought to transform Singapore into a cosmopolitan and inclusive global city. The resulting culture war has seen the state and the citizenry caught between the increasingly vocal antagonism between conservatives and progressives, and the space of protests reflects this. Paradoxically, the spectacular nature of protest means that the political and social middle ground is being crowded out in public discourse, at the same time as activists with radical conservative and progressive views are looking beyond mainstream protest space to express their discontent.

THE STATE AND THE MORALITY OF ARTISTIC PROTESTS

Sociology has sought to understand protests as unpredictable outbursts of collective sentiments or as a collective action tool for the pursuit of group interests. James Jasper argued that protests should be best understood as public and collective articulations of moral beliefs and feelings.[4] This is a decidedly Durkheimian approach that sees society as a normative order in which its underpinning moral beliefs and sentiments have to be contested and tested regularly to ensure societal values reflect individual consciences. As such, protests are needed because modern institutions are rationalized and thus fail to allow for moral contests and tests to become the vehicle for the re-enactment of social order. But beyond the Durkheimian base, Jasper makes the case that culture as shared understanding and practices of communication is a crucial dimension of protests and the fundamental moral beliefs and feelings have to be expressed through culture. Protest organizers are therefore "very much like artists", creating new cultural perspectives and affections that encapsulate the moral intuitions of individuals, allowing these individuals to coalesce into a social movement and identify themselves as a social group.[5]

This is useful for understanding the situation in Singapore in the 1990s. For more than two decades after independence in 1965, the developmental state deployed draconian political instruments to suppress dissent and emasculate civil society. Coupled with extensive resettlement of the population into public housing estates with modern amenities under the rubric of urban redevelopment, the state directed the energies of the citizenry towards becoming a modern workforce for industrialization. Memories of the political chaos experienced during decolonization in the 1950s and 1960s, marked by public demonstrations, violent strikes and fatal racial riots, were used to justify authoritarian order. Protests were thus treated as imminent threats to the fragile social order of independent Singapore.

Conditioned by the overemphasis on public order and extreme sanctions on dissent, ordinary citizens were not able to overcome the cultivated fear to engage the liberalization of politics and society that the Goh Chok Tong government began in the early 1990s. Civil society groups, representing special causes in nature conservation, heritage preservation, women's rights and minority rights, made strides but stayed clear of protests and, instead, channelled their work into advocacy and lobbying. Artists were the ones who waded into protests, not as organizers of protest movements, but as individual voices of conscience calling out attention to grievous injustices in the liberalizing climate. From Jasper's work, we can explain why this was so. With the political discourse and shared understandings dominated by the hegemonic party-state, it took especial and daring creativity to challenge and protest the established normative culture, so as to open up the social space for new ways of thinking and feeling.

On New Year's Eve in 1993, performance artist Josef Ng staged the rare public protest in the form of performance art and provoked a major backlash from the liberalizing state. A month earlier, the police staged an entrapment operation in Tanjong Rhu, a well-known gay cruising area, and arrested and charged a dozen homosexual men with outraging the modesty of their "victims" who were actually undercover officers. Six of the men pleaded guilty and received sentences of a few months as well as three strokes of the cane. At a service corridor in a large suburban mall in the Prime Minister's ward of Marine Parade, Ng's performance, which he called *Brother Cane*, alluded to the big brother state and the cane. Dressed in a black robe, Ng laid out twelve tiles on the floor to represent the twelve men arrested at Tanjong Rhu. He placed a newspaper cutting of the report of the arrests, a block of tofu and a small bag of red dye on each tile. Josef then picked up a small cane and struck the floor in a rhythm. He then performed a dance, tapped the cane on each block and whipped the tofu and bag of dye.

His ritualistic violence evoked popular Taoist spirit-medium practices in Singapore, but the protest moment came after the splattering of white tofu and red paint. Ng spoke, saying that he heard clipping hair was a form of silent protest. He walked to the far end, faced a wall, took off his robe to reveal his bare body clad only in black briefs, lowered his briefs slightly to reveal the top of his buttocks, and purportedly snipped off some of his pubic hair, which he scattered on a tile back in the performance area. Ng asked for a cigarette, lit it and smoked a few puffs. He then said that, sometimes, silent protest was not enough, stubbed out his cigarette on his arm, thanked the audience to end the performance and put his robe back on.[6] The snipping of the pubic hair with buttocks part-revealed was a provocative gesture using borderline obscenity to protest the oppression and social castration of gay men. But the terrifying part of the performance was actually the inflicting of self-injury when Ng burned his arm with the cigarette, alluding to the practice of torture and expressing his solidarity with the caned men beyond the mere silent protest that Singaporeans were reduced to by political circumstances and the regime.

In response, the government came down hard on the fledging arts scene. The police raided the 5th Passage, an avant-garde arts centre which organized the performance, and arrested Ng and others. A pro-government tabloid newspaper ran a headline story complete with Ng's bare back and partly revealed buttocks to paint the performance as an obscene act.[7] Ng was charged as such, pleaded guilty and sentenced with a fine. The mall evicted the 5th Passage. The National Arts Council condemned the performances as "vulgar and completely distasteful", deserving of "public condemnation" and not to be construed as art.[8]

As the performance took place during the a 12-hour art festival called The Artists' General Assembly organized by 5th Passage and The Artists Village, an artist colony whose performance artists were beginning to define the contemporary arts scene in Singapore, performance art came into the spotlight. The government announced that it was "concerned that new art forms such as 'performance art' and 'forum theatre' which have no script and encourage spontaneous audience participation pose dangers to public order, security and decency", and could be "exploited to agitate the audience on volatile social issues, or to propagate the beliefs and messages of deviant social or religious groups, or as a means of subversion".[9] Governmental funding for performance art and forum theatre pieces were withdrawn, which along with new licensing conditions, practically banned their performances. The Necessary Stage was soon mired in the controversy that they were bringing Marxist elements into the arts scene by way of forum theatre.

Tang Da Wu, founder of The Artists Village, protested the curbs by performing a piece, slipping on a black jacket with the words "Don't Give Money To The Arts" embroidered on the back, when he was introduced to the President of Singapore, Mr Ong Teng Cheong, at the opening ceremony of *Singapore Art '95*, a major event held to showcase Singapore art in celebration of Singapore's 30th anniversary and the United Nations' 50th anniversary. As Lee Wen notes, Tang was pointing to the very contradiction of the state's funding of performance art, it "being anti-establishment, provocative, interventionist, and an opposition to the commodification of art".[10] But it was interesting that the crackdown had shifted the original focus of Josef Ng's moral protest of the injustices experienced by homosexual men in Singapore to the tensions concerning the moral function and purpose of art in society undergoing market transformation, which Tang's protest cleverly highlighted.

My aim here is not to recover the original and authentic moment of moral protest. The Josef Ng episode has been pressed into service for the critique of Singapore's political economy and illiberal regime and as an emblem for the gay rights movement in Singapore,[11] in which the impetus for the moral protest by Ng—neither democratic freedoms nor gay rights, but social injustice and state corporeal violence—has been largely bypassed. The episode marked a turning point in the state's treatment of protest, as it came to realize two things.

First, through this episode, the state found a better way to deal with the restless intelligentsia, by turning the discursive table on the protesting groups, marking them as moral renegades threatening the normative order of society and placing the onus on them to debate and defend their social purpose. Thus, the displacement from the moral outrage at systemic injustice in Ng's protest to grievances concerning the morality of art in Tang's protest, caused the artists to turn inwards to look at themselves rather than outwards to society. In effect, the sting of the original protest by Ng was taken out, replaced by self-concerned angst with one's own craft in relation to society.

As a result of the displacement from moral outrage to moral introspection, the artists sought to enter into mainstream spaces and to mainstream their practices, just as the state increasingly opened up mainstream spaces to accommodate the artists and their protests. This is the second thing that the state came to realize: it was better to offer regulated and contained spaces of protest rather than to suppress protests altogether and cause them to spring up in unexpected spaces and in unpredictable ways. The spatiality of protest mattered, and in the decade to come after the Josef Ng episode, the state sought to produce spaces of protest that limited these protests to publicity actions rather than moral acts.

THE SPATIALITY OF PROTEST FROM PRIVATIZATION TO PUBLICITY

Returning to the 2001 forum on "Protest, Provocation, Process", theatre doyen Kuo Pao Kun made another intuitive observation that he could not quite explicate:

> The recent events like *Talaq* are most telling. Ms S. Thenmoli was arrested but there was no charge. Can you imagine something like this ten years ago? They did such a stupid thing to Josef when something happened in the 5th Passage gallery—a gallery you can't even find if you try—hidden away in Parkway Parade and yet this was blown up into something so ridiculous. The arrest of S. Thenmoli was captured on television and even reported upon in the international press, and yet in the end she was just released. I think there is a *big change* here.[12]

Kuo's point about the not-quite-public, hidden character of the moral protest is actually an important question. Furthermore, especially since the 5th Passage was located in an obscure corner of a shopping mall, the audience was small and self-selected. Why did the state bother about a practically private performance for a specialized audience? Was the government trying to make an example of Josef Ng to put the brakes on the fledging experiments in new improvised art forms by artists in theatre and the visual arts? Asking this question would assume the government had the cultural nous to understand and fear the anti-establishmentarian thrust of performance art and forum theatre. It would be more valid to argue that it was precisely because the government *did not* understand the new art forms, particularly their illegibility due to their unscripted character, that they therefore feared these new art forms. The government was not able to *read* the performances and could not therefore calculate and predict their social effects.

However, this does not fully answer the first question. The nature of performance art is such that photographic and videographic documentation of the improvised performance would not capture the experiential moment and visceral gravity of the live act. Corporeal interaction, once mediatized, takes on a very different affection. If the government feared its social impact, whether it understood Josef Ng's performance or not, then it would have made more sense for the government to let the performance pass into ephemeral memory among the small and specialized audience in an obscure space, rather than to blow it up, which gave the performance the publicity it would otherwise not have and, in the process, sealing its place as a landmark event in the history of Singapore art. That the government reacted so quickly and strongly, even before the performance could pass into memory, meant that the government felt the performance had crossed the line and intruded into the prerogatives of the state.

What prerogatives of the state was there in an obscure service corridor in Parkway Parade, a private commercial mall? Josef Ng's protest was taking place at a time when the developmental state was beginning to introduce the practices of neoliberal marketization into its political economy. The government began an extensive privatization exercise across broad sectors. State-owned companies were part privatized. The downtown Central Business District was being redeveloped into a global city centre, in which the mobility of finance capital and cosmopolitan residents was being greatly facilitated.[13] The public housing sector was liberalized to allow cross-ownership of public housing apartments and private property. More land was parcelled out for condominium development to cater to the rising aspirations of Singaporeans for private property ownership. Town centres also began to privatize, with privately managed shopping centres or private malls replacing public shophouse complexes, and in many cases, small family-owned businesses. Built in 1984, Parkway Parade was a pioneer in this trend, and its success in Marine Parade, PM Goh's ward, helped drive the trend in other towns.

While more private spaces were produced through state urban planning, the government also sought the choreographing of global city lifestyles through urban design, in which art was beginning to be deployed to cultivate citizen consumers.[14] The problem was that people did not conform to the idealized citizen-consumer subjects. After the Josef Ng episode, a section of the democratic opposition began to deploy moral protest tactics. The Singapore Democratic Party (SDP), which won three parliamentary seats in 1991, the biggest win for the opposition in two decades, was on the ascendency. Academic Chee Soon Juan subsequently seized the party leadership and placed the SDP on a more antagonistic path. He took to the international circuit and made moral claims of fighting for human rights in Singapore to overseas audiences. Under his leadership, the party failed to win any seats in 1997, and Chee was defeated at the polls by a junior ruling party candidate. He proceeded to adopt street protest tactics. In 1999, he was jailed for giving two political speeches with a microphone and speaker at Raffles Place, a pedestrian square in the heart of the downtown financial district, without a licence, and was named as a prisoner of conscience by Amnesty International.

Under international pressure to accommodate the democratic opposition and in seeking to contain the green shoots of street protests, the government decided to designate the downtown Hong Lim Park as a space for regulated protests in 2000, otherwise known as Speakers' Corner. This was around the same time as the *Talaq* incident that Kuo alluded to. *Talaq* was an acclaimed Tamil-language play by controversial playwright Elangovan about marital rape experienced by an Indian Muslim woman. However, the play's questioning of Islamic law led to strong protests from Muslim religious groups. It had no difficulties staging the play in Tamil but when the theatre company wanted to stage the play in English and Malay, it ran into licensing hurdles with the authorities and they were worried about racial and religious sensitivities being provoked. A public dress rehearsal was staged, almost like a protest, which led to the arrest of the company president, S. Thenmoli. Thenmoli was very shortly released after an international outcry embarrassed the government, which was then pursuing a vaunted Renaissance City Plan to turn Singapore into a global city for the arts and the cultural centre for the coming Asian Renaissance in the twenty-first century.

In both the Chee and Thenmoli incidents, the state was running into the society of the spectacle,[15] which it embraced when it embarked on a concerted effort to brand Singapore as a global city. By 2000, Singapore already boasted a well-connected economy with networked infrastructure, but it was deemed a globalized "cultural desert".[16] The arts afforded the cultural makeover that the government hoped would turn the dull, pragmatic and strait-laced city-state into a hip and cool place for global jetsetters and well-heeled visitors. The city-state had commodity power but suffered an image problem in an advanced global capitalism driven by spectacles. Contemporary art as the sublime combination of commodity and image seemed like the perfect medium for bridging the gap.

The biggest opportunity for branding and marketing came in 2002, when it was announced that Singapore was to host the 2006 International Monetary Fund (IMF)-World Bank annual meetings. An elaborate programme with the tagline "Singapore 2006: Global City, World of Opportunities" was enacted to welcome the international dignitaries and place Singapore under the world spotlight. Importantly, the de facto ban on performance art was lifted. The first Singapore Biennale of contemporary art, which included static exhibits and performance pieces by local and foreign artists spread over the city's civic and religious heritage buildings to highlight Singapore's cultural diversity, was organized to coincide with the meetings.

The flowering of expressive freedom posed a quandary for the government. The IMF-World Bank meetings regularly attract a coterie of activists protesting against global capitalism. Singapore 2006 marked the second time public demonstrations could not be held in conjunction with the meetings, the first being Dubai 2003. The IMF and the World Bank pressured the Singapore government for a compromise, especially with regards to accredited non-governmental organization (NGO) representatives.[17] The government relented and cordoned off an area of 14 by 8 metres on the ground floor of the convention centre where the meetings were held, just outside the Starbucks coffee shop. With international media camped around the rectangle, registered protesters would get the immediate media publicity spotlight. Activists objected to the arrangement, which was not only limiting, but also staged the protests as media circus shows, making them part of the spectacle of Singapore 2006. The state was, in fact, imposing its own narrative on these protests and protesters, namely that it was a global city that could accommodate such protests while at the same time maintaining strict law and order. In effect, these protesters were props for the state's desired brand of publicity for the international meetings. Some 1,000 activists decided to hold their own protest forum meetings and demonstrations in the neighbouring island of Batam in Indonesia instead.

Despite the severe restrictions, dozens of activists vouched for by the IMF and World Bank were denied entry into Singapore. This was because, the government claimed, they had previously participated in violent demonstrations elsewhere involving occupation of public spaces and break-ins, and as such would not likely conform to the state's desired narrative. The IMF and World Bank openly criticized the government for reneging on its agreement to let the protesters enter, stating that they valued the protesters' role and worked with them though they disagreed. This negative publicity led to the government to compromise by lifting the ban on the majority of the activists who were denied entry.

At the event, Chee saw the opportunity to escalate the protests that he had been carrying out with his party activists. He had made use of Hong Lim Park on several occasions and had on one occasion went against the advice of police to apply for a licence to speak on a controversial racial-religious topic. He was also convicted for speaking without a licence and disqualified from standing in the 2006 general election. For the Singapore 2006 event, he sought to organize a march that would start from Speakers' Corner, include the Parliament and the IMF-World Bank convention, and end at the presidential palace. The march was blocked by the authorities, but Chee's group continued the protests at Hong Lim Park for a few days which subsided when the Prime Minister, Lee Hsien Loong, gave his speech at the IMF-World Bank meeting.

In other words, Hong Lim Park became the local counterpart to the indoor protest rectangle at the IMF-World Bank meetings' convention centre, both of them operating as publicity spaces for Singapore 2006 to show that the aspiring global city was not as illiberally governed as it had been portrayed. Instead, protests could take place in Singapore as long as they conformed to the morality of public order, as long as protestors took to the stage set up by the state, where protests were no longer moral acts in themselves, but acts to publicize the causes the groups were championing.

RED, WHITE AND PINK: THE SPECTACLE OF THE CULTURE WAR

After Singapore 2006, the government moved to institutionalize the publicity containment that it thought it had successfully experimented with during the meetings. In 2008, major changes were made to the regulation of Hong Lim Park. In addition to speaking, exhibiting and performing, citizens could now hold demonstrations at the park. The police withdrew from the park and left interested organizers to register with the National Parks Board, the agency in charge of the upkeep of all parks on the island. They could even register online. Events could be held around the clock and voice amplification equipment could be used from 9:00 a.m. to 10:30 p.m. However, citizens who wanted to speak, exhibit or demonstrate on racially or religiously sensitive matters still had to obtain a police permit. Nevertheless, this was a substantial liberalization that saw almost a dozen groups stage protests in the first month of the changes. Since then, protests in Hong Lim Park have become so commonplace that organizers have had to find creative means to attract publicity from the government-sanctioned media in Singapore. The most successful in this respect has been the annual Pink Dot rallies organized in support of LGBT (lesbian, gay, bisexual and transgender) rights.

After the Josef Ng incident, gay activists employed various creative ways to organize and mobilize themselves, with a keen eye on engaging the law to normalize homosexuality.[18] Activists used the fledgling Internet and growing gay social consciousness to increase pressure on the government to change its stance towards LGBT peoples. In 1998, in response to a question on homosexuality in Singapore in a live interview on CNN International, former Prime Minister Lee Kuan Yew said that the government would leave people to lead private lives, as long as their actions did not impose on others. This decidedly liberal statement became the informal policy principle for the government, which satisfied some in the LGBT movement but caused a growing backlash from Christian conservatives. In the early 2000s, governmental figures showed growing support for tolerance of LGBT peoples, which some saw as reeking of the economic motive for cultivating the pink dollar in the creative, cultural and service industries.[19]

Christian objections to the normalization of homosexuality grew in tandem, most notably when the National Council of Churches Singapore issued a statement opposing homosexuality in 2003. The debate on homosexuality blew into the open in 2007 during the review of the Penal Code and the decriminalization of anal and oral sex. After heated exchanges in Parliament as well as in the public sphere between pro-LGBT and anti-LGBT supporters, the government decided to reaffirm its support of the heterosexual nuclear family and left the provision making "any act of gross indecency" committed between consenting men, whether in public or private, a crime on the Code. However, in line with the stance on the privatization of sexual norms, the government promised not to actively enforce the law on consenting gay men.

This compromise brought on a brief truce on the LGBT front but in 2009 the issue exploded in a spectacular way. A group of conservative Christian women, many from a single church known for its vocal activism against LGBT rights, joined an established feminist advocacy organization, Association of Women for Action and Research (AWARE), just before its annual general meeting and launched a takeover bid by getting their leaders elected to the executive committee.[20] The conservative group saw itself as a vanguard acting to remove what conservative critics call "secular fundamentalism" from AWARE as well as its perceived pro-gay agenda.[21] AWARE thus became a battleground for the pro-LGBT and anti-LGBT activists. An extraordinary general meeting was called to address the takeover and its membership burgeoned by supporters from both camps in the run-up to the meeting. It was not just a showdown of opinions and will, but a media event as well, with live coverage of the meeting by the local media. The conservatives wore red T-shirts emblazoned with the white words "Pro Woman, Pro Family, Pro Singapore", while the liberals wore white T-shirts with a red box with white letters arranged to mean "We are Aware", thus enacting protests at the downtown shopping mall where the meeting was held.

The latter won the battle, but it may have been a Pyrrhic victory, as the Christian conservatives had raised the issue in the most public manner possible, generating much publicity for its cause than it otherwise would if they had just issued statements objecting to homosexuality. This point is important because the option of using Hong Lim Park was not available to these conservatives as their objections to the LBGT issue was intimately linked to religion. In fact, the AWARE coup and the subsequent battle was far more spectacular and provided a lot more publicity. On the other hand, even though AWARE managed to purge the Christian conservatives from its leadership positions, it was subsequently cut off from providing family and sexuality education in public schools.

It was during the AWARE saga that a group of gay activists was planning to take advantage of the liberalized regulations by holding Singapore's very own gay pride parade at Hong Lim Park. Internal discussions revolved around whether to stage a parade to champion LGBT rights in a direct and overt manner, or to mobilize as many supporters as possible to raise consciousness to seek to normalize homosexuality. Some activists felt that many Singaporeans would be turned off by protest-like marches and conventional gay pride parades, fearing it would alienate sympathetic or fence-sitting non-LGBT peoples. Additionally, Hong Lim Park was too small for such a parade as it would force the marchers to go around in circles with little orientation and purpose. In the end, the activists decided on calling for people to simply come together to form a human pink dot that could be photographed from a building overlooking the park.[22] Spurred on by the AWARE saga, the activists believed they could get the numbers to form the pink dot.

In the Pink Dot event, the gay activists understood the logic of the new society of spectacle that Singapore was becoming. To gain maximum publicity and support for the cause, one needed a powerful image that could evoke feel-good sentiments and symbolize the cause in an emblematic way. The logic of the spectacular defined the other promotional elements of Pink Dot. The event was accompanied by a campaign video that played on the national colours, which both camps at the AWARE saga also wore, with the colours red and white mixing to form pink. Local arts and media celebrities were co-opted to become Pink Dot ambassadors. According to the organizers, 2,500 people participated in the 2009 event, the largest an event had attracted to Hong Lim Park at that time. The event ended with the participants forming the pink dot, the image of which attracted widespread local and international media coverage.

Better organized and bigger Pink Dot events followed the successful inaugural event. The growing entourage of celebrity ambassadors was matched by a growing coterie of international corporate sponsors,[23] which included key players in global capitalism such as Google, Barclays, JP Morgan, Goldman Sachs, and BP. By 2014, the event had evolved into a concert attracting a record 26,000 participants with international franchises organized in cities around the world, including Hong Kong, Montreal, Okinawa and Salt Lake City. The themes varied minimally as reiterations of the message that LGBT people were family-friendly and normal people who just sought the freedom to love. This messaging was a peculiar and clever adaptation of the hegemonic heterosexual family-centred discourse in Singapore in order to portray LGBT people and pro-LGBT supporters as progressive and cosmopolitan citizens of the global city who valued family life as much as everyone else.[24] Such messaging was particularly disarming for anti-LGBT Christian conservatives who carried the pro-family flag because they now appeared as close-minded moralistic reactionaries trying to undermine loving relationships.

In 2014, the Christian conservatives regrouped. The LoveSingapore network of evangelical churches organized the Red Dot Family Movement to hold a counter-event called FamFest at the Padang on the same day as the annual Pink Dot event. The government turned down the application, finding the location unsuitable. The event was held as a virtual rally on

Facebook instead. However, the failed spectacularization received a boost when some Muslim activists called for a Wear White campaign to protest Pink Dot and reaffirm traditional family values. Pink Dot 2014 took place on the eve of the fasting month, Ramadan, and Muslim activists took the opportunity to stage the protest, ostensibly against Muslims attending and supporting the event. It was disingenuous on their part, as it was traditional practice for Muslims going to mosques on the eve of Ramadan to wear white anyway.

Nevertheless, Christian conservatives joined the Muslim protesters in wearing white clothes in protest. The Pink Dot spectacle that year saw another spectacle of 6,000 Christians wearing white to Sunday service at the Faith Community Baptist Church in solidarity with Muslim conservatives, as the intrepid pastor of the church, Lawrence Khong, emerged as the leading anti-LGBT voice for the Christian conservatives. With this move, Khong found renewed purpose for the flagging LoveSingapore movement he had led.[25] In effect, the Wear White campaign became the successful rallying counterpoint to Pink Dot, matching spectacle with spectacle.

CONCLUSIONS: THE PROBLEM WITH SPECTACLES

The ongoing clash between LGBT rights advocates and religious fundamentalists is the most visible example of the culture war manifesting in Singapore. It is not to be misrecognized as a transplant of a Western or American problem, though the influence is obvious. The culture war in Singapore takes place in the conservative but liberalizing social milieu of public morality grounded in the ideology of Asian family values. Thus, the protests by both sides have revolved around what define these family values. The protests in Singapore differ significantly from marches and demonstrations in Western cities. The former take on creative but spectacular forms, as the Singapore state has shaped local protests through tentative containment by way of delineating bounded public spaces for regulated protests. Finally, the state settled on the framing of spectacles for particular narratives and carefully crafted publicity in which the media performed the role of regulation and the state itself faded into the background. Thus, in the AWARE saga and the Pink Dot versus Wear White rallies, the state merely warned activists on all sides to not allow their actions to escalate into open social conflict, thus allowing it to claim the moral high ground as grand arbiter of disputes to maintain social order.

While the state may have found the equilibrium for maintaining a disciplined society and allowing for protests to relieve political pressure, the configuration of protest spaces as spectacles poses three problems in the emerging culture war. The first is the dissatisfaction with the protest spaces felt by progressives of a more radical bent. For these activists, protest spaces are increasingly seen as spaces of disciplinary co-optation. Going back to Kuo at the 2001 forum on protests, he articulated the discomforting sentiment best, "So I have the leisure and pleasure to complain and do oppositional things and in the end, I am still part of the system. This is the thing that eats into our very existence, in the end it will probably subvert our own autonomy we have built in the first place."[26] Thus, some activists are looking beyond Hong Lim Park and other regulated protest channels to enact their moral protests. One such example is when former migrant worker rights activist Jolovan Wham led eight others to enact a silent protest against the 1987 "Marxist Conspiracy" crackdowns on board a subway train on the occasion of its thirtieth anniversary.

The second problem is that even though the spectacular in contained protest spaces may well be a buffer for the state, it can also be used to provoke and draw the state's attention. For example, other than Pink Dot events, significant protests involving thousands of participants to date include investor protests against the Lehman Brothers Minibond default in 2008, protests against the immigration targets of the Population White Paper in 2013, and the "Return Our CPF" protests calling for reforms of the public pension fund system in 2014. However, these protests came and went, exerting some pressure on the government but with very little response. Frustrated, and starved of publicity for the lack of media attention, the organizers of the "Return Our CPF" protests took to marching, shouting slogans and disrupting a charity carnival taking place at Hong Lim Park. They achieved the publicity they sought by being charged with causing public nuisance, but lost a lot of credibility for their anti-social actions.

Nevertheless, it shows that even within the contained protest spaces, spectacles can turn ugly against the state and produce unexpected political effects. This could be especially deleterious for multiracialism and multiculturalism if racially charged protests against immigration policies and immigrant groups get out of hand. This threatened to happen in 2014 when some Singaporeans took umbrage at plans by the Filipino diaspora to celebrate Philippine Independence Day in an outdoor space in a downtown shopping area popular with Filipino domestic workers. This provoked an online firestorm of xenophobic attacks on the Philippine Day organizers.

The third problem is that different groups have different degrees of access to the spectacle of protests. Religious conservatives, because of state proscriptions on religious outreach and publicity in public spaces, are not able to enact their counter-protests on social issues at Hong Lim Park. They have tried instead to hold religiously neutral carnivals and charity walks to express their views, but these, as with the FamFest in 2014, have also been increasingly discouraged and proscribed by the authorities. Exclusion from protest spaces could push the conservative groups into activism in cyberspace instead, where the spectacle is far less regulated and the culture war gets more virulent, possibly involving foreign support for both sides.

Beyond the citizenry, there have been many protests involving lowly paid foreign workers taking place in public but hidden from the public view. Some of these protests have slipped through to the media as stories when they become spectacular. These include individual workers staging sit-ins in construction cranes, scores of unpaid workers protesting outside the Ministry of Manpower, and most spectacularly, when around a hundred Chinese bus drivers went on strike to protest low wages and when hundreds of Indian workers rioted in Little India after a worker was knocked down and killed by the bus he was ejected from. These involve a different kind of spatiality associated with migrant labour,[27] but they are linked to the culture war as progressive activists are also associated with the championing of migrant rights, while religious conservatives have made inroads in proselytization outreach to the different migrant groups. This combination, far from the regulated spectacle of contained protest spaces, would be the most destabilizing threat to a multicultural Singapore dependent on migrant workers.

Notes

1. The initial draft of this chapter was presented as a paper at the Workshop on Protest Spaces and Social Movements in Asia, School of Arts and Social Sciences, Monash University Malaysia, 14–15 January 2016. My thanks to Yeoh Seng Guan, Terence Chong and John Choo for their critical comments.

2. "Protest, Provocation, Process: Cultural Activism in Singapore", forum transcript, The Necessary Stage, 21 January 2001, in *focas: Forum on Contemporary Art & Society* (Singapore: The Necessary Stage, 2001) p. 99.

3. Singapore Parliamentary Reports (Hansard), 21 March 2018, Vol. 94, http://sprs.parl.gov.sg

4. James M. Jasper, *The Art of Moral Protest: Culture, Biography, and Creativity in Social Movements* (Chicago: University of Chicago Press, 1997), p. 369.

5. Ibid.

6. Ray Langenbach, "Looking Back at Brother Cane: Performance Art and State Performance", in *Space, Spaces and Spacing: The Substation Conference 1995*, edited by Lee Weng Choy (Singapore: The Substation, 1996) pp. 132–47.

7. "Public Protest", *The New Paper*, 31 December 1993.

8. "Singapore Arts Council Attacks Vomiting Act", *South China Morning Post*, 6 January 1994.

9. "Government Acts against 5th Passage over Performance Art", *Straits Times*, 22 January 1994.

10. Lee Wen, "Performance Art Performing," in *Singapore Shifting Boundaries: Social Change in the Early 21st Century*, edited by William S.W. Lim, Sharon Siddique and Tan Dan Feng (Singapore: Asian Urban Lab, 2011) p. 181.

11. Garry Rodan, "State-Society Relations and Political Opposition in Singapore", in *Political Oppositions in Industrialising Asia*, edited by Garry Rodan (London: Routledge, 1996), pp. 78–103; Cherian George, "Silence and Protest in Singapore's Censorship Debates", in *Popular Culture and the State in East and Southeast Asia*, edited by Nissim Otmazgin and Eyal Ben-Ari (London: Routledge, 2012), pp. 191–202; Eng-Beng Lim, "Glocalqueering in New Asia: The Politics of Performing Gay in Singapore", *Theater Journal* 57, no. 3 (2005): 383–405; Kenneth Paul Tan and Gary Lee Jack Jin, "Imagining the Gay Community in Singapore", *Critical Asian Studies* 39, no. 2 (2007): 179–204.

12. "Protest, Provocation, Process", p. 98.

13. Daniel P.S. Goh, "Capital and the Transfiguring Monumentality of Raffles Hotel", *Mobilities* 5, no. 2 (2010): 175–95.

14. Daniel P.S. Goh, "Choreographing Utopia by the Bay in Singapore", in *Tourist Utopias*, edited by Tim Simpson (Amsterdam: University of Amsterdam Press, 2017), pp. 97–120.

15. Guy Debord, *Society of the Spectacle*, translated by Donald Nicholson-Smith (New York: Zone Books, 1994).

16. C.J. W.-L. Wee, "Creating High Culture in the Globalized 'Cultural Desert' of Singapore", *Drama Review* 47, no. 4 (2003): 84–97.

17. "IMF and World Bank Rebuke Singapore", *Financial Times*, 9 September 2006.

18. Lynette J. Chua, *Mobilizing Gay Singapore: Rights and Resistance in an Authoritarian State* (Singapore: NUS Press, 2014).

19. Kean Fan Lim, "Where Love Dares (Not) Speak Its Name: The Expression of Homosexuality in Singapore", *Urban Studies* 41, no. 9 (2004): 1759–88; Meredith Weiss, "Who Sets Social Policy in Metropolis? Economic Positioning and Social Reform in Singapore", *New Political Science* 7, no. 3 (2005): 267–89.

20. Terence Chong, ed., *The AWARE Saga: Civil Society and Public Morality in Singapore* (Singapore: NUS Press, 2011).

21. Borrowed from the culture war in the West, the term was used by then nominated member of parliament and law professor Thio Li-ann to refer to anti-religion atheism that demand for the strict separation of state and religion (Thio Li-ann, "Secularism, the Singapore Way", *Straits Times*, 30 October 2007). A conservative who has written a theological treatise on the need for Christians to participate in public affairs to defend Singapore from secular fundamentalism, Thio opposed the decriminalization of homosexual acts during her stint in Parliament.

22. Lynette J. Chua, *Mobilizing Gay Singapore*, p. 121.
23. In 2016, the Ministry of Home Affairs disallowed foreign sponsors for Pink Dot and other events at Speakers' Corner, announcing that it would "take steps to make it clear that foreign entities should not fund, support or influence" Speakers' Corner events (Yuen Sin, "MHA Says Foreign Sponsors Not Allowed for Pink Dot, or Other Events, at Speakers' Corner", *Straits Times*, 7 June 2016).
24. Natalie Oswin, "Queer Time in Global City Singapore: Neoliberal Futures and the 'Freedom to Love'", *Sexualities* 17, no. 4 (2014): 412–33.
25. Daniel P.S. Goh, "Pluralist Secularism and the Displacements of Christian Proselytizing in Singapore", in *Proselytizing and the Limits of Religious Pluralism in Contemporary Asia*, edited by Michael Feener and Juliana Finucane (Springer, 2014), pp. 125–46.
26. "Protest, Provocation, Process", p. 109.
27. Daniel P.S. Goh, "Super-Diversity and the Bio-Politics of Migrant Worker Exclusion in Singapore", *Identities: Global Studies in Culture and Power* 26, no. 3 (2019): 356–73.

9

People's Action Party in Government
The Pole for "Big Tent" Singapore

Kenneth Paul Tan

Introduction

As political society in Singapore matures, it has also become more diverse, presenting a significant challenge to the ruling People's Action Party (PAP) government's ongoing post-colonial nation-building project. The fact that Singapore is both a nation-state and a global city, a fundamental contradiction that has become more profound since the neoliberal developments of the 1990s, makes it imperative to go beyond the more conservative goal of national integration when it comes to ensuring Singapore's continued survival. What the PAP government should aim for, far beyond straightforward integration, is national resilience.[1]

I will argue here that, as its context changes, the PAP itself needs to become more resilient as a party that, for about sixty years, has been at the centre of Singapore's political, governmental, and even—some might argue—social and cultural life.[2] This will, among other things, mean that the PAP should embrace diversity more profoundly and become a "big tent" party,[3] not only to better represent and be relevant and responsive to the evolving needs and interests of a more diverse society, but also to draw from a wider, deeper, and richer pool of talent and ideas in its endeavour to maintain high standards of governance and effective policymaking. Otherwise, the PAP runs the risk of becoming shackled to formulas that have delivered success in the past but could lead to failure in the future, if they do not adapt to changing circumstances.

This is not to say that a transformed and more resilient PAP in government will need to jettison a fundamental goal of keeping Singaporeans safe so that all who have a stake in the country can contribute to its material prosperity and be equally capable of enjoying the fruit of their labour. However, a resilient PAP government will need seriously to consider shedding its paternalist legacy of making life in Singapore so "safe" that it stifles creativity and variety, cultivates conformity and risk-aversion, encourages intolerance of change and difference, and entrenches an inactive culture of complaint. These qualities, when embedded in the system, can lead to its downfall. This is partly because such qualities work against resilience and partly because they do not adequately reflect the changing profile of a more diverse and cosmopolitan society.

Under this big tent managed by the PAP in government, all who have a stake in Singapore and who contribute to its well-being should be recognized and be given the space to pursue a life that they individually discover to be meaningful and valuable. People should not simply impose their views on others. Nor should they simply coexist in a disengaged and superficially pragmatic way, to each their own. Instead, under this tent, people with diverse perspectives and values should engage with one another constructively, with an open mind and heart, according to acceptable norms of deliberation aimed at reaching the best conclusions rather than winning arguments, taking credit, or assigning blame. All this has to be done in good faith.[4] It cannot just happen when we want it to. Thus, the PAP government should take the lead in efforts to build the necessary levels of generalized trust and social capital required for such a diverse and deliberative national community to thrive. In this spirit, the PAP government should revisit those policies and their underlying philosophy that may, today, have the unintended consequence of being divisive or encouraging chauvinistic notions about what it means to be a good person, a true Singaporean, and so on.

In this chapter, I will discuss how the PAP has, over the decades, managed to secure and maintain its leading position in a dominant party system. Then I will paint a possible future scenario in which PAP dominance unravels as a result of the degradation of those very same qualities that have led the PAP to success in earlier decades. And finally, I will discuss how such a scenario might be avoided, focusing on the question of what is required for a more resilient PAP in government and a more resilient Singapore.

THE NEW NORMAL

The four years between parliamentary elections of 2011 and 2015, popularly dubbed GE2011 and GE2015 respectively, were triumphantly described as the "new normal". The label, short-lived as it turned out, signified an expectation that the PAP would be confronted with more challenging and effective oppositional politics, civil society activism, private citizens who were more demanding and articulate, and—perhaps most importantly—an electorate that was able to use their votes more tactically to get what they wanted.[5]

In GE2011, the PAP won only 60.1 per cent of the total votes, its worst performance since Singapore gained independence. The leading opposition Workers' Party, which had successfully slated a few highly credentialed and charismatic candidates, was able to win Aljunied Group Representation Constituency (GRC), unseating two Cabinet Ministers. These results seemed to follow a trend signalling an erosion of electoral support for the PAP: from 75.3 per cent of the total votes in 2001 (when 35 per cent of the seats were contested) to 66.6 per cent in 2006 (when 56 per cent of the seats were contested) and then 60.1 per cent in 2011 (when 94 per cent of the seats were contested). Subsequently, by-elections in 2012 and 2013 brought two more Workers' Party candidates into Parliament, both by a convincing majority of the vote.

Social media, a somewhat anarchic space, had turned into the premier site where people argued with one another, sometimes with very little civility, and organized themselves on ideological and political grounds. Public intellectuals provided insight, theorizing Singapore's political and social condition and diagnosing its problems, and then—most importantly—formulating a shared and accessible language that appealed to ordinary people who could express through it what they hitherto could only feel. The public also seemed more divided, even polarized, into those who were more conservative and those who were more liberal. The former had, for a long time, been ideologically constructed as a silent majority and the latter a vocal minority to produce the ideological limits of political change. And yet, many in the so-called silent majority—supposedly materialistic, conventional, apathetic, and inexpressive—were becoming less satisfied with the government and its policies,[6] learning and adopting through their participation in social media clearly articulated ideological perspectives and vocabularies that were alternative and even oppositional to the established view.

Thus, there was widespread expectation that GE2015, when 100 per cent of the seats were contested, would yield an even narrower margin of victory for the PAP. To the surprise of many, the PAP won 69.9 per cent of the votes, and eighty-three of the eighty-nine contested seats in Parliament, by most accounts a landslide victory and a national swing back to the PAP. The Workers' Party lost a single-member constituency and retained its Aljunied GRC by only a slim margin. The new normal, it seemed, had come to an abrupt end.

PAP DOMINANCE

There are numerous historical examples of authoritarian regimes that have become more democratic, even liberal democratic, with capitalist economic growth and development, and a rising middle class.[7] But why does the PAP continue to be entrenched at the centre of a dominant party system in an economically advanced and successful Singapore? There are at least four reasons for this: performance legitimacy, moral authority, electoral advantages, and the fear factor.

1. Performance Legitimacy

The first reason relates to performance legitimacy, which the PAP has secured while in government, mainly by being recognized as responsible for Singapore's material success. That Singapore is a safe and prosperous city-state where its citizens are provided with resources and opportunities to live well is hard to deny. That most of the credit for this should go to the PAP in government, a rather more political claim, is also hard to deny. These claims, situated at the heart of the PAP's credibility, form a powerful basis for a transactional relationship between the PAP government and the people, a social compact securing the tacit obedience of the people in exchange for material benefit that relates to values most Singaporeans share.

The PAP's heroic post-colonial era, led by its first Prime Minister and founding father Lee Kuan Yew, saw dramatic progress from a low base, giving rise to the popular slogan "from third world to first", the title of the second volume of Lee's influential memoirs.[8] Now that Singapore has a more advanced economy with a more mature and diverse citizenry, policies have become more complicated and difficult to get right. Choices incur harder trade-offs, benefitting some citizens at the expense of others. The idea that the "administrative state", altruistic and insulated from political pressure, can continue to formulate and implement technically rational and far-sighted policies in the long-term interests of Singapore, and sometimes against the short-term wants of the people, seems rather anachronistic, even naïve, today.[9] The PAP government is more susceptible to making mistakes and, when it does, will find it harder to shield them from the critical glare of public scrutiny, not least because of social media. A straightforwardly transactional basis of authority is a necessary but increasingly insufficient condition for the PAP's durability in government.

2. Moral Authority

In addition, the PAP requires moral authority as a transformational basis of its leadership, the second reason for its long-standing dominance in government. Transformational leadership refers to the ability to motivate and inspire followers through elevated values and principles. One of these relates to paranoia, arising from an often-hyperbolic public rhetoric of survival, permanent vulnerability, and fragile success. In the light of Singapore's multiracial and multireligious society, lack of resources, geo-strategic vulnerabilities, and threat of being overtaken by its competitors, Prime Minister Lee Hsien Loong has proudly described his proactive and far-sighted government as a "paranoid government", worrying all the time about Singapore's future.[10]

A second contributor to the PAP government's moral authority is its demonstrated political will to stamp out corruption. The specialized and independent Corrupt Practices Investigation Bureau (CPIB) answers to the Prime Minister's Office. Corruption cases, even those involving high-level members of the PAP establishment, are dealt with openly, which generates strong public confidence and deters others from corruption.[11] High public sector salaries mean that the opportunity cost of corruption, and not just the risk of getting caught for it, is also high. Singapore's successful anti-corruption record has been acknowledged by the Political and Economic Risk Consultancy (PERC), which has ranked Singapore the least corrupt country in Asia continuously for numerous years, and by Transparency International, which continuously ranks Singapore among the least corrupt countries in the world.

A third contributor to the PAP government's moral authority is the value it places on meritocracy. Behind Singapore's material success is the widespread view that public service and leadership, amounting to a high-capacity state, are of paramount importance and thus Singapore's most talented people, usually signalled by academic accomplishment, should be encouraged to join the government. This has been achieved through a rigorously meritocratic system, featuring key institutions such as a highly competitive education system, public sector scholarships for top students to study at the best universities around the world and that tie them to public sector careers, a prestigious corps of Administrative Service officers, and some of the highest public service salaries in the world. These meritocratic institutions, coupled with a tough stance against corruption, have produced and reproduced a clean and elite government that could not only draw up highly rational policies and programmes in ivory-tower-like conditions, but also effectively implement these policies and programmes in conditions that were relatively unconstrained by popular pressure.

For meritocracy to work, there must be social mobility, enabling those who are endowed with socially valued talent and are willing to work hard to rise to the top. It also means that those at the top who no longer perform must make way for others who do. Adequate reward for performance provides an extrinsic incentive for people to be competitive and perhaps even to innovate. But rewards should not then create inequalities of resources and opportunities, structurally embedded in ways that make it impossible for the disadvantaged to compete fairly and rise if they do well. Thus, in practice, meritocracy will require a redistribution of resources and opportunities to maintain a reasonably level playing field, particularly in favour of newcomers to the game who may have inherited disadvantages. And it should only take into account such things as race, religion, language, gender, sexuality, age, and others, if they are found to be the basis of structural inequalities. Otherwise, meritocracy calls for a non-discriminatory focus on ability, effort and outcomes.[12]

What role does the PAP, as a party, play in meritocratic government? A quick inspection of the backgrounds of the Prime Minister and Cabinet Ministers, the de facto pinnacle of executive power, reveals very impressive academic and professional credentials. By convention, the Prime Minister is also the Secretary-General of the PAP's Central Executive Committee (CEC), the party's inner sanctum and most powerful committee. This makes him the de facto party leader. Out of the CEC's current eighteen members, fifteen of them are also Cabinet Ministers. CEC members are elected through a closed cadre system, in which the CEC appoints over 1,000 elite party members, who then have the right to vote in the CEC elections. Thus, the most powerful in the party and in government overlap, are visibly meritorious, and have devised a system that concentrates power and keeps it in their hands.

But the PAP is also a parliamentary party and therefore needs to represent the broader range of voters in their national policy debates as well as their constituency work. PAP members of parliament (MPs), who are not Cabinet Ministers, are appropriately more diverse, even though their selection for candidature is done with great care. Among them are also successful individuals from the business community, labour unions, the Chinese-educated, and so on.

Perhaps most interesting, in the context of meritocratic government, is the role of the PAP grassroots at the constituency level. Populated by ordinary members and grassroots leaders, the PAP is not a mass party, so membership is relatively low and most members are inactive until election campaign periods when some of them emerge to assist. Active members turn out at public occasions such as ministerial walkabouts and ceremonial events to simulate public support. Grassroots leaders are mostly party stalwarts whose authority is based on charisma, tradition, and seniority, rather than more narrowly meritocratic qualities like academic achievement and career success. They keep an eye on residents and they also help to explain policy changes to them. Most importantly perhaps is the role that grassroots members play in the weekly Meet-the-People Sessions (MPS), when ordinary Singaporeans come to see their MPs, often for help to solve their day-to-day problems. Party members provide valuable support to their MPs by organizing the logistics of the meetings, conducting pre-interviews before residents see their MPs, advising their MPs on possible solutions, and following up on and monitoring each case. Thus, they help to give the PAP a compassionate and sympathetic human face, a necessary counterpoint to an elite government that exudes a cold hard technical logic and erudite sophistication that can often be alienating if not off-putting.[13]

A fourth contributor to the PAP government's moral authority is the principle of multiracialism, which combines an integrationist impetus to build national identity—"Singaporean-ness"—with a pluralist impetus to retain colonial-legacy ethnic categorization—Chinese, Malays, Indians, and Others (the so-called CMIO model)—and its numerical proportions.[14] According to this CMIO model, Singaporeans are encouraged to engage with their deep ethnic cultures in the private sphere as long as this does not affect other Singaporeans' ability to engage with their own ethnic cultures. In the public sphere, meritocracy should prevail: the principle of non-discrimination should apply unless recognizing ethnic differences is necessary to level the playing field. The PAP fashions itself as a multiracial party, its leadership visibly including Singaporeans from each racial group. Thus, Singapore's party system is cast in contradistinction with the image of a communally organized party system in Malaysia, which The Singapore Story, particularly in the merger and separation episode, features as a means of securing communal Malaysia as multiracial Singapore's other.

A fifth contributor to the PAP government's moral authority is the value it places on pragmatism. Lee Kuan Yew, whose understanding of pragmatism was particularly materialistic, solution-oriented, and results-focused, described it this way: "If a thing works, let's work it ... Our test was: Does it work? Does it bring benefits to the people?"[15] Over the decades, the PAP government's pragmatism has, in practice, taken various forms. Policymaking has not generally been constrained by patience for philosophical, theoretical, or academic nuances and sophistication, or strict adherence to ideological dogma or any comprehensive moral-cultural frameworks.[16] On the rare occasion, PAP leaders might make passing reference to the party's founding democratic socialist values, but these references tend to go over the heads and around the hearts of ordinary Singaporeans for whom grand theories mean very little. Instead, culture and morality have sometimes been conveniently deconstructed, repurposed, vulgarized, and instrumentalized in order to achieve economic, social, or political outcomes. The top-down inculcation of Confucian values and later Asian values is an example of the pragmatic appropriation of culture as economic, social, and political resource.[17]

What really connects the value that the PAP government places on paranoia, integrity, meritocracy, multiracialism, and pragmatism to the hearts and minds of the people is the national narrative, commonly known as The Singapore Story. By reshaping Singapore's history into a narrative of national founding, permanent existential challenges, and common destiny, The Singapore Story—essentially a victor's history—positions the PAP government as chief protagonist and its political opponents as the nation's antagonists. At its most powerful, the national narrative melds the party, government, state, and nation into one sanctified entity. The basic narrative is told and retold in school syllabi, national day parades, official speeches, television programmes, and the framing of news and debates in the mainstream media.[18]

3. Electoral Advantages

Although Singapore has inherited the basic Westminster model of representative government, parliamentary elections have not been competitive, yielding a PAP-centred dominant party system since Singapore's independence. This is all in spite of universal suffrage and compulsory voting, and has much to do with the power of incumbency to influence the rules of the game in ways that are above board, justifiable in terms of the values espoused in The Singapore Story, and yet disadvantageous to opposition parties. At the crudest level, the incumbent party has enjoyed the power to influence the way electoral boundaries are redrawn and the power to determine which constituencies will be given priority in the use of public funds to upgrade residential facilities. At a more sophisticated level, its overwhelming majority in Parliament has enabled the PAP to amend the Constitution without much obstruction or delay. Thus, it has been able to gradually introduce institutional changes with the effect of strengthening the party's electoral dominance and continued control of Parliament.

One example of this is the Group Representation Constituencies (GRCs) scheme, which came into effect in 1988, creating multimember constituencies to ensure adequate minority representation in Parliament. Each GRC needs to have at least one MP from a designated ethnic minority group. While the scheme has made it more challenging for opposition parties to assemble credible candidates to field teams to contest and win GRCs, and has given the PAP an advantage in being able to shepherd into Parliament its newer candidates through GRCs helmed by ministerial heavyweights, the PAP government justifies the scheme in terms of the principle of multiracialism, here seemingly compatible with the need to provide what amounts to a form of positive discrimination in order to level the political playing field for minorities.

A second example involves the introduction of two types of non-elected MPs. Non-constituency MPs (NCMPs), introduced in 1984, are appointed from among unsuccessful opposition candidates who are able to win the highest number of votes in parliamentary elections, thus guaranteeing a minimum number of opposition MPs. Nominated MPs (NMPs), introduced in 1990, are appointed parliamentarians who are not affiliated to any political party, are not representative of any constituency, and have distinguished themselves in various fields such as the arts and sports, women's and youth issues, environmental issues, labour unions, business, social enterprise, and so on. The justification for both schemes points to the importance of ensuring adequate opposition presence in Parliament and raising the standard of debate.

However, these non-elected MPs have limited voting powers and their presence in Parliament may reduce the incentive for the electorate to use their vote to get more alternative voices into Parliament. This is based on a long-standing assumption that the Singapore electorate generally wants the PAP to stay in power, but it also desires more alternative and oppositional voices in Parliament that can stand up against an inadequately checked monopoly on power. If this assumption were true, then many risk-averse voters who wish to vote for an opposition candidate might choose not to do so out of a concern that there will be a "freak election", in which the electorate over-votes for the opposition and ends up with the unintended consequence of toppling the PAP.[19] Furthermore, voters who want more opposition in Parliament might still want to live in a PAP constituency, so they can enjoy priority in governmental decisions that bring them material benefit. This is a form of the free-rider problem where voters who want more opposition in Parliament will rationally choose to leave other voters to be responsible for achieving it.

4. Fear Factor

The political risk-aversion that characterizes the electorate's fear of a "freak election" relates to a conventional wisdom that more broadly links popular paranoia about Singapore's national survival with the indispensable role of a clean, elite, multiracial and results-oriented PAP government, buttressed by its successful track record. As Singaporeans connect their individual prospects with the survival and prosperity of the nation, they cannot imagine what it would be like without the PAP in power. They wonder if the opposition would be ready to take over the reins of government if they were to win. They wonder if the civil service, working so seamlessly for so long with the PAP political leadership, will be willing or even able to cooperate with opposition politicians who come to power. Opposition parties themselves have not mounted a shadow government, which almost suggests they see themselves as a permanent opposition.

But the fear factor also operates at another level. While the PAP government's authority rests mostly on transactional and transformational bases, the government does also resort to more forceful measures against those who offend it, usually as a last resort or as a periodic gesture of deterrence. The government has sued several opposition politicians and journalists for defamation, always underscored by the need to protect its integrity and reputation. An earlier generation of Singaporeans would also remember the PAP government's use of detention without trial against those who were labelled communalists or communists. Although such explicitly forceful acts are today much less common, the lingering memory of these often-traumatic episodes creates a low-frequency atmosphere of anxiety that puts limits on what people dare to do.

A FUTURE SCENARIO: THE UNRAVELLING OF PAP DOMINANCE

Given how secure these four reasons for PAP dominance seem to be, does GE2015 (the first fully contested general elections in Singapore's history) confirm that the PAP has little to fear when it comes to staying in power in the foreseeable future? After all, there had been similar "watershed" general elections in 1984 and 1991 when the fortunes of the political opposition seemed to be on the rise but the PAP was able to regain popular support soon after.

Those who say no have at least two reasons for saying so. First, they observe that 2015 was a special year. Lee Kuan Yew had passed away only a few months before the elections. It was also Singapore's fiftieth year of independence, celebrated lavishly with a year-long series of high-profile events, branded as SG50, which created a wave of public nostalgia. Lee's state funeral and SG50 were public spectacles that raised a groundswell of emotion, not least of which were patriotism and national pride, associated readily with the PAP's historic role in transforming Singapore from third world to first.

The second reason for saying that the PAP will not rest on its laurels has to do with the policy concessions it had made during the new normal. Responding to public pressure arising from a widely articulated criticism of Singapore's cost of living, income inequality, and emerging levels of poverty particularly among the elderly, the PAP government put in place after GE2011 directly redistributive programmes such as the Pioneer Generation Package (PGP) that benefitted 450,000 senior citizens who received lifetime assistance with their healthcare costs. The government also increased taxes on the top earners and instituted a higher eligibility ceiling for public housing. The government's shift to the left gave the impression that it was sensitive to the needs of ordinary Singaporeans and enabled the PAP to outdo the redistributive postures of the opposition parties. However, for a government with strong neoliberal tendencies and a negative view of the comprehensive welfare state, it is unlikely that such directly redistributive policies—which it has usually attacked as irresponsibly populist—will, in its view, be sustainable.

Quite aside from the specificity of GE2015, it is not impossible that the PAP itself starts to degenerate and lose political legitimacy in the process. What follows is a three-stage account of how PAP dominance could unravel. It is deliberately written in a hyperbolic fashion to bring the factors leading to such a development into sharp relief.

1. Pragmatism Degrades

For the most part, pragmatism has served the Singapore leadership well as a practical mindset that is non-binary, non-totalizing, dynamic, adaptive, open to new techniques, and oriented to solving problems. In years to come, pragmatism starts to harden into habits of the mind and heart. Resourceful, creative, and effective policymaking degrades into success formulas that shackle the imagination, encourage bureaucratic routine, promote managerial groupthink, and ultimately lead to mediocrity.

Even as people become more sophisticated, life more varied, and values more wide-ranging in global-city Singapore, the PAP government's policies become even more narrowly obsessed with a long-standing economic growth agenda that relegates other important public goods such as equity, cultural flourishing, nature preservation, and human emotional and psychological well-being to secondary importance. The government adheres more dogmatically to the demands of the market and the needs of corporate capital, foreign investors, and the wealthy class. Pragmatism degenerates into a barely disguised practice of neoliberal capitalism, indistinguishable in some cases from market fundamentalism.

In its effort to keep the economy competitive, the PAP government tightens up on social investment and assistance, even as the pool of unemployed and unemployable Singaporeans widens, mainly the result of automation and artificial intelligence, hallmarks of the Smart Nation, taking over the more mechanical and routine work performed by the labour force. The government focuses on strengthening its financial reserves rather than spending more generously on mounting social needs and developing less effable though essential human capabilities. Its pragmatism contains realist assumptions about human nature that policy has to work around rather than attempt to change. For instance, the government's reluctance to provide a more comprehensive state welfare system is based on the assumption that people will abuse the system if there are "free lunches". Over time, these assumptions harden into dogmas. The idea that social welfare can actually build social cohesion and resilience in a diverse multiracial society is instead blindsided. The government introduces numerous new workfare and skills upgrading schemes, and adapts the rhetoric of meritocracy to reinforce the belief that people are responsible for their own success and failure, and should be self-reliant. Ordinary Singaporeans, already leading stressful lives, come to experience deeper ontological insecurity.

Pragmatism's focus on outcomes also degenerates into a desire for quick results, establishing a policy preference for attracting even more migrant workers, foreign talent, and the super-rich. In the shorter term, this exacerbates inequality and poverty in an ever-more expensive city. Existing racial, religious, language, gender and generational cleavages are also aggravated by these developments. In the longer term, it slows down a more authentic nurturing and anchoring of local talent and capabilities. The government continues to argue that more and more economic growth, achieved by augmented efforts to attract foreign investment and talent, will yield benefits that will trickle down to the least advantaged, thus mitigating the problem of inequality and even poverty. And yet, to many Singaporeans at the day-to-day level, the sense of widening disparities becomes more palpable in the densely populated city. Meanwhile, Singapore's image as one of the wealthiest countries in the world jars against the experience of many ordinary Singaporeans who find it a challenge to live and work comfortably in their country.

2. Meritocracy Degrades

Meritocracy similarly starts to degenerate into elitism, where society is more sharply divided into winners and losers. Rising inequality and poverty hamper social mobility. The poor and the unemployed, pushed further away from the starting line, are made to feel fully responsible for their "failures" through a more unforgiving and winner-focused rhetoric of meritocracy. Those at the bottom start to disengage from the competitive society and become cynical, or they become envious and resentful.

Those at the top dwell on their success with a bloated sense of self-importance, their need to protect their elite status dressed up as an aristocratic obligation to lead the masses who do not understand what is good for them. As social mobility decreases, members of the elite start to look very similar in background. They think, speak, and act in the same ways and continue to do so habitually. Those from a different background, who extraordinarily made it into the elite circle, are pressured to comport with the values and affectations of the elite, forced to shed whatever insights and competencies they may have usefully brought from their diverse backgrounds. To the rest, including the grassroots base of the PAP, the elite starts to look and sound insensitive, unrelatable, high-handed, and arrogant. Lacking empathy and emotional intelligence, the elite is quick to dismiss popular emotions and the experience of ordinary life as irrelevant or mistaken. They make it a point to defeat differing perspectives from the ground with technical analysis, cold hard data, and sometimes even a humiliating and bullying style that seems less interested in engagement than in winning arguments.

Apart from public image issues and its inability to engage the wider society, the elite also faces the threat of internal rot. Success breeds overconfidence, even as circumstances are changing. Groupthink provides a zone of comfort and strength in numbers, of which individuals do not feel the need to step out. Since the electoral system fails to provide a strong enough challenge to the incumbent, the government continues to do things in the same old ways, losing sensitivity to changing circumstances, as it ignores alternative points of view and signals coming from outside the political and policymaking ivory tower. Overconfident in the extent of public trust it enjoys, the PAP government becomes prone to making major mistakes, which it will find much more difficult to explain to a sceptical, even cynical, electorate.

The rot also leads the government down the slippery slope of corruption. The elites come to believe that because they are special and have made such extraordinary contributions to Singapore's success, they deserve more. Not only is this about political and public sector salaries, it can also morph into the taking of liberties with rules and privileges. Members of the elite push the boundaries of what is legally acceptable and justify to themselves why it is reasonable to do so. Before too long, norms and standards of integrity start to slip, perhaps without the elite even noticing it.

Finally, the internal rot also takes the form of factions developing within the party and splinter groups forming out of them. Without a strongman like Lee Kuan Yew at the helm securing a united front, egos start to rise, rivalries form, and infighting ensues. As the electorate witnesses the erosion of the PAP government's electoral and performance legitimacy, they express their dissatisfaction at the ballot box in ways that are more consequential than GE2011. Seeing its dominance crumble, the government resorts to forceful authoritarian measures, which in turn provoke social unrest.

3. Public Trust Erodes, Giving Rise to Authoritarian Populism

Elite, technocratic and paternalistic, the PAP government has not invested sufficiently in building social capital, without adequate amounts of which, national disenchantment and social unrest will be nearly impossible to manage peacefully. The Singapore Story no longer resonates and, to the ordinary Singaporean, sounds increasingly like fiction told in order to placate and even deceive.

Popular cynicism and mistrust present a fertile ground for a demagogue—either from civil society, the opposition parties, or a PAP splinter group—to emerge and inspire the masses with populist language, appealing to an anti-establishment mood, a mobilized sense of victimhood, and an impulse to find scapegoats that explain all of society's ills, including foreigners and minorities of all kinds. Both mainstream and social media platforms amplify the outrage provoked by the demagogue, profiting from an angry public that has had enough.

The demagogue extracts loyalty and support from the old establishment elite, by offering them basic protection from the masses that the demagogue now controls. Benevolent authoritarian government in independent

Singapore's founding decades degenerates into crude authoritarian populism.

AVOIDING THIS ROUTE

The PAP in government can today do a number of things to reduce the possibility of going down this route.

First, it needs to change its thinking—and also transform the public's thinking—on a number of things that relate to performance legitimacy. The PAP does not need to seek and claim full credit for Singapore's success as the basis of its political legitimacy, because this will exclude valuable talent, energy, and ideas outside of the establishment; reduce the extent to which citizens feel they should share in the responsibility for their nation's well-being; and ultimately put the blame for any major problems—nearly unavoidable in a more complex future—squarely on the shoulders of the PAP government. Sharing credit for success does not mean the PAP government will be viewed as less competent. But by taking the lead in being more genuinely collaborative, it can demonstrate open-mindedness, confidence, and strength. Similarly, being responsive to even inconvenient ideas does not mean giving in to public or sectarian pressure, and teaching the public that pressure works. If the PAP government desires the trust of the people, it needs not only to earn it, but also to trust the people in return. Future Prime Ministers and Cabinet Ministers will need to be more powerfully motivational and transformational, not through a singular Singapore Story that they author, but by inviting Singaporeans whose diversity greatly exceeds the CMIO model to collaboratively narrate multi-perspective Singapore Stories that inspire.

Thus, the PAP government should aim to be the leader in bringing voices, even contrarian ones, together and exchanging fresh perspectives under a big tent. The government should not attempt to harden up in the face of a more challenging set of circumstances. Resilience is not achieved that way. Instead, it should authentically absorb and include diversity and difference. This has to exceed the more superficial—and sometimes patronizing—efforts to engage in safe conversation or even pseudo-conversation with a clinically engineered cross-section of people, designed not to rock the boat.

Under a resilient big tent held up by the PAP government, engagement needs to be empathetic, imaginative, and critical so that difficult differences that matter are not politely sidestepped. To achieve this, the government needs to take the lead in generating social capital to sustain levels of good faith necessary for diverse people to communicate, collaborate, and care for one another. It has to free up the education system and the arts from commercial and political restraints so that they can do the job of helping people develop human and social capabilities to the fullest, and thus be able to participate fully in a resilient society.

Undergirding all of this is the importance of rebalancing meritocracy. The PAP government needs to return to its social democratic roots and make a more wholehearted attempt to reduce the debilitating material inequalities in society through substantive redistributive measures. By helping to equalize starting points for all Singaporeans, not only will social mobility be re-energized, but also more Singaporeans from different backgrounds will be able to contribute valuable ideas, perspectives and actions in the PAP government's big tent.

Singaporeans are preparing for the transition to its fourth-generation leadership. Many will remember Singapore's second Prime Minister Goh Chok Tong describing his approach to government as kinder, gentler, and more participatory and consultative, as compared to the tough and no-nonsense approach of the first Prime Minister Lee Kuan Yew. They will perhaps remember third Prime Minister Lee Hsien Loong describing his approach as more inclusive. Thus, a government strong and confident enough to support a big tent under which a greater diversity of perspectives, values, and goals can thrive and contribute creatively and productively to Singapore's advancement, would not seem like an unreasonable next stage.

Notes

1. Kenneth Paul Tan, *Governing Global-City Singapore: Legacies and Futures After Lee Kuan Yew* (London: Routledge, 2017).
2. I also assume here, for the sake of argument, that a dominant party system is compatible with a resilient Singapore. Whether it is the best thing for a resilient Singapore is a question for another occasion.
3. Kishore Mahbubani, *Can Singapore Survive?* (Singapore: Straits Times Press, 2015).
4. Kenneth Paul Tan, "Civic Education and Deliberative Democracy in Singapore", in *Civil Society and the State in Singapore*, edited by Carol Soon and Gillian Koh (Singapore: World Scientific, 2017), pp. 203–28.
5. Elvin Ong and Mou Hui Tim, "Singapore's 2011 General Elections and Beyond: Beating the PAP at Its Own Game", *Asian Survey* 54, no. 4 (2014): 749–72.
6. Derek da Cunha, *Breakthrough: Roadmap for Singapore's Political Future* (Singapore: Straits Times Press, 2012).
7. Francis Fukuyama, *The End of History and the Last Man* (London: Hamish Hamilton, 1992).

8. Lee Kuan Yew, *From Third World to First: The Singapore Story: 1965–2000* (Singapore: Times Editions, 2000).

9. Sudhir Thomas Vadaketh and Donald Low, *Hard Choices: Challenging the Singapore Consensus* (Singapore: NUS Press, 2014).

10. Lee Hsien Loong, "Civil Service Salary Revisions", Singapore Parliamentary Reports (Hansard), 11 April 2007, Vol. 83, http://sprs.parl.gov.sg

11. Jon S.T. Quah, *Curbing Corruption in Asia: A Comparative Study of Six Countries* (Singapore: Eastern Universities Press, 2003).

12. Kenneth Paul Tan, *Governing Global-City Singapore*.

13. Kenneth Paul Tan, "Democracy and the Grassroots Sector in Singapore", *Space and Polity* 7, no. 1 (2003): 3–20.

14. Daniel P.S. Goh, "Multiculturalism and the Problem of Solidarity", in *Management of Success: Singapore Revisited*, edited by Terence Chong (Singapore: Institute of Southeast Asian Studies, 2010), pp. 561–78.

15. Lee Kuan Yew, "Speech in Parliament on the White Paper on Ministerial Salaries on 1 November 1994", in *Lee Kuan Yew: The Man and His Ideas*, edited by Han Fook Kwang, Warren Fernandez, and Sumiko Tan (Singapore: Times Editions, 1998).

16. Kenneth Paul Tan, *Governing Global-City Singapore*.

17. Ian Patrick Austin, *Pragmatism and Public Policy in East Asia: Origins, Adaptations, and Developments* (Singapore: Fairmont International, 2001).

18. Kenneth Paul Tan, *Governing Global-City Singapore*.

19. Han Fook Kwang, "What Caused the GE Vote Swing?", *Straits Times*, 20 September 2015.

10

The Burdens of Ethnicity
Chinese Communities in Singapore and Their Relations with China

Ja Ian Chong[1]

INTRODUCTION

Tension between ethnic Chinese in Singapore and the People's Republic of China (PRC) was on open display over the two-year period from 2015 to 2017. A series of incidents brought out unprecedented friction between Singapore and the PRC. They range from Singapore's stress on rule of law to address disputes in the South China Sea involving the PRC to Beijing's unhappiness over Singapore's close security ties with the United States and the seizure of Singaporean military equipment in Hong Kong.[2] Public and quasi-official opinion in the PRC displayed displeasure towards Singapore for not siding with the PRC internationally despite the city-state's ethnic Chinese majority population.[3] Almost concurrently, some Singaporeans voiced their concerns over rising PRC immigration on both temporary and permanent bases, citing difficulties in integration due to differing values.[4]

Communities in Singapore who trace their roots to what is today the PRC have a complex and sometimes difficult relationship with their place of ancestral origin. This was the case since migration to Singapore began en masse in the early nineteenth century. Much of the complication comes from how these communities and their diverse interests intersect with the concerns of other groups in Singapore, as well as politics and economics both locally and in China. The PRC's recent global prominence and the efforts of its government to exercise influence externally muddies matters further for ethnic Chinese in Singapore. A solution is to develop a stronger sense of citizenship based around reasonable, substantive, and meaningful civic values and rights that transcend ethnicity, religion, and other narrower concerns.

Awkwardness in the relationship between Singaporean Chinese and today's PRC nationals originates from two distinct nation-building projects that at times cross paths. The PRC is the culmination of efforts to create a Chinese national state, built on an idea that this entity is historically synonymous with and represents all Chinese persons—a category that historically included those living all over the world.[5] The concept of "Chinese" is largely conflated with being ethnically Han. It was for these reasons that early nationalists like Sun Yat-sen targeted ethnic Chinese in Singapore for recruitment into and mobilization for revolution against the Manchu-ruled Qing Empire.[6] The Singapore state, itself a product of decolonization, seeks accommodation between the majority ethnic Chinese and other communities—sometimes imperfectly—while learning to live with its immediate neighbours.[7]

Examining the relationships between ethnic Chinese communities in Singapore and China necessarily raises questions about what "China" and "Chinese" mean. The answer is not clear-cut. One standard view of being "Chinese" is that of being a national or citizen of a state called "China". Cultural practices of supposed ethnic Han peoples and Sinitic languages, particularly Mandarin, define the people who unproblematically constitute the population of this Chinese sovereign state.[8] China, the state, is the ultimate political expression of being Chinese even though the modern, sovereign state is, of course, an institution with early modern European origins.[9] A further extension of this view is that there can only be a single political entity called "China". This is the basic Chinese nationalist interpretation of "China", and the one that informed efforts at popular mobilization by nationalist Chinese leaders from Sun Yat-sen to Chiang Kai-shek, Mao Zedong, and even Xi Jinping today.[10]

"China" as a single political entity that represents "Chinese" people in all their plurality is the product of political imagination, albeit a powerful one. This is despite the existence of ethnic minorities within China's borders, as well as significant cultural and linguistic variations within the ostensibly Han population.[11] The Manchu Qing Empire (大清國) that from 1644 to 1911 broadly controlled territories similar to today's PRC and beyond was, as its name suggests, a multiethnic empire for instance.[12]

The idea that "Chinese" are a single people or ethnicity that should rule over a unitary polity was one that gained popularity starting in the late nineteenth century. Much traction for this idea came from popular mobilization efforts by nineteenth century revolutionaries as they sought to overthrow Manchu rule using the banner of nationalism.[13] Until then, populations under Manchu rule generally accepted their role as subjects, especially those in areas firmly under Qing control since the mid-seventeenth century. With the exception of literati and gentry with ambitions for taking the imperial examinations and entering political office, most people were largely content speaking their own regional languages and engaging in local cultural practices.[14] Few communicated in Mandarin—then known as *Guanhua* （官話） or "official-speak"—the language of administration and fewer still in *Manju Bithe*, the language of the rulers.

DIVERSITY AND ETHNIC CHINESE IN SINGAPORE

Even though the Chinese in Singapore share cultural and linguistic similarities with the communities from which they originated, their experiences and sensitivities diverge substantially from those of PRC nationals today. Chinese communities in Singapore did not have to go through first-hand events like the Great Leap Forward, the Cultural Revolution, struggles of the reform era, and demands of national unification. Cold War restrictions on travel to and from the PRC from the 1950s through the 1980s insulated Singapore Chinese communities from the PRC's tumultuous formative experiences. That said, some associated Communist-run China with negative images of backwardness based on accounts of relatives living there. Instead, Singaporean Chinese underwent the throes of state- and nation-building, which included the marginalization and recasting of their culture, language, and traditions. They also shared more popular culture and interactions with Sinophone societies in Taiwan, Hong Kong, and Malaysia, compared to communist-ruled China. It is against this backdrop that Singaporean Chinese now interact with new PRC immigrants as well as the PRC state.

Indeed, the historical layers of ethnic Chinese immigrants to Southeast Asia make the communities very complex. A majority of immigrants to Singapore between the early nineteenth to mid-twentieth centuries came from locales in and around what are today southeastern Fujian, eastern Guangdong, and Hainan provinces.[15] Political loyalties and conceptions of China among these groups historically tended to centre on their native villages, clans, and temple networks rather than a strong conception of some national state.[16]

The descendants of earlier ethnic Chinese immigrants to Southeast Asia who later moved to Singapore from places like Malacca, Penang, and various parts of the Indonesian archipelago saw themselves as distinct from the groups mentioned above. These communities trace their arrival in Malaya and the Indonesian archipelago to the fifteenth century. They partially assimilated with indigenous communities through intermarriage and call themselves Peranakan, or local-born, in contrast to later arrivals, whom they called *sinkeh* (新客) or "new visitors" in Hokkien and *totok* in Malay.[17] Peranakan identify with a culture that combines elements from their points of origin with those from their adoptive land, and speak Baba Malay, a language that mixes Malay with Hokkien.[18] Under British colonial rule, many Peranakan saw themselves as "the King's Chinese", while others identified with being Qing subjects.[19]

On top of the already complex social setting described above are the various state-building efforts that tried to mobilize and organize ethnic Chinese communities in Singapore. As previously mentioned, ethnic Chinese in Singapore were targets for mobilization by anti-Manchu revolutionaries and later Chinese nationalists like the Revolutionary Alliance and KMT.[20] British and Japanese imperial projects in Singapore sought to make ethnic Chinese in Singapore pliant colonial populations.[21] Then there were the various left- and right-wing anti-colonial efforts that sought to win over ethnic Chinese communities, successively trying to convince them to become Malayan, Malaysian, and Singaporean.[22] Finally, post-independence nation-building and political consolidation attempts under the People's Action Party (PAP) replaced education in Mandarin and other Sinitic languages with English-oriented bilingual education.[23]

The Second World War highlighted further complications in the ties ethnic Chinese in Singapore have with the predecessor of the PRC, the KMT-led Republic of China. Ethnic Chinese in colonial Singapore mobilized to donate money and even volunteer to fight for the KMT government against Japan, most notably along the Burma-Yunnan border.[24] Such efforts angered the Japanese Imperial government to the extent that they massacred ethnic Chinese in Singapore and demanded reparations once they occupied the island in 1942.[25] Surviving ethnic Chinese tried to eke out a living under Japanese occupation, while the Japanese sought to turn them into Japanese subjects and the collaborationist KMT splinter government in Nanjing tried to win their loyalties.[26] Others escaped into the jungle to join the Malayan People's Anti-Japanese Army among whose members became the backbone of the CCP-inspired communist armed insurgency led by the Malayan Communist Party (MCP) after the Second World War.[27]

Furthermore, there are members of one or two generations of Singaporean Chinese who bear the scars of being targeted by the state during the Cold War. The decades immediately leading to and from Singapore's independence dovetailed with the height of the Cold War in Asia and the Vietnam War. Working-class anti-colonial and labour movements between the 1950s and 1970s had close ties with left-leaning unions.[28] British colonial authorities as well as the Labour Front and People's Action Party administrations of the period saw these movements and their affiliated organizations as communist-controlled or at least sympathizers.[29] These unions and movements included large numbers of the Chinese-educated, many of whom were subject to suspicion, surveillance, and even detention without trial.[30] The trauma of this period lives on with a number of older Singaporean Chinese.

As Singapore opened its doors to engage the PRC economically and to welcome new PRC immigrants from the late 1970s and particularly since the early 2000s, Singaporean Chinese faced yet another round of pressures. Part of this pressure came from having to respond to unfamiliar expectations from the PRC state and people from the PRC themselves.[31] For example, PRC officials and people who grew up under the CCP tend to hold implicit beliefs about the universality of Chinese struggle against Western imperialism. This anti-imperialist struggle shapes Chinese nationalism and is believed by many people from the PRC to be a globally shared Chinese experience, given the way nationalist sentiments permeate the education system and popular culture in China.[32] That such understandings are distant, if not alien, to most Singaporean Chinese—especially younger generations—creates friction during interactions and in efforts to integrate new PRC immigrants.

A New Round of Interactions
China's rise to prominence over the past four decades has further convoluted its relationship with Singaporean Chinese in light of the material opportunities available. The PRC government, taking advantage of the ethnic affinity many Chinese overseas have for their ancestral homeland, welcomed Chinese capital and expertise from outside China at the start of its ambitious economic reform programme. Recent years witnessed the PRC state blurring lines between its citizens living overseas and persons of ethnic Chinese origin as Beijing sought support for advancing its national interests and foreign policy abroad.

Today, China is Singapore's largest trading partner, while Singapore is the largest foreign investor in China.[33] To seize market and investment opportunities in China, Singaporean Chinese business people unsurprisingly leverage on their cultural, linguistic, and other similarities with the PRC's population.[34] In this sense, Singaporean Chinese act in ways that parallel their counterparts from Taiwan, Hong Kong, Malaysia, and elsewhere; and may, over time, blur the distinction between the ethnic Chinese communities of Singapore, Malaysia, Hong Kong, and Taiwan in China. Such a development may prove politically salient given Beijing's desire to exert control over ethnic Chinese populations in Hong Kong and Taiwan.

The PRC government has encouraged local business connections with Chinese communities in Singapore and elsewhere since the start of Deng Xiaoping's "Opening and Reform" programme in 1978. Leaders in Beijing actively sought the advice, expertise, and experience of Chinese business people from around the world, as well as their capital, to jump-start economic reform. It was partially for such reasons that Deng met repeatedly with Singapore's then Prime Minister Lee Kuan Yew over the course of the 1980s and early 1990s.[35] China's welcoming attitude towards Singaporean businesses, many of which are ethnic Chinese-led simply due to Singapore's population make-up, helped re-establish connections with China that were cut off during the Cold War. Such exchanges paved the way for Singapore to engage in large-scale intergovernmental cooperation in China, characterized today by the Suzhou Industrial Park and subsequently Tianjin Eco-City and the Chongqing Connectivity Initiative.[36]

For some Singaporean Chinese who feel that the Singapore state's past de-emphasis on Chinese language education was unfair or wrong, China's economic success is vindication of their insistence on the promotion of Chinese culture. This group lamented the redirection of attention and resources to English-language–based instruction and the corresponding decline in Mandarin standards in Singapore as repudiation of the cultural roots of ethnic Chinese in the country.[37] Moreover, many faced employment difficulties and even discrimination as past PAP administrations focused on raising English standards and closed Chinese-medium schools between the 1970s and 1980s.[38] For some, their earlier emphasis on Chinese languages and cultures put them under suspicion for being resistant to nation-building and even "Chinese chauvinism".[39]

Economic liberalization in China alongside Singapore's demand for labour also led to the increased flow of PRC emigrants into Singapore, although the results of this interaction are more fraught.[40] High-income, high-net-worth individuals see Singapore as a safe place to park their money, including by investing in property, leading to accusations that they drive up property prices at the expense of locals through speculation. Another reaction to the highly visible PRC migrant labour population in Singapore is that they are depriving locals of middle-income jobs while driving down wages and adding to overcrowding. Singaporeans sometimes see PRC students as depriving local students of already limited places in educational institutions. There is the highly unfair association of low-wage PRC workers with unruliness and low-wage PRC female immigrants with vice as well.

Friction between Singaporeans of different ethnicities and recent immigrants from China is part of a larger wariness towards immigration that developed in Singapore from the early 2000s.[41] Differences in social mores, cultural references, and the fact that many non-Chinese, as well as Chinese, Singaporeans do not speak Mandarin make integration and mutual accommodation more trying for PRC immigrants. Among some Singaporeans, there is the lingering suspicion of communism, which they project on new PRC immigrants given that China remains ruled by the CCP. As Singaporeans tend to have vague notions of common social and political values and citizenship rights, they may be less confident and more apprehensive when facing groups with a strongly articulated sense of political identity such as PRC citizens.

Furthermore, cases of PRC citizens and new Singaporeans originally from China using fake documents to obtain local residency and citizenship foster suspicions among Singaporeans about PRC migrants.[42] This magnifies the unease and, among some people, xenophobia towards PRC migrants thus reinforcing existing negative views of China amongst Singaporeans.

About Political Influence

To complicate matters, there are concerns over the PRC government's renewed efforts to mobilize Singaporean Chinese, including both those locally born and raised as well as new immigrants. This issue came to light in late 2017, when a PRC-born academic holding a US passport was expelled from Singapore for allegedly trying to illicitly influence Singapore politics via individuals at his institution with high-level official access.[43] Even though the Ministry of Home Affairs, which issued the expulsion, did not explicitly state the foreign government the individual was supposedly working for, suspicions fell on China. This was partially due to this individual's pro-China positions and long-standing suspicions that Beijing has been trying to use Chinese business people, academics, and other socially prominent individuals to advance its interests inside Singapore. Such perspectives became particularly widespread as differences between Singapore and Beijing grew over interpretations of rule of law as applied to behaviour in disputed parts of the South China Sea.[44]

Suspicions about China's efforts to galvanize Singaporean Chinese to serve its political aims also come from Beijing's policies towards Singapore and ethnic Chinese outside the PRC more broadly. The PRC government-backed China Cultural Centre in Singapore, which President Xi Jinping officially opened in 2015, emphasizes Chinese culture as understood by PRC nationals.[45] The China Cultural Centre seeks to be a platform to project the PRC's national image outwards. The apparent official response by the Singapore state seems to be to underscore the uniqueness of ethnic Chinese experiences in Singapore, as seen in the accounts surrounding the creation of a Singapore Chinese Cultural Centre (SCCC) in 2017.[46] The key point in Singapore Prime Minister Lee Hsien Loong's speech opening the SCCC was that Singaporean Chinese culture is different from China's national culture.[47]

President Xi's administration's repeated official statements about the need to bring newly emigrated Chinese together with "older" Chinese communities to serve China's national interests abroad have also raised concerns over Beijing's intentions. For instance, reform plans for the All-China Federation of Returned Overseas Chinese in 2017 declare a need to emphasize:

> [M]utual reinforcement of domestic and overseas work, work on older and newer Chinese overseas to deepen and widen overseas work … to activate their [Chinese overseas] love for country and hometown to the greatest extent … so that they can contribute to the glorious restoration that is the China Dream.[48]

This statement follows PRC Premier Li Keqiang's call for Chinese abroad to help:

> [A]dvance the economic development of the nation, to guard and advance national unification, facilitate the PRC's foreign cooperation, raise PRC soft power and expand other such functions to realize a moderately prosperous society and provide new contributions to the realization of the Chinese people's glorious restoration.[49]

Such language indicates a new willingness to activate ethnic Chinese communities to influence foreign governments and societies over matters of China's security and economic interests, possibly even at some expense to the host country's position.[50] Issues may include exporting Beijing's position on areas such as Taiwan, Hong Kong, Tibet, Xinjiang, the South

China Sea, and even topics such as the US role in Asia as they relate to Beijing's concerns or points of national pride.[51]

Part of such outreach efforts is the extension of special residential status to ethnic Chinese abroad, including those from Singapore. A person who can prove his or her Chinese ancestry will be afforded ethnic Chinese status which qualifies him or her for five years of visa-free entry into China along with extended residency rights.[52] Nonetheless, this ethnic-based visa category may be of higher propaganda than practical value, since there remains some vagueness over its implementation. It may also apply more to former PRC citizens than individuals whose families left China before 1949. Beijing, too, invites participation from ethnic Chinese community and business leaders from overseas—including Singapore—into official and quasi-official activities. Some of these include World Chinese Entrepreneurs Conference, China Overseas Friendship Association, National Chinese People's Political Consultative Conference, and National People's Congress.[53] These policies parallel programmes for Taiwanese and Hong Kongers, which blur the lines between people China wants to claim as nationals and their place of legal origin.[54]

There are also calls by the Overseas Chinese Affairs Office (OCAO), the official body overseeing relations with ethnic Chinese outside China, to have Chinese overseas communities serve the PRC state. The United Front Work Department (UFWD) of the CCP, a body historically implicated in supporting underground agitation and insurgency, made similar statements about winning over ethnic Chinese communities abroad to advance China's interests.[55] These outreach efforts, however, appear to go beyond building ties with a diaspora and may tend towards efforts to interfere in the politics and societies of foreign countries to advance China's interests. The UFWD absorbed the OCAO along with the State Administration for Religious Affairs in early 2018.[56] Then, there are the allegedly illicit, even illegal, PRC influence operations using businesses, academics, and students around the world that contribute to worries about Beijing's approach to ethnic Chinese communities in Singapore.[57]

Adding to concerns about relations with China and its ties with local Chinese communities is the fact that such connections can have direct implications for Singapore's foreign affairs. Singapore's immediate neighbours, Malaysia and Indonesia, both have of histories of strong anti-Chinese sentiment, which have resulted in communal violence on several occasions, the most recent of these being the anti-Chinese riots in Indonesia that came with the fall of the Soeharto regime in 1998. Indonesian politicians also accuse Singapore of providing safe harbour for ill-gotten gains and evaded taxes by ethnic Chinese Indonesian business people.[58] For much of independent Singapore's history, it has sought to convince both Kuala Lumpur and Jakarta that it is not a "Chinese fifth column" despite its majority ethnic Chinese population and has had considerable success in doing so.[59] The Singapore state worries that a rekindling of a public image in Indonesia and Malaysia that ethnic Chinese majority Singapore is Beijing's stooge can easily invite tensions with its neighbours that it wishes to avoid.

Responding to Influence

Importing notions of "Chinese-ness" into Singapore that emphasize cultural and political convergence with China can sharpen local communal tensions if championed with sufficient vigour by segments of Singaporean Chinese. Numerical preponderance already means that Singapore society too easily emphasizes ethnic Chinese preferences over its ethnic minorities.[60] These include persistent doubts over the loyalty of Malay citizens given their predominant religious affiliation and debates over respect for minority religious and cultural practices.[61] Moreover, there is general inattention to and insufficient awareness about the structural socio-economic disadvantages minorities face, particularly given that the widespread association of failure with personal or family inadequacy.[62] Greater emphasis on ethnic Chinese concerns can come at further expense of recognizing and adequately addressing minority needs.

Singapore already lacks systematic ways to address discrimination towards minorities. Singapore's Chinese-Malay-Indian-Others (CMIO) policy for handling communal relations enforces in principle legal parity among official ethnic groups with some special allowances for recognized minorities, particularly Malays.[63] However, the CMIO approach does not sufficiently convey understandings about discrimination or minority rights. Playing up and focusing on concerns particular to ethnic Chinese communities can inadvertently promote prejudice and discrimination towards minorities even as it prompts anti-foreign sentiment towards those with China ties. There are few channels of legal redress in Singapore when it comes to discrimination towards ethnic minorities and new immigrants, notably in areas such as employment and in the rental housing market.[64]

Importing or sympathizing with China's sensitivities over issues as territorial claims and its nationalist proclivities does not serve Singapore's standing on the international stage. Among Singapore's qualities is an ability to play the role of an honest broker and to be able to assert its voice over issues like the rule of law.[65] This creates value in Singapore being a dialogue partner and a site for international engagement such as the June 2018 Singapore Summit between US President Trump and North Korean leader Kim Jong-un, while creating a global stake in Singapore's continued autonomy. If Singaporeans allows Beijing to limit Singapore's independence of action, the city-state may find itself facing declining international value and becoming more dependent on major powers like China. Note that Beijing's recent unhappiness over Singapore's fidelity to the Hague arbitral tribunal process over the South China Sea prompted calls from some Singaporeans for acceptance of, if not support for, Beijing's position.[66]

A Singapore that appears too close to Beijing can present other problems for foreign policy as well. Singapore spent decades convincing its neighbours that it is not a Southeast Asian proxy for China. A Singapore whose foreign policy or public position is muddied by domestic voices calling for greater conformity with Beijing's preferences can reverse previous efforts to allay concerns about Singapore's position.[67] Given the potential for the manipulation of anti-Chinese and anti-China sentiments in Southeast Asia, seeming too pliant to Beijing is not in Singapore's long-term interest.[68] The Singapore state needs to be wary of situations where pro-Beijing positions dominate domestic discourse at the expense of other voices, especially given Singaporeans' general inexperience with political debate and their usual public silence.

A stronger sense of nationally-shared civic and political values can encourage Singaporeans to rise above communal and sectarian particularities. This does not mean erasing features that characterize different communities. Rather, clear civic and political values should enable Singaporeans from all ethnic groups to move beyond communal and sectarian distinctions while being respectful of their own cultures and those of others. Imbuing the concept of citizenship in Singapore with such meaning requires practising and holding each other, as well as politicians, state institutions, and corporations, to actual standards—including legal ones—beyond the purely aspirational. Principles of democracy, justice, and equality as enshrined in the National Pledge, flag, and present in the education system are obvious starting points, given their familiarity.[69] Shared values people can reasonably and consistently expect to shape laws, policy, as well as behaviour are critical for grounding citizenship, since there can always be greater material incentives and temptations from elsewhere.

Enhancing the ability to dialogue and live with disagreement can reduce the urge to dominate others, while limiting the likelihood of disagreement resulting in denigration and animosity. By enabling meaningful public participation and encouraging mutually respectful disagreement, citizens can better overcome ethnic, cultural, class, and other differences. Regulating and requiring disclosure of lobbying activities, along with regular audits—as is common in other jurisdictions—are ways to oversee entities that wish to engage in political discussions for good reason and ensure that they do so in good faith.[70] Local and foreign actors with an interest in entering public discourse will be clearer about permissible behaviour and understand that their participation occurs under open public scrutiny, reducing risks from undue or inappropriate influence. Instead of fearing the foreign and myriad other types of actors Singapore's open economy and society requires, there exist appropriate means to manage the risks associated with their engagement in local political processes.

CONCLUSION

The relationship Singaporean Chinese have with China has been a complex and sometimes difficult one and will continue to be so as the latter develops its role as a major global actor. Ups and downs in their interactions are invariably tied with successive political projects in both Singapore and China. Diluting the political relationship between China and Singaporean Chinese is central to making both official and unofficial ties between Beijing and Singapore less fraught.

Links between Singaporean Chinese and China began with the history of Chinese migration to Singapore in search of opportunity from the nineteenth century. Many Chinese migrants then believed that this sojourn was temporary and they would return home in their lifetimes. In the meantime, these Chinese migrants to Singapore would send earnings back to families in their hometowns. As they settled permanently, they became targets for activation, mobilization, as well as political and financial support by political actors in China. Later, links with China became reason for suspicion with the establishment of the PRC and the onset of the Cold War before becoming an opportunity for enrichment once China began to reform. Such dynamics continue to colour interaction between ethnic Chinese in Singapore and China as the PRC continues to establish global prominence and Singapore opens itself again to large-scale immigration.

Ethnic Chinese communities in Singapore can have fruitful relationships with China, provided that there is sufficient mindfulness to mitigate the associated risks. Certainly, cooperative commercial and cultural exchanges can benefit both sides, as indeed they have in the decades of the PRC's reform period. However, China is today a major global power that is ready to pursue its interests even at the expense of greater friction with its neighbours and other world actors, and unafraid of using ethnic Chinese communities abroad to do so. Such efforts, even if not directed against Singapore, can still put pressure on Singapore's multiethnic society and her ties with neighbours. Nonetheless, Singapore can adequately respond to these challenges with confidence and prudence, particularly if its reactions rest on careful consideration of evidence, rather than fear, insinuation, or anxieties over conspiracy.

Notes

1. The author would like to acknowledge the Singapore Social Science Research Council Thematic Grant project, "Making Identities Count in Asia", and the Identities Cluster at the Asia Research Institute (ARI), National University of Singapore for research support that went into this chapter. Some of the description on broader trends draw from the Singapore national identity reports produced by "Making Identities Count in Asia" and the ARI Identities Cluster.

2. Ai Jun, "Singapore's Hypocrisy Exposed by Seized Military Vehicles", *Global Times*, 27 November 2016, http://www.globaltimes.cn/content/1020583.shtml (accessed 16 April 2018); "Singapore's Mixing into the South China Sea Leads to China's Displeasure: Online Claims that It Is Flirting with the United States" [新加坡攬和南海令中國不滿 網民稱其諂媚美國 *Xinjiapo jiaohuo nanhai ling zhongguo buman wangmin chengqi chanmei meiguo*], *People Daily Online*, 30 September 2016, http://military.people.com.cn/n1/2016/0930/c1011-28753695.html (accessed 16 April 2018).

3. "Singapore's Attitude to China Is 'Complicated and Complex'" [新加坡對中國態度"複雜而微妙" *Xinjiapo dui zhongguo taidu 'fuza er weimiao'*] *Global Times*, 27 September 2013, http://world.huanqiu.com/depth_report/2013-09/4398968. html (accessed 16 April 2018); "Online Responses to Lee Kuan Yew from the Global Times" [中國環球網友回應李光耀 *Zhongguo huanqiu wangyou huiying liguangyao*], *Singapore Documents*, 2 November 2009, https://www.sginsight.com/xjp/index.php?id=3601 (accessed 16 April 2018).

4. Brenda S.A. Yeoh and Weiqiang Lin, "Chinese Migration to Singapore: Discourses and Discontents in a Globalizing Nation-State", *Asian and Pacific Migration Journal* 22, no. 1 (2013): 31–54.

5. For a discussion of a national state, see Charles Tilly, *Coercion, Capital, and European States, AD 990–1992* (New York: Wiley-Blackwell, 1992), Ch. 5.

6. Huang Jianli, "'Chinese Overseas Are the Mother of Revolution': The Origins and Narratives of Praise" ["華僑為革命之母": 讚譽之來歷與敘述 *'Huaqiao wei gemingzhimu': Zanyu zhi laili yu xushu*], *International Journal of Diasporic Studies* 3, no. 2 (2011): 21–56.

7. Christine Han, "The 'Myth' of Singaporeanness: Values and Identity in Citizenship Education", in *Living with Myths in Singapore*, edited by Loh Kah Seng, Thum Ping-Tjin, and Jack Meng-Tat Chia (Singapore: Ethos Books, 2017), pp. 41–52; Laavanya Kathiravelu, "Rethinking Race: Beyond the CMIO Categorisation", in *Living with Myths in Singapore*, pp. 159–68; Loh Kah Seng, Thum Ping-Tjin, and Jack Meng-Tat Chia, "Introduction: Singapore as a Mythic Nation", in *Living with Myths in Singapore*, pp. 1–14.

8. Allen Chun, "Fuck Chineseness: On the Ambiguities of Ethnicity as Culture as Identity", *boundary 2*, vol. 23, no. 2 (1996): 111–38.

9. Ja Ian Chong, *External Intervention and the Politics of State Formation: China, Indonesia, Thailand—1893-1952* (Cambridge: Cambridge University Press, 2012), pp. 4–16.

10. Chiang Kai-shek, *China's Destiny* [中國之命運 *Zhongguo zhi mingyun*] (Taipei: Zhongzheng Shuju, 1953); Sun Yat-sen, *Three People's Principles* [三民主義 *Sanminzhuyi*] (Changsha: Yuelu Shushe, 2001); Sun Yat-sen, *Strategy for Building a Nation* [建國方略 *Jianguofanglue*] (Beijing: Huaxia Chubanshe, 2002); Jin Binggao, "Mao Zedong's Great Contribution to the Marxist Theory of Nationalism" [毛澤東對馬克思主義民族理論的偉大貢獻 *Maozedong dui makesizhuyi minzulilun de weida gongxian*], http://cpc.people.com.cn/BIG5/69112/70190/70194/5235504.html

11. Philip A. Kuhn, *Origins of the Modern Chinese State* (Stanford: Stanford University Press, 2003); Pamela Kyle Crossley, Helen F. Siu, and Donald S. Sutton, eds., *Empire at the Margins: Culture, Ethnicity, and Frontier in Early Modern China* (Berkeley: University of California Press, 2006).

12. Pamela Kyle Crossley, *A Translucent Mirror: History and Identity in Qing Imperial Ideology* (Berkeley: University of California Press, 2002); Mark C. Elliot, *The Manchu Way: The Eight Banners and Ethnic Identity in Late Imperial China* (Stanford: Stanford University Press, 2001); Evelyn S. Rawski, *The Last Emperors: A Social History of Qing Imperial Institutions* (Berkeley: University of California Press, 2001).

13. Prasenjit Duara, "Nationalists among Transnationals: Overseas Chinese and the Idea of China, 1900–1911", in *Underground Empires: The Cultural Politics of Modern Chinese Transnationalism*, edited by Aihwa Ong and Donald Nonini (London: Routledge, 1996), pp. 39–61; Edward J.M. Rhoads, *Manchus and Han: Ethnic Relations and Political Power in Late Qing and Early Republican China, 1861-1928* (Seattle: University of Washington Press, 2000); Sun Yat-sen, *Three People's Principles*, pp. 27–36.

14. Victor H. Mair, "The Classification of Sinitic Languages: What is 'Chinese?'", in *Breaking Down the Barriers: Interdisciplinary Studies in Chinese Linguistics and Beyond*, edited by Guangshun Cao, Hilary Chappell, Redouane Djamouri, and Thekla Wiebusch (Taipei: Institute of Linguistics, Academia Sinica, 2013), pp. 735–54.

15. Joyce Ee, "Chinese Migration to Singapore, 1896–1941", *Journal of Southeast Asian*

History 2, no. 1 (1961): 33–51; Brenda S.A. Yeoh and Weiqiang Lin, "Chinese Migration to Singapore".

16. Maurice Freedman, "Immigrants and Associations: Chinese in Nineteenth Century Singapore", *Comparative Studies in Society and History* 3, no. 1 (1960): 25–48; Hong Liu, "Old Linkages, New Networks: The Globalization of Overseas Chinese Voluntary Associations", *China Quarterly* 155 (1998): 588–609; Yen Ching-Hwang, "Early Chinese Clan Associations in Singapore and Malaya, 1819–1911", *Journal of Southeast Asian Studies* 12, no. 1 (1981): 62–91.

17. Leo Suryadinata, *Chinese and Nation-Building in Southeast Asia* (Singapore: Singapore Society of Asian Studies, 1997), pp. 9–10.

18. Lisa Lim, "Migrants and 'Mother Tongues': Extralinguistic Forces in the Ecology of English in Singapore", in *English in Singapore: Modernity and Management*, edited by Lisa Lim, Anne Pakir and Lionel Wee (Hong Kong: Hong Kong University Press, 2010), pp. 24–25.

19. Prasenjit Duara, "Nationalists among Transnationals"; Stuart Heaver, "High Society", *South China Morning Post*, 10 May 2014, http://www.scmp.com/magazines/post-magazine/article/1506517/high-society-preserving-peranakan-culture (accessed 16 April 2018).

20. Prasenjit Duara, "Nationalists among Transnationals".

21. Lee Geok Boi, *The Syonan Years: Singapore Under Japanese Rule, 1942-1945* (Singapore: National Archives of Singapore, 2005), Chs. 5 and 7; Carl A. Trocki, *Singapore: Wealth, Power and the Culture of Control* (London: Routledge, 2005), Chs. 1–3.

22. Carl A. Trocki, *Singapore*, Ch. 4.

23. Bilingual education in Singapore is based around English with language classes and several minor subjects taught in the "mother tongue" of the pupil. "Mother tongue" broadly falls into the four main "races" along which the Singapore state categorizes its population—Chinese, Malay, Indian and Others. The mother tongue for "Chinese" is Mandarin, officially *Huayu*（華語）or "Chinese language", in contrast to *Guoyu*（國語）and *Putonghua*（普通話）used respectively in Taiwan and the PRC. See Lisa Lim, "Migrants and 'Mother Tongues'".

24. Pang Wing Sing, "The 'Double Seventh' Incident, 1937: Singapore Chinese Response to the Outbreak of the Sino-Japanese War", *Journal of Southeast Asian Studies* 4, no. 2 (1973): 269–99.

25. Yoji Akashi, "Japanese Policy toward the Malayan Chinese", *Journal of Southeast Asian Studies* 1, no. 2 (1970): 61–89; Lee Geok Boi, *The Syonan Years*, pp. 105–16.

26. Lee Geok Boi, *The Syonan Years*, Chs. 5–7; Lee Yinghui, "Resistance and Association with Japan: Chinese Overseas, the Nationalist Government, and the Wang Regime" [抗日與附日——華僑、國民政府、汪政權 *Kangri yu furi - huaqiao, guominzhengfu, wangzhengquan*] (Taipei: Shuiniu Chubanshe, 2003).

27. Chin Peng, *My Side of History* (Singapore: Media Masters, 2003), Chs. 5–7; Lee Geok Boi, *The Syonan Years*, pp. 218–19.

28. Kevin Hewison and Garry Rodan, "The Ebb and Flow of Civil Society and the

Decline of the Left in Southeast Asia", in *Political Oppositions in Industrialising Asia*, edited by Garry Rodan (London: Routledge, 1996), pp. 49–57.

29. Garry Rodan, *The Political Economy of Singapore's Industrialization: National State and International Capital* (London: Palgrave Macmillan, 1989), Ch. 3.

30. Huang Jianli, "Positioning the Student Political Activism of Singapore: Articulation, Contestation, and Omission", *Inter-Asia Cultural Studies* 7, no. 3 (2006): 403–30; Kwok Kian-Woon, "Chinese-Educated Intellectuals in Singapore: Marginality, Memory, and Modernity", *Asian Journal of Social Science* 29, no. 3 (2001): 495–519.

31. Andrew Jacobs, "In Singapore, Vitriol Against Chinese Newcomers", *New York Times*, 26 July 2012, https://www.nytimes.com/2012/07/27/world/asia/in-singapore-vitriol-against-newcomers-from-mainland-china.html (accessed 18 April 2018).

32. Christopher R. Hughes, *Chinese Nationalism in the Global Era* (London: Routledge, 2006).

33. "News Release of National Assimilation of FDI From January to November 2016", *Invest in China*, http://www.fdi.gov.cn/1800000121_49_4473_0_7.html (accessed 18 April 2018); Department of Statistics Singapore, "Singapore's International Trade", https://www.singstat.gov.sg/modules/infographics/singapore-international-trade (accessed 18 April 2018).

34. Min Ye, *Diasporas and Foreign Direct Investment in China and India* (New York: Cambridge University Press, 2014), Ch. 3.

35. Arif Dirlik, "Critical Reflections on 'Chinese Capitalism' Paradigm", *Identities: Global Studies in Culture and Power* 3, no. 3 (1997): 303–30.

36. "Singapore Has Great Expectations for Inter-Connectivity Cooperation with China: PM", *Xinhua*, 18 September 2017, http://www.xinhuanet.com/english/2017-09/18/c_136618742.htm (accessed 18 April 2018).

37. See, for example, Shen Zewei, "'Speak Mandarin Campaign' Ought to be Renamed 'Rescue Mandarin Campaign'" ["講華語運動"應改為"搶救華語運動" *Jiang Huayu Yundong' ying gaiwei 'Qiangjiu Huayu Yundong'*], *Redants*, 14 August 2017, http://www.redants.sg/perspective/story20170814-106 (accessed 18 April 2018); Chen Dingyuan, "Singaporean Chinese or Just Singaporean?" [新加坡華人乎新加坡人？ *Xinjiapohuaren hu xinjiaporen?*], *Sin Chew Jit Poh*, 23 July 2017, http://www.sinchew.com.my/node/1665537 (accessed 18 April 2018); Xinjing Yi'ersan, "Singapore's Awkwardness" [新加坡的尷尬 *Xinjiapo de gangga*], *The Paper*, 12 June 2016, https://www.thepaper.cn/newsDetail_forward_1482095 (accessed 18 April 2018).

38. Kwok Kian-Woon, "Chinese-Educated Intellectuals in Singapore".

39. James Chin, "Anti-Christian Chinese Chauvinists and HDB Upgrades", *Southeast Asia Research* 5, no. 3 (1997): 217–41; Kwok Kian-Woon, "Chinese-Educated Intellectuals in Singapore", pp. 498–99; Charles Pendley, "Language Policy and Social Transformation in Singapore", *Southeast Asian Journal of Social Science* 11, no. 2 (1983): 46–58; Marvin L. Rogers, "Malaysia and Singapore: 1971 Developments", *Asian Survey* 12, no. 3 (1972): 175–76.

40. Andrew Jacobs, "In Singapore, Vitriol Against Chinese Newcomers"; Brenda S.A. Yeoh and Weiqiang Lin, "Chinese Migration to Singapore".

41. Brenda S.A. Yeoh and Weiqiang Lin, "Chinese Migration to Singapore".

42. See, for example, Elena Chong, "Student Agent Fined $72K Over Fake Certs Obtained from China", *Straits Times*, 23 December 2013, http://www.straitstimes. com/singapore/student-agent-fined-72k-over-forged-certs-obtained-from-china (accessed 18 April 2018); Yang Peidong, "Why Chinese Nationals and Singaporeans Don't Get Along", *AsiaOne*, 27 March 2013, http://news.asiaone.com/News/ Latest+News/Singapore/Story/A1Story20130327-411776.html (accessed 18 April 2018); "Fake Passport, Fake Qualifications: Former Tycoon Stripped of Singapore Citizenship", *Today*, 5 March 2018, https://www.todayonline.com/singapore/fake-passport-fake-qualifications-former-tycoon-stripped-spore-citizenship (accessed 18 April 2018).

43. Singapore Ministry of Home Affairs, "Cancellation of Singapore Permanent Resident (SPR) Status: Huang Jing and Yang Xiuping", 6 August 2017, https://www.mha.gov. sg/newsroom/press-release/news/cancellation-of-singapore-permanent-residence-(spr)-status---huang-jing-and-yang-xiuping (accessed 18 April 2018).

44. Zuraidah Ibrahim, "What Singapore Is Saying by Expelling China Hand Huang Jing", *South China Morning Post*, 12 August 2017, http://www.scmp.com/week-asia/ opinion/article/2106497/what-singapore-saying-expelling-china-hand-huang-jing (accessed 18 April 2018).

45. China Cultural Centre, "About Us", http://www.cccsingapore.org/index.php?s=/ home/index/jieshao.html (accessed 18 April 2018).

46. "'Competing Stages' for Two Major Chinese Cultural Centres in Singapore" [新加 坡兩大華族文化中心"打擂台" *Xinjiapo liangdahuazu wenhuazhongxin 'daleitai'*], *Nanyang Post*, 21 November 2015, http://news.nanyangpost.com/2015/11/21_1. html (accessed 18 April 2018).

47. Singapore Prime Minister's Office, "PM Lee Hsien Loong at the Official Opening of the Singapore Chinese Cultural Centre", 19 May 2017, http://www.pmo.gov.sg/ newsroom/pm-lee-hsien-loong-official-opening-singapore-chinese-cultural-centre (accessed 18 April 2018).

48. Author's translation. All-China Federation of Returned Overseas Chinese, "Explanation of the Reform Plan for the All-China Federation of Returned Overseas Chinese" [中國僑聯改革方案解讀 *Zhongguoqiaolian gaigefangan jiedu*], (Beijing: All-China Federation of Returned Overseas Chinese, 2017), p. 5.

49. Author's translation. "Xi Jinping Gives Important Directives on Chinese Overseas Work; Li Keqiang Provides Instructions" [習近平對僑務工作作出重要指示 李 克強作出批示 *Xijinping dui qiaowugongzuo zuochu zhongyaozhishi likeqiang zuochu pishi*], *Xinhua News Agency*, 17 February 2017, http://news.xinhuanet. com/politics/2017-02/17/c_1120486778.htm (accessed 16 January 2018).

50. Leo Suryadinata, *The Rise of China and the Chinese Overseas: A Study of Beijing's Changing Policy in Southeast Asia and Beyond* (Singapore: ISEAS – Yusof Ishak Institute, 2017).

51. Ibid., Chs. 9–12.

52. "PRC Permits Ethnic Chinese to Apply for Five-Year Visas, Multiple Entry with Right of Residency" [中國準華裔申請五年簽證 多次往返並擁有居留權 *Zhongguo zhun huayi shenqing wunianqianzheng duociwangfan bing yongyou juliuquan*], *Yazhou Zhoukan* 32, no. 7, 18 February 2018, http://www.yzzk.com/cfm/content_archive.cfm?id=1518060205372&docissue=2018-07&fb_comment_id=1493418040781316_1498113206978466#fde7e318c3a7e (accessed 18 April 2018); "Foreign Media Claims that PRC Permission for Chinese Overseas to Apply for Five-Year Visas Very 'Tempting': Recognising One's Forefathers and Returning to One's Ancestors" [外媒稱中國允許海外華人申請五年簽證很"動情"：認祖歸宗 *Waimei cheng zhongguo yunxu haiwaihuaren shenqing wunianqianzheng hen 'dongqing': Renzuguizong*], *Reference Information*, 6 February 2018, http://www.cankaoxiaoxi.com/china/20180206/2254718.shtml (accessed 18 April 2018).

53. Leo Suryadinata, *The Rise of China and the Chinese Overseas*, pp. 15–18, 154–63; Wang Lili, "Special Interview: Putting in an Effort to Contribute to the China Dream—Speaking with Head of the Singapore Huayuan Association Wang Quancheng Who Will Be A Delegate at the First Session of the 13th National Political Consultative Conference" [專訪：為實現中國夢貢獻一份力量——訪即將列席全國政協十三屆一次會議的新加坡華源會會長王泉成 *Zhuanfang: Weishixian zhongguomeng gongxian yifenliliang – fang jijiang liexi quanguozhengxie shisanjieyicihuiyi de xinjiapo huayuanhui huizhang wangquancheng*], *Xinhua*, 3 March 2018, http://www.xinhuanet.com/2018-03/03/c_1122481843.htm (accessed 20 April 2018); "Association Leadership" [本會領導 *benhui lingdao*], Zhonghua Haiwai Lianyihui], http://www.cofa.org.cn/bhld.jhtml (accessed 5 April 2020).

54. State Council of the People's Republic of China, "Order No. 661 of the State Council of the People's Republic of China" [中華人民共和國國務院令第661號 *Zhonghuarenmingongheguo guowuyuanling di 661 hao*], 14 June 2015, http://www.gov.cn/zhengce/content/2015-06/18/content_9862.htm (accessed 18 April 2018); Chinese People's Political Consultative Committee National Committee, "Hong Kong, Macau, and Taiwan Overseas Committee" [港澳台僑委員會 *Gangaotaiqiao weiyuanhui*], http://www.cppcc.gov.cn/zxww/zxww/gatqwyh/ (accessed 20 April 2018); "Hong Kongers Returning to Reside in Hometowns Enjoy Citizen Treatment" [港人回鄉定居 倡享國民待遇 *Gangren huixiangdingju changxiang guomindaiyu*], *Wenweipo*, 5 March 2014, http://paper.wenweipo.com/2014/03/05/CH1403050045.htm (accessed 18 April 2018).

55. Gerry Groot, *Managing Transitions: The Chinese Communist Party, United Front Work, Corporatism, and Hegemony* (London: Routledge, 2003); Mai Yanting, "The United Front Work Department's Growing Power: Using Chinese Overseas to Expand Its Soft Power, the Next Phase Is an Alliance with Taiwan" [統戰部擴權：藉華僑擴軟實力 下階段期與台灣結盟 *Tongzhanbu kuoquan: Ji huaqiao kuoruanshili xiajieduanqi yu taiwan jiemeng*], *Radio France International*, 22 March 2018, http://trad.cn.rfi.fr/中國/20180322-統戰部擴權藉華僑擴軟實力-下階段期

與台灣結盟 (accessed 19 April 2018); "Central United Front Work Department: Hopes Chinese Overseas and Ethnic Chinese Respect Laws of Host Countries" [中央統戰部: 希望華僑華人尊重住在國法律 *Zhongyangtongzhanbu: Xiwang huaqiaohuaren zunzhong zhuzaiguo falü*], *Phoenix News*, 21 October 2017, http:// news.ifeng.com/a/20171021/52734518_0.shtml?_cpb_pindaotj2 (accessed 19 April 2018); "Main Functions of the United Front Work Department" [統戰部門的主要職能 *Tongzhanbumen de zhuyaozhineng*], *People's Daily Online*, http://cpc.people. com.cn/GB/64162/64171/65717/65718/4455937.html (accessed 19 April 2018); "Press Conference: CPC's United Front and International Relations" ["黨的統一戰線工作和黨的對外交往情況"記者會 *Dang de tongyizhanxiangongzuo he dang de duiwaijiaowangqingkuang' jizhehui*], *China.org.cn*, 21 October 2017, http://www. china.com.cn/zhibo/2017-10/21/content_41765498.htm (accessed 20 April 2018).

56. Zhang Qian, "Overseas Chinese Affairs Office Reportedly to Merge into United Front Work Department of the Chinese Communist Party" [中國僑辦傳將併入中共統戰部 *Zhongguoqiaoban chuan jiang bingru zhonggongtongzhanbu*], *United Daily News*, 8 March 2018, http://www.cna.com.tw/news/acn/201803080063-1. aspx (accessed 19 April 2018); "Overseas Chinese Affairs Office: Will Only Get Better with Merger into the Central United Front Work Department, the Maternal Home is the Maternal Home" [國僑辦: 併入中央統戰部只會更好, 娘家人還是娘家人 *Guoqiaoban: Bingru zhongyangtongzhanbu zhihui genghao, niangjiaren haishi niangjiaren*], *Phoenix News*, 24 March 2018, http://news.ifeng. com/a/20180324/57012167_0.shtml (accessed 19 April 2018).

57. Bethany Allen-Ebrahimian, "China's Long Arm Reaches into American Campuses", *Foreign Policy*, 7 March 2018, http://foreignpolicy.com/2018/03/07/chinas-long-arm-reaches-into-a...-chinese-students-scholars-association-university-communist-party/ (accessed 19 April 2018); Bethany Allen-Ebrahimian, "The Chinese Communist Party is Setting Up Cells at Universities Across America", *Foreign Policy*, 18 April 2018, http://foreignpolicy.com/2018/04/18/the-chinese-communist-party-is-setting-up-cells-at-universities-across-america-china-students-beijing-surveillance/ (accessed 19 April 2018); Thorsten Benner, Jan Gaspers, Marieke Ohlberg, Lucrezia Poggetti, and Kristen Shi-Kupfer, *Authoritarian Advance: Responding to China's Growing Political Influence in Europe*, Report by the Global Public Policy Institute and Mercator Institute for China Studies, February 2018; Anne-Marie Brady, "Magic Weapons: China's Political Influence Activities under Xi Jinping", presented at The Corrosion of Democracy under China's Global Influence conference, 16–17 September 2017; Clive Hamilton and Alex Joske, "Submission to the Parliamentary Joint Committee on Intelligence and Security", Submission 20. Review of the National Security Legislation Amendment (Espionage and Foreign Intervention) Bill 2017, Parliament of Australia, 2018; Sam Sachdeva, "Ardern to Query Chinese Links to Break-In", *Newsroom*, 19 February 2018, https:// www.newsroom.co.nz/2018/02/19/89724/draft-brady (accessed 19 April 2018).

58. Barry Desker, "Challenging Times in Singapore-Indonesia Relations", *RSIS Commentaries*, 14 October 2015, https://www.rsis.edu.sg/rsis-publication/rsis/

co15216-challenging-times-in-singapore-indonesia-relations/#.WthpzC-p25c (accessed 19 April 2018).

59. Chen Nahui and Xue Li, "Lee Kuan Yew's Legacy for Singapore-China Relations", *The Diplomat*, 5 December 2016, https://thediplomat.com/2016/12/lee-kuan-yews-legacy-for-china-singapore-relations/ (accessed 19 April 2018); National Library Singapore, "Prof Wang Gungwu: Chinese Identity and Loyalty in Singapore in the 19th and 20th Centuries", [Video file] National Library Prominent Speaker Series, 29 July 2017, https://www.youtube.com/watch?v=-SvvA_ku-Zg (accessed 19 April 2018).

60. Petra Dierkis-Thrun, Adeline Koh, and Sangeetha Thanapal, "Chinese Privilege, Gender, and Intersectionality: A Conversation with Adeline Koh and Sangeetha Thanapal", *b2o: The Online Community of the Boundary 2 Editorial Collective*, 4 March 2015, https://www.boundary2.org/2015/03/chinese-privilege-gender-and-intersectionality-in-singapore-a-conversation-between-adeline-koh-and-sangeetha-thanapal/ (accessed 18 April 2018); Surekha A. Yadav, "Is Singapore a Racist Country?", *Malay Mail*, 31 August 2014, http://www.themalaymailonline.com/opinion/surekha-a-yadav/article/is-singapore-a-racist-country (accessed 18 April 2018).

61. See aspects of these debates in, for example, Masturah Alatas, "The Double Captivity of 'Chinese Privilege'", *New Mandala*, 22 April 2015, http://www.newmandala.org/the-double-captivity-of-chinese-privilege/ (accessed 20 April 2018); Hydar Saharudin, "Confronting 'Chinese Privilege' in Singapore", *New Mandala*, 2 November 2016, http://www.newmandala.org/brief-history-chinese-privilege-singapore/ (accessed 20 April 2018); Sean P. Walsh, "The Roar of the Lion City: Ethnicity, Gender, and Culture in the Singapore Armed Forces", *Armed Forces and Society* 33, no. 2 (2007): 265–85.

62. Association of Muslim Professionals, *Third Convention Journal* (2017), Chs. 4–5, https://www.amp.org.sg/publications/#ert_panel-1 (accessed 6 June 2018); Singapore Ministry of Community, Culture, and Youth, *Progress of the Malay Community since 1980* (Singapore: Ministry of Community, Culture, and Youth, 2015).

63. Articles 152–54, Constitution of the Republic of Singapore. Refer to https://sso.agc.gov.sg/Act/CONS1963 (accessed 6 June 2018); Norman Vasu, "Governing through Difference in Singapore: Corporatism's Composition, Characteristics, and Complications", *Asian Survey*, 52, no. 4 (2012): 737–39.

64. Asyraf Kamil, "Muslim Group Wants Body to Be Set Up to Handle Discrimination Cases", *Today*, 4 May 2016, https://www.todayonline.com/singapore/association-muslim-professionals-calls-formation-central-body-address-discriminatory (accessed 7 June 2018); Nyshka Chandran and Michelle Loh, "Even in Weak Market, Racial Bias Trumps Profit for Many Singapore Landlords", *CNBC*, 2 March 2017, https://www.cnbc.com/2017/03/02/singapore-rental-racism-prc-and-indian-tenants-often-deemed-undesirable.html (accessed 7 June 2018).

65. Vivian Balakrishnan, "Commentary: Singapore Is at an Inflection Point", *Channel*

NewsAsia, 5 February 2018, https://www.channelnewsasia.com/news/asia/commentary-asean-is-at-an-inflection-point-9926476 (accessed 7 June 2018); Singapore Ministry of Foreign Affairs, "Transcript of Minister of Foreign Affairs Dr Vivian Balakrishnan's Media Doorstop in Washington, DC, 5 June 2018", 6 June 2018, https://www1.mfa.gov.sg/Newsroom/Press-Statements-Transcripts-and-Photos/2018/06/06062018TranscriptMinWashington (accessed 7 June 2018).

66. Tan Weizhen, "S'pore Businesses Quizzed by Chinese Counterparts over Stand on South China Sea", *Today*, 9 October 2016, https://www.todayonline.com/business/spore-businesses-quizzed-chinese-counterparts-over-their-stand-south-china-sea-issue (accessed 7 June 2018).

67. C.P. Fitzgerald, *The Third China: The Chinese Communities in Southeast Asia* (Vancouver: University of British Columbia Press, 1965); David S.G. Goodman, "Are Asia's 'Ethnic Chinese' a Regional Security Threat?", *Survival*, 39, no. 4 (1997–98): 140–55.

68. Chen Nahui and Xue Li, "Lee Kuan Yew's Legacy for China-Singapore Relations"; "A Little Red Dot in a Sea of Green", *The Economist*, 16 July 2015, https://www.economist.com/special-report/2015/07/16/a-little-red-dot-in-a-sea-of-green (accessed 7 June 2018).

69. Viswa Sadasivan, "Nation Building Tenets (motion)", Singapore Parliamentary Reports (Hansard), 18 August 2009, Vol. 86, http://sprs.parl.gov.sg; Hydar Saharudin, "Confronting 'Chinese Privilege' in Singapore".

70. An example of such legislation is the United States' Foreign Agents Registration Act (FARA). See United States Congress, Foreign Agents Registration Act, 22 U.S.C. § 611 *et seq. United States Code* (1938), https://www.justice.gov/nsd-fara/fara-index-and-act (accessed 20 April 2018); United States Congress, Administration and Enforcement of Foreign Agents Registration Act of 1938, as Amended. Title 28 C.F.R. Part 5. *Judicial Administration* (2007), https://www.gpo.gov/fdsys/pkg/CFR-2016-title28-vol1/pdf/CFR-2016-title28-vol1-part5.pdf (accessed 20 April 2018).

Part IV

DIVERGING ECONOMIC WORLDS

11

Self-Reliant Wealth and Trickle-Down Welfare
The Singapore Story in 200 Years?

IRENE Y.H. NG

WEALTH AND WELFARE SINCE BRITISH RULE

Wealth generation is steeped in Singapore's history. When Stamford Raffles established a trading post in Singapore in 1819, this entrepôt trading outpost of the East India Company attracted not just British colonials, but migrants from China and India for its promise of wealth. Welfare, in terms of personal well-being, improved because of their economic gains from being part of the commerce that took place in this thriving port. Welfare is thus strongly tied to personal wealth generation. On the other hand, institutional welfare in terms of government policy was minimal because the bulk of infrastructural support was devoted to encouraging commerce and the building of the Empire. Hence any improvement in personal well-being was not the outcome of any policy from the colonial authorities but that of personal savings and sacrifices within these immigrant communities.[1]

Interestingly, the conditions and philosophies surrounding notions of wealth and welfare in Singapore some 200 years ago continue to prevail in the Singapore of 2019. With regard to wealth, Singapore is said to have one of the highest concentration of wealthy individuals in the world.[2] With regard to welfare, in a speech in 2006, Prime Minister Lee Hsien Loong asserted that in Singapore, we treat welfare as a dirty word.[3] By this, he meant that the Singapore government rejected the policy of welfare handouts to improve personal economic well-being. Repeatedly, Singaporeans are called on to be self-reliant, to work hard and turn to the government for assistance only as a last resort. Often accompanying this call is the belief that any erosion of work ethic and self-reliance would lead to the demise of Singapore, a small vulnerable island economy dependent on its human resource and deep port as the only natural resources.[4] In addition, it is often asserted that the establishment of a welfare state, taken here to mean a form of government that sees itself as the main promoter and protector of its citizens' economic well-being, would result in high taxes. If this happens, "talent and businesses will leave, no investments will come".[5]

INCOME INEQUALITY: WHAT DO THE NUMBERS SAY?

Given the resistance to "welfare", it is unsurprising that Singapore's income inequality has been observed to be high throughout most of its development.[6] In the last decade, with more aggressive employment-based policies such as the Workfare Income Supplement (WIS) and the Progressive Wage Model (PWM), income inequality in the country has moderated. However, it remains higher than pre-2000s levels.[7]

For an international comparison, Figures 11.1a and 11.11b show Singapore's position in the Gini index, a measure of income inequality where 1 indicates complete inequality and 0 indicates complete equality, relative to a range of countries. These Gini indices are from the Standardized World Income Inequality Database,[8] harmonized to maximize comparability in Gini indices. The countries are selected to represent a range of comparable countries such as neighbouring countries in Asia, European welfare states, and Anglophone countries. Figure 11.1a shows that for market Gini (Gini index before accounting for taxes and transfers), Singapore's index is lower than many developed countries. It also shows rising inequality in most of the countries, and Singapore's moderating levels in the last decade. However, Figure 11.1b shows that Singapore's index becomes the second highest after only Hong Kong and Malaysia when government taxes and transfers are accounted for.

Thus, based on the harmonized measure of Gini indices, Singapore's income inequality is not as severe as many developed countries, including Sweden, Germany, and the United States which have been experiencing widening inequality.[9] However, given the Singapore government's resistance towards welfare handouts, the country's income inequality, after taking into account taxes and transfers, remains extremely high.

THE EXPERIENCE OF INEQUALITY: EXAMINING OUR SOCIAL INSTITUTIONS

Beyond the challenges of economic inequality, many local academics and experts have pointed to increasing social inequality and its consequences in

FIGURE 11.1a

Comparison of Market Gini Coefficient of Several Countries, 1960–2016

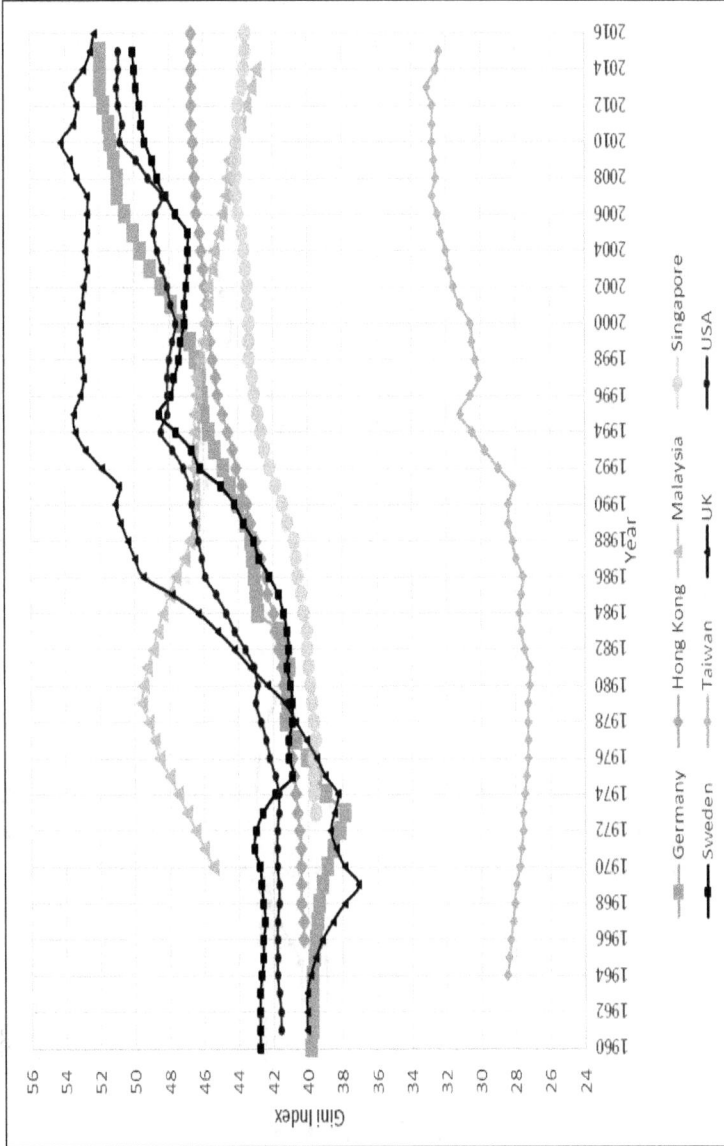

Source: Frederick Solt, "The Standardized World Income Inequality Database", *Social Science Quarterly* 97, no. 5 (2016): 1267–81. SWIID Version 7.1, August 2018 (2018-08-14).

FIGURE 11.1b

Comparison of Disposable Gini Coefficient of Several Countries, 1960–2016

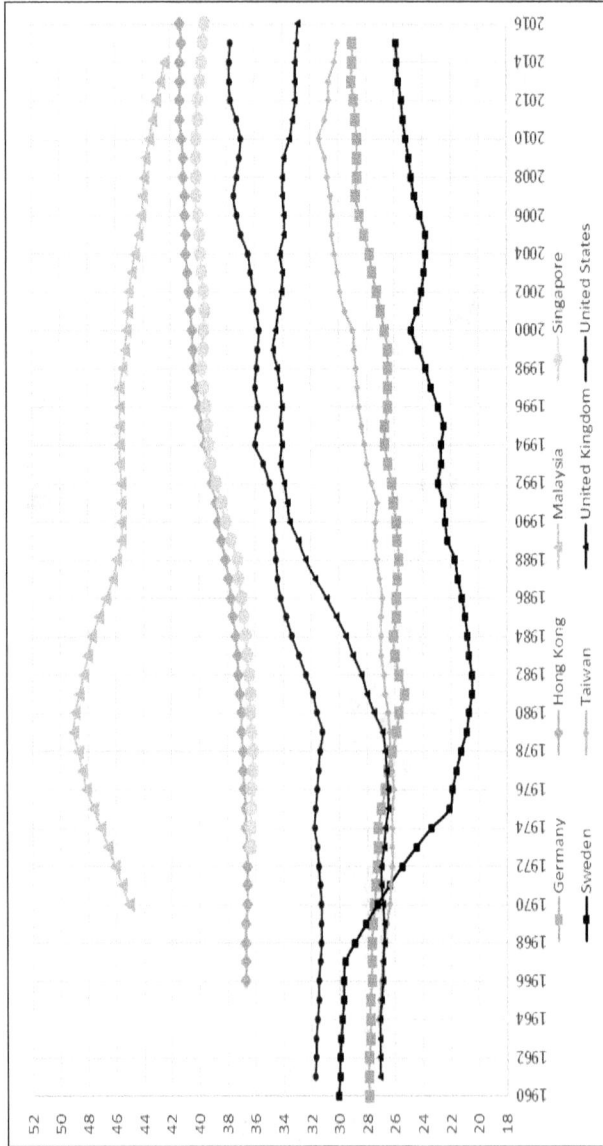

Legend: Germany — Hong Kong — Malaysia — Singapore
Sweden — Taiwan — United Kingdom — United States

Source: Frederick Solt, "The Standardized World Income Inequality Database", *Social Science Quarterly* 97, no. 5 (2016): 1267–81. SWIID Version 7.1, August 2018 (2018-08-14).

Singapore. Teo (2018)'s book *This is What Inequality Looks Like*[10] detailed her ethnographic work among more than 200 low-income households. It contrasted the lives of the women in these households to higher-income families based on several dimensions, including the home environment, work, childcare, and children's school. In their study of social capital, Chua, Tan and Koh (2017)[11] found that one's exclusive social networks depended on whether one lives in a condominium or public housing, and on whether one attended an elite or neighbourhood school.

In 1989, economist Linda Lim observed that privatizing healthcare and education had made them regressive.[12] In 2015, Ng repeated this observation that the main systems of social development, namely housing, healthcare, and education, now segregated Singaporeans rather than integrating them.[13] Ng posited that while economic stratification is expected as a society matures and as social structures become entrenched, they should not be allowed to divide society.[14] The case for addressing inequality becomes more compelling when the intergenerational dimension is considered. For instance, if inequality influences the rate of intergenerational mobility, that is to say the ability of children from lower-income families to transcend their class background, then inequality perpetuates through generations and the issue of inequality deserves a national response.

Indeed, as a nation we have recently become nervous about inequality. Perhaps triggered by the recent studies of Teo (2018) and Chua, Tan and Koh (2017), or perhaps by warning signs from other countries such as the Umbrella Movement in Hong Kong or the election of US President Donald Trump, who rode on the wave of deep unhappiness over economic disparity in certain parts of the United States, 2018 saw an unprecedented public discussion of social inequality in Singapore. In her inaugural President's Address in Parliament on 7 May 2018, Halimah Yacob made "tackl[ing] inequality vigorously" her main theme.[15] This theme took centre stage in the subsequent parliamentary debates over the President's Address which, in turn, saw local media outlets offer robust analyses and debates in the form of special features and opinion pieces from experts on inequality and how to tackle it.

With the surge in public interest in inequality, the question is whether there will be substantive changes. I believe this might take a while. The government's emphasis on self-reliance has decreased in the last decade. For example, in his 2013 National Day Rally speech, Prime Minister Lee Hsien Loong said, "Today, the situation has changed. If we rely too heavily on the individual, their efforts alone will not be enough, especially among the vulnerable like the low-income families … The community and the government will have to do more to support individuals."[16] However, its preference for trickle-down economics remains strong. In his concluding speech at the 2018 Budget Debate, Finance Minister Heng Swee Keat reminded everyone that "rather than focus on how the pie is divided, we should grow the pie so that we can all enjoy a larger slice".[17] Although the government has rolled out many policies to uplift low wages and support low-income families, these transfers are still small when compared to other countries[18] and other forms of government expenditures.[19] All these suggest that there are other important policy goals which prevent greater redistribution or lead to greater inequality. Some concrete examples of such policies can be found in the areas of the tax regime, the labour market, education, housing, and healthcare. Before we look at each in turn, I should emphasize that the following discussion is not to explain the specific goals of the policies, but their impact on inequality.

Firstly, with regard to Singapore's tax regime, the city-state has one of the lowest tax rates among industrialized and neighbouring countries, and does not impose an inheritance tax.[20] A competitive tax regime keeps business and individual investments in Singapore, but in terms of inequality, it means that the wealthy can pass on their wealth within their organization or intergenerationally without returning a proportionate share to society. In addition to the statutory tax rates, incentives are also given such that effective tax rates are lower.[21] At the bottom end of the economic spectrum, while the introduction of transfers such as the WIS and Silver Support have made the tax system more progressive, Singapore's spending on social security and social protection continues to be low compared to other countries.[22]

It is important to emphasize that the point of the tax and transfers comparisons is not to suggest that Singapore should become a high tax regime such as those in Scandinavia. Instead, the much lower taxes in Singapore signal the low policy priority to redistribution. Repeated analyses have shown that countries with more redistributive tax systems have less income inequality.[23] Thus, if we are to commit to reducing inequality, the tax system would have to be more redistributive. In this context, the government has been preparing the local population for the possibility of rising taxes, although the one that has been announced thus far has been the regressive Goods and Services Tax (GST) meant to kick in between 2021 and 2025.[24] The International Monetary Fund[25] has proposed that efficient regressive taxes can be used to fund social transfers for a net redistributive effect. The question is how much of the GST revenue will be channelled towards social transfers, and looking further into the future, the extent to which the government will commit more taxes and transfers to tackle inequality. Although policy leaders have been signalling the inevitability of higher taxes, actual tax changes have been incremental, accompanied by continued warnings that higher taxes would lead to business flight and emigration. Such narratives, from both the government and the private sector, seems to signal that the vitality of the economy, to which the interests of capital and business owners are tied, continue to be prioritized over redistribution.

Secondly, the labour market in Singapore has eschewed unemployment insurance or a minimum wage. Driving the rationale of these labour policies are the economic principles of incentives and moral hazard, where there are fears that policy changes would lead to undesirable social behaviour. On one hand, low corporate and income taxes and zero inheritance tax attract business and wealth into Singapore and dissuade them from offshoring elsewhere. On the other hand, the absence of unemployment insurance pushes the unemployed to actively look for jobs instead of being incentivized to stay unemployed if such insurance were available. The textbook argument against a minimum wage is that the higher manpower cost would lead employers to decrease demand for labour, leading to unemployment.

Thus, we have implemented uniquely Singaporean schemes such as the WIS and the PWM. WIS is an earnings supplement for low-wage workers without increasing their employers' business cost, whereas the PWM provides different levels of minimum wage for different job types. PWM is currently legally enforced in three industries, namely cleaning and sanitary; security; and landscaping, with plans to roll out the scheme to other sectors. While seemingly similar to a general minimum wage, it is substantively different because it applies only to stipulated industries and is tied to training and productivity improvements that the government will work with these sectors to improve. While clearly advantageous in meeting multiple and perhaps longer term goals for sector transformation, the disadvantage of this incremental approach is that the overhaul of low wages runs only at a pace that corporations are comfortable with while not addressing the immediate needs of low-income workers not employed in PWM-covered sectors.

Besides low and stagnant wages, the nature of employment has become more precarious at the lower end of the economic ladder. Ng, Ng and Lee (2018)[26] document some of these trends. They found that low-wage incidence (defined as the percentage of employees earning below two-thirds of median) in Singapore was high compared to other developed countries, and that the use of part-time and short-term contracts have increased greatly among labourers and service jobs. In 2015, 34 per cent of cleaners, labourers and related workers, as well as 21 per cent of service and sales workers in Singapore were in part-time employment arrangements. These percentages were thrice and twice, respectively, that of all types of other workers. Similarly, in 2015, 15 per cent of cleaners, labourers and related workers, as well as 12 per cent of service and sales workers were on employment contracts of less than three months. These were respectively thrice and twice that of all types of workers. In their case-study of the local food and beverage (F&B) industry, various forms of poor job conditions were found.

Thirdly, education has been an important policy arena in the inequality debate and rightly so. International intergenerational mobility research shows that more homogeneous educational regimes with more progressive spending lead to higher intergenerational mobility, and that the effects accumulate through the course of one's life.[27] In particular, streaming or sorting students based on academic ability leads to the widening of the achievement gap.[28]

Meanwhile, a wide range of local scholars and government leaders have noted the increased educational stratification in Singapore as a result of children from different social-economic statuses (SES) attending different types of schools and educational streams. While Singapore's students top international tests, their achievement gap and the dependence of their scores on parents' SES are relatively high.[29] Several local studies have shown that the education gap might be related to educational segregation. Using the National Youth Survey (NYS) 2013, Ng and Choo (2018)[30] found that the effect of parents' education on youths' educational aspiration is mediated through educational stream. Specifically, students in the technical stream had lower educational aspirations and had parents with lower educational qualifications. One interpretation of this statistical finding is that parents with low educational qualifications are more likely to place their children in the technical stream, which in turn leads to their children having lower educational aspirations. Using the NYS 2016, Ng and Nursila (2018)[31] found a similar result but at the opposite end of the spectrum. Educational stream that mediates the effect of parents' education on aspiration is now significant for students in the International Baccalaureate or Integrated Programmes (IB/IP). That is, parents with higher educational qualifications are more likely to place their children in the IB/IP, which in turn leads to the children aspiring towards a higher level of education.

Strikingly, in focus group discussions conducted with Singapore youths, Nursila Senin (2018)[32] found that higher SES youths referred to attaining university education as the norm, but lower SES youths referred to attaining polytechnic education as the norm. Finally, using the Programme for International Student Assessment (PISA), Ker (2018)[33] found that there is a correlation between the level of autonomy and resources enjoyed by a school on the one hand, and its students' PISA scores and SES on the other. Students in schools with more autonomy to set their curriculum and a wider variety of co-curricular activities (CCAs) (an indication of resources) have higher-SES parents and better PISA scores. Thus, in the case of Singapore students, who their parents are matters to what schools they attend, and what schools they attend matters to their achievements, aspirations and, ultimately, careers.

Fourthly, housing inequality contributes to social inequality. Ninety-one per cent of households in Singapore own their homes, with 79 per cent of households living in Housing and Development Board (HDB) flats.[34] While this topline statistic looks homogeneous, the variety of flat types is, however, diverse, as Figure 11.2 shows. Further, different flat types are concentrated in different neighbourhoods and are clustered differently. For example, the more expensive executive and five-room flats tend to be in the same blocks, whereas the cheaper two-room flexi

FIGURE 11.2
Distribution of Housing Types

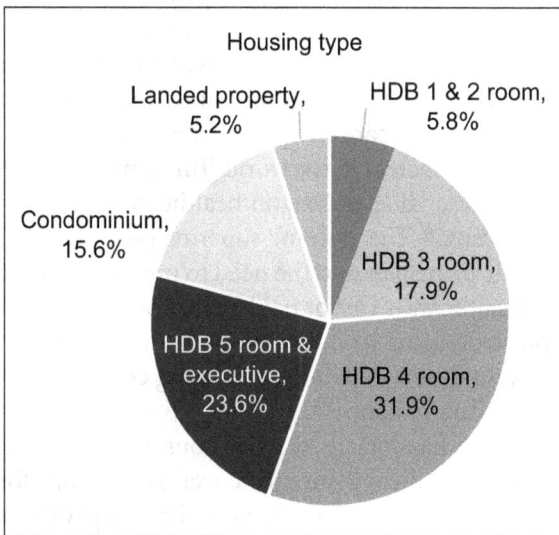

Source: Department of Statistics Singapore, 2019, "Households", https://www.singstat.gov.sg/find-data/search-by-theme/households/households/latest-data

and three-room flats tend to be in the same blocks. Four-room flats are in the same blocks as a wider variety of flat sizes. The most expensive condominiums are located in central Singapore and are more highly populated by expatriate residents.

While there have been attempts to locate different flat sizes in the same or nearby neighbourhoods, there are clear stratifications of higher-income and lower-income neighbourhoods because of the clustering of the same types of flats, thus resulting in social segregation. Chua, Tan and Koh (2017)[35] found that private housing dwellers (those who live in condominiums or landed property) have ties to an average of 3.05 fellow private housing dwellers and only 2.6 public housing dwellers. In contrast, public housing dwellers have ties to only 0.8 private housing dwellers and 4.3 public housing dwellers. Using GIS maps, Leong, Teng and Ko (2020)[36] also show the higher concentration of Chinese in the central area of Singapore versus the higher concentration of Malays in the outskirts of towns such as Woodlands and Pasir Ris. The latter two areas tend to also have lower proportions of high-income households. Such stratification patterns have emerged despite HDB ethnic quota policies which ensure that the ethnic representation in each residential area is generally reflective of the national ethnic proportion.

Arguably, the existing class concentration in residential neighbourhoods could be worse without intentional town planning to ensure a mix of housing types. However, the way we mix the housing types is also stratified as the previous paragraphs suggest. No matter the cause, despite the high density in small Singapore, housing segregation is evident. The rich and poor live and move around in very different communities that often do not intersect.

The fifth issue is healthcare inequality. Singapore's healthcare system ranks among the most efficient in the world. This is measured by comparing life expectancy to personal spending on healthcare and the share of GDP to healthcare spending.[37] The system's superior performance is anchored on strong economic principles and the need to prevent the moral hazard of overspending if healthcare is free or paid by insurance. Hence, by requiring co-payment and structuring health services on one's ability or willingness to pay, we are said to have avoided the escalating costs or long queues that plague other healthcare systems.[38]

Yet, such a system has socially divisive consequences. People who buy more comprehensive medical insurance coverage, or work for companies that provide comprehensive coverage, or are willing to pay the unsubsidized price for healthcare will invariably receive faster care from senior doctors. They may also opt to receive treatment in private hospitals and clinics.

For others, subsidized care may mean waiting months for an appointment at a restructured hospital, and on the day of the appointment, waiting considerably longer to see a doctor who is more likely to be a junior doctor rather than a senior consultant. In the case of some middle-class patients who may require urgent medical treatment such as a cancer biopsy or a fracture surgery, they may decide not to wait for these appointments by forgoing the subsidy and paying private fees to receive earlier treatment. For hospitalization, one stays in different-sized wards depending on one's pay category.

While the design of the local healthcare system is to prevent moral hazard and overconsumption of health resources, some have argued that people do not demand healthcare unless they require medical attention, and that supply-induced overconsumption can be contained with regulation.[39] Whatever the merits of either side of the debate, Singapore's healthcare system, which is based on a co-payment model, has become an area in which existing social inequality and segregation can be witnessed and accentuated.

Each of the above examples of stratification is tied closely to income inequality because one's income level determines the treatment one receives in each sphere. Low income thus becomes a key determinant of a citizen's life chances and experience. For example, a Singaporean in a low-paying job is more likely to experience stagnant wages and employment insecurity. A student from a lower-income family is more likely to attend a non-elite school and be assigned a lower academic track, thus shaping his employment opportunities and his future income. A lower-income Singaporean living in a smaller flat will see his or her asset appreciate at a slower rate in contrast to owners of five-room flats and executive flats. A Singaporean who relies on subsidized healthcare will have to wait longer to receive medical treatment and cannot choose his or her doctor because he or she cannot afford to purchase additional integrated insurance coverage.

In other words, while inequality is often couched in economic terms, the experience of inequality is very much social. Singapore has reached a stage of development and maturity where the wealthy and poor need never cross paths. They go to different schools, go on to climb different job ladders, live in different communities, and when they fall ill, go to different hospitals and wards. Our lives are stratified by where we work, study, live and fall ill. To cross into the other's world will be very uncomfortable. So the natural reaction will be to remain in our comfort zone, secure our inner circle and keep out the outsiders. As we do so, we have less and less understanding of and empathy for one another. To be sure, social and economic stratification exists in every country. The question is the extent of such stratifications, society's attitude towards these divides, and how policy choices may accelerate or decelerate the pace of disparity. For example, although the plight of low-wage workers can be said to be more precarious in Singapore compared to many other developed countries, we collectively choose an income redistribution model that emphasizes the dangers of moral hazard because we believe that this is necessary to prevent overspending and to retain our ethos of self-reliance.

Worst Case Scenario: A Patronage Culture that Divides

I am asked to imagine a worst case scenario if social inequality continues to rise. Asking this of an economist and a social work academic like myself is tricky. It is said that if you ask ten economists for their predictions, they will give you eleven. Social workers, on the other hand, tend to give "it depends" answers. Because of the systems ecological perspective in the discipline of social work, the various systems in a person's life need to be taken into account. Thus, what is worst depends on what angle is taken (or what systems are taken into account) to view the issue.

Forced to take a stand, I will highlight three scenarios, only one of which is ultimately the worst case to me. Two extreme scenarios that uncontrolled inequality might lead to but which I think are not worst case scenarios are the following. First, an increasing social divide in Singapore might lead to a political coup and reformation. This to me is not the worst case scenario because it shows that people have enough hope that things can improve to take action. Second, too wide an inequality might lead to the collapse of Singapore as a nation. This is also not a worst case scenario because to me, such a divided nation that somehow pushes its people away from one another might as well not be a nation.

To me, the worst case scenario goes to the core of what I began with in this chapter—well-being. The worst case scenario in terms of unabated inequality and segregation in Singapore is when our efforts to tackle them fail, resulting in their acceleration and intergenerational entrenchment. I fear the impact of this scenario on our sense of humanity and our human spirit. It is when stratification is so complete and entrenched in Singapore that we are able to accept the ruling elite running the country only for self-serving interests, thus widening the normalized gap between those of their class and the rest of society. It is when the ruled masses lose hope and confidence to strive and to seek a better future, accepting that their lowly station in life is where they deserve to be. The disappearing middle class either takes flight to other countries, or stays on only to serve the ruling elites and keep out the poor working class. It is when the working class simply subjects itself to exploitation by the ruling class. Many of the working class are powerless, but they do not have the resources to leave for greener pastures. It is when self-reliance means self-centredness and selfish individualism, we will then have come full circle. It will be a return to 200 years ago when the British colonials were the ruling elites, and our forefathers the unruly masses to be managed. Only this time, the economic opportunities that drew Chinese and Indians immigrants will no longer be there. To me, a slow slide to such a society is the worst case scenario, more disconcerting than a political coup or national collapse. In these latter scenarios, Singaporeans may continue to strive, to fight for a cause, and their inherent dignity is preserved.

The worst case scenario I have painted is made possible by the strong patronage culture in Asia, including Singapore. Syn (2017) defines patronage as a system that involves "a power figure who is in a position—a patron—to give security, inducements, or both, and his persona followers, who in return for such benefits, contribute their loyalty and personal assistance to the patron's designs".[40] While some scholars paint patronage in a negative light, others suggest that patronage systems might not propagate inequality, but can in fact promote social mobility and political participation.[41] For better or worse, both views note that patronage systems contribute to the perpetuation of political stability by accepting local hierarchies and thus reaffirming the status quo. As Syn opines, "patronage is a relationship model that fits comfortably into an Asian context".[42]

Patronage in Singapore is seen in examples such as the appointment of a patron (often a political or business leader) to a cause or a community organization, and small benefits such as priority Primary 1 admission and special parking labels to community volunteers in residential committees. These illustrations are given not to criticize current practices, but to show the practice of patronage in Singapore. However, in the development towards my worst case scenario, a patronage culture might create the conditions favourable to elite rulers who preside over a divided society in which the masses are in servitude. This is because under a patronage system, the patron-rulers can take advantage of the way hierarchies and the status quo are accepted as the natural order and dispense minimal but sufficient favours to their client-subjects in order to prevent meaningful opposition.

A possible indication of this is in Figure 11.3, which gives the difference between the market and disposable Gini indices shown previously in Figures 11.1a and 11.1b. Noticeably, all the Asian economies of Hong Kong, Malaysia, Singapore and Taiwan are at the bottom of the graphs with the least change in the Gini index through taxes and transfers. Although Malaysia and Hong Kong have recently experienced political upheaval, their extent of distribution is still substantially lower than the Western economies. Apparently, Asian economies have a higher tolerance for smaller efforts at redistribution or narrowing inequality. This might reflect greater acceptance of hierarchy and power imbalance in Asia.

Conclusion

In summary, this chapter makes two points which lead to two opposing conclusions. First, self-reliance with minimal welfare as a governing principle started with the British colonial rulers. This was embraced by the post-independence government and continues until today. Second, with self-reliance and minimal welfare as key tenets, as well as ensuring that incentives for hard work will undergird our economic growth, it is clear that our institutions not only distribute less welfare than other developed countries but perhaps even reinforce inequality.

As social inequality continues to worsen worldwide, and appreciably so in Singapore, one conclusion is to awaken to the challenges of inequality. From the recent public debates in Singapore, it appears that more Singaporeans have become uncomfortable with the increasing entrenchment of social stratification in society. Addressing this complex issue will require an ideological review of the *raison d'être* and priorities of many of our main institutions. For example, should our education system start to prioritize redistribution and equity over human capital development? Should our healthcare system start to prioritize high-quality basic care for all citizens, regardless of income, over concerns of moral hazard?

The opposing conclusion, however, is to accept inequality as a way of life. Social and economic inequalities have been the unavoidable consequences of an economic model of development that has driven the Singapore story. It is a story not just of survival but of an economic miracle that saw a little British outpost without any natural resources flourish as one of the world's leading financial centres. This story has been possible because of fiscal prudence, political stability and the ensuring of economic competitiveness. Although this story is riddled with inequality, the incremental, measured and targeted steps taken by the government along the way have mitigated

FIGURE 11.3

Comparison of Differences between Market Gini Coefficient and Disposable GINI Coefficient of Several Countries, 1960–2016

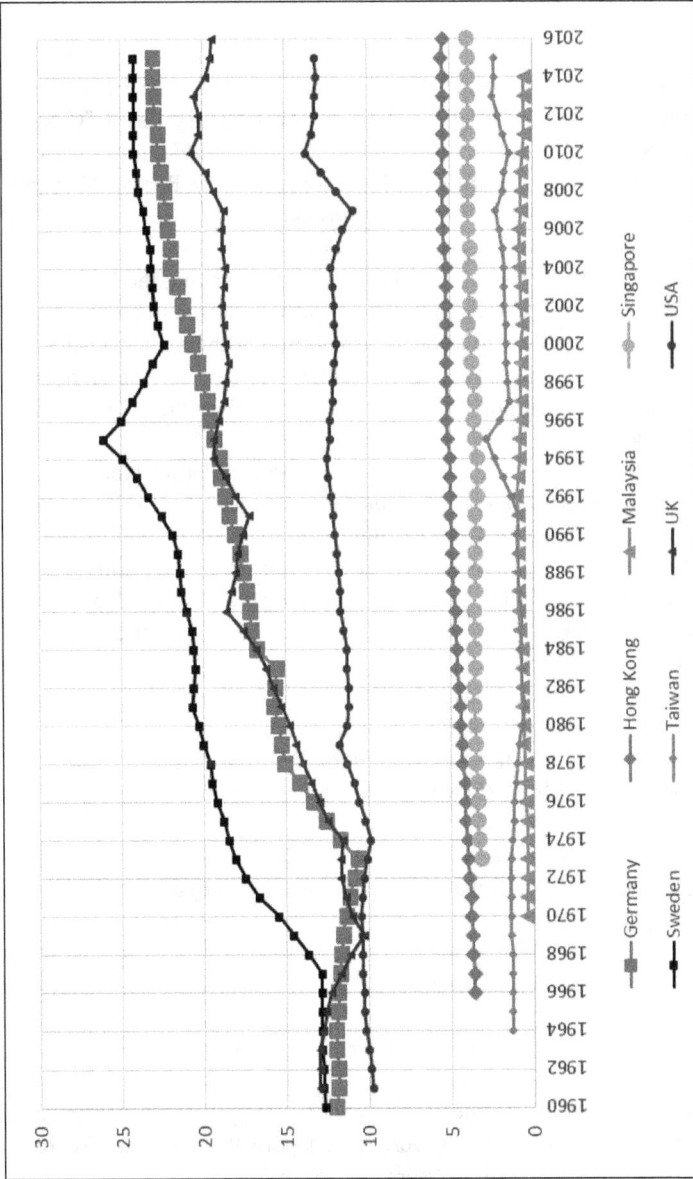

Source: Frederick Solt, "The Standardized World Income Inequality Database", *Social Science Quarterly* 97, no. 5 (2016): 1267–81. SWIID Version 7.1, August 2018 (2018-08-14).

some of its effects. After 200 years since the founding of modern Singapore by Raffles and the East India Company, it appears that Singaporeans are at a decision point with regard to inequality and its place in our society.

Notes

1. Ho Chi Tim and Ann Wee, *Singapore Chronicles: Social Services* (Singapore: Institute of Policy Studies, 2016); National Library Board, "Colonial Port City 1819–1945", *HistorySG: An Online Resource Guide,* http://eresources.nlb.gov. sg/history/timeline/1819–1945; National Library Board, "Singapore Treaty Is Signed", *HistorySG: An Online Resource Guide,* http://eresources.nlb.gov.sg/history/ events/72da3f9a-186a-4234-83d1-7dcaca27cfa9

2. Claire Huang, "Singapore's Wealth Per Adult Among the Highest in the World", *Business Times,* 23 November 2016, https://www.businesstimes.com.sg/government-economy/singapores-wealth-per-adult-among-the-highest-in-the-world

3. Lee Hsien Loong, "President's Address (Debate on the Address)", Singapore Parliamentary Reports (Hansard), 13 November 2006, Vol. 82, http://sprs.parl. gov.sg

4. Organization for Economic Co-operation and Development, *Singapore: Rapid Improvement Followed by Strong Performance* (2010), https://www.oecd.org/ countries/singapore/46581101.pdf

5. Lee Hsien Loong, "President's Address (Debate on the Address)".

6. Irene Y.H. Ng, "Being Poor in a Rich 'Nanny State': Developments in Singapore Social Welfare", *Singapore Economic Review* 60, no. 3 (2015): 1–17.

7. Ibid.

8. Frederick Solt, "The Standardized World Income Inequality Database", *Social Science Quarterly* 97, no. 5 (2016): 1267–81.

9. Ibid.; International Monetary Fund, *IMF Fiscal Monitor: Tackling Inequality,* October 2017, https://www.imf.org/en/Publications/FM/Issues/2017/10/05/fiscal-monitor-october-2017

10. Teo You Yenn, *This Is What Inequality Looks Like* (Singapore: Ethos Books, 2018).

11. Vincent Chua, Tan Ern Ser, and Gillian Koh, *A Study on Social Capital in Singapore* (Singapore: Institute of Policy Studies, 2017).

12. Linda Y.C. Lim, "Social Welfare", in *Management of Success: The Moulding of Modern Singapore,* edited by Kernial Singh Sandhu and Paul Wheatley (Singapore: Institute of Southeast Asian Studies, 1989), pp. 171–97.

13. Irene Y.H. Ng, "Being Poor in a Rich 'Nanny State'".

14. Ibid.

15. Halimah Yacob, "President's Address (A Strong People-Government Partnership, to Build our Future Singapore)", Singapore Parliamentary Reports (Hansard), 7 May 2018, vol. 94, http://sprs.parl.gov.sg

16. Singapore Prime Minister's Office, "Prime Minister Lee Hsien Loong's National Day Rally 2013 (English)", 18 August 2013, https://www.pmo.gov.sg/newsroom/ prime-minister-lee-hsien-loongs-national-day-rally-2013-english

17. Heng Swee Keat, "Debate on Annual Budget Statement (Round-Up Speech)", Singapore Parliamentary Reports (Hansard), 1 March 2018, vol. 94, http://sprs.parl.gov.sg

18. David Tay, "Balancing Social Spending with Financial Prudence", *Straits Times*, 30 April 2018, https://www.straitstimes.com/opinion/balancing-social-spending-with-financial-prudence

19. Ng Kok Hoe, "To Tackle Inequality, Policy Mindsets Must Change", *Straits Times*, 11 May 2018, https://www.straitstimes.com/opinion/tackling-inequality-vigorously

20. KPMG, "Individual Income Tax Rates Table" (2018), https://home.kpmg/xx/en/home/services/tax/tax-tools-and-resources/tax-rates-online/individual-income-tax-rates-table.html; Siow Li Sen, "Wealth Taxes May Hit the Rich but Other Factors Can Mitigate Impact", *Straits Times*, 25 January 2018, https://www.straitstimes.com/business/economy/wealth-taxes-may-hit-the-rich-but-other-factors-can-mitigate-impact; John Geddie and Masayuki Kitano, "As Singapore Ages, Low Tax Model Creaks", *Reuters*, 23 January 2018, https://www.reuters.com/article/us-singapore-taxes-analysis/as-singapore-ages-low-tax-model-creaks-idUSKBN1FC0TP

21. PricewaterhouseCoopers, *Singapore: Sovereignty, Society, Substance, Success: White Paper on Singapore's Tax Policy* (2015), https://www.pwc.com/sg/en/publications/assets/tax-policy-white-paper.pdf

22. David Tay, "Balancing Social Spending with Financial Prudence".

23. Luiz de Mello and Erwin R. Tiongson, "Income Inequality and Redistributive Government Spending", *Public Finance Review* 34, no. 3 (2006): 282–305; Rune Ervik, *The Redistributive Aim of Social Policy: A Comparative Analysis of Taxes, Tax Expenditure Transfers and Direct Transfers in Eight Countries*, LIS Working Paper, no. 184, 1998.

24. Heng Swee Keat, "Annual Budget Statement", Singapore Parliamentary Reports (Hansard), 19 February 2018, vol. 94, http://sprs.parl.gov.sg

25. International Monetary Fund, *IMF Fiscal Monitor: Tackling Inequality*, October 2017.

26. Irene Y.H. Ng, Yi Ying Ng and Poh Choo Lee, "Singapore's Restructuring of Low-Wage Work: Have Cleaning Job Conditions Improved?", *Economic and Labour Relations Review* 29, no. 3 (2018): 308–27.

27. See, for example, John Ermisch, Markus Jänitti and Timothy M. Smeeding, *From Parents to Children: The Intergenerational Transmission of Advantage* (New York: Russell Sage Foundation, 2012).

28. Chen-Lin C. Kulik and James A. Kulik, "Effects of Ability Grouping on Secondary School Students: A Meta-Analysis of Evaluation Findings", *American Educational Research Journal* 19, no. 3 (1982): 415–28; Robert E. Slavin, "Achievement Effects of Ability Grouping in Secondary Schools: A Best-Evidence Synthesis", *Review of Educational Research* 60, no. 3 (1990): 471–99; Ermisch, Jänitti and Smeeding, *From Parents to Children*.

29. Organization for Economic Co-operation and Development. *Equity in Education: Breaking Down Barriers to Social Mobility* (2018); Irene Y.H. Ng and Nursila Senin,

"Effects of SES and Tracking on Students", in *Working with Low-income Families Through the Life Course: Challenges to Social Services* (Singapore: National University of Singapore, forthcoming).

30. Irene Y.H. Ng and Choo Hyekyung, "Parental Background and Youth Educational Aspiration in Singapore: A Path Analysis in Institutional and Psychological Context" (2018). Manuscript under review.

31. Irene Y.H. Ng and Nursila Senin, *Educational Pathways, Youth Well-Being & Outlook* (Singapore: National Youth Council, 2018).

32. Nursila Senin, *Youth Aspirations: Uncovering Patterns and Understanding Stories of Class and Ethnicity*, (MSoc. Sci. Thesis, National University of Singapore, 2018).

33. Rachel Ker, *The Role of School in the Relationship between Parental Socioeconomic Status (SES) and the Child's Achievement and Aspiration* (Honours Thesis, National University of Singapore, 2018).

34. Department of Statistics Singapore, "Households", https://www.singstat.gov.sg/find-data/search-by-theme/households/households/latest-data

35. Vincent Chua, Tan Ern Ser, and Gillian Koh, *A Study on Social Capital in Singapore*.

36. Leong Chan-Hoong, Eugene Teng and William Weiliang Ko, "Thirty Years of Ethnic Management in Neighbourhoods: Evaluating the Success of the Ethnic Integration Policy", in *Building Resilient Neighbourhoods: The Convergence of Policies, Research, and Practice*, edited by Leong Chan-Hoong and Lai-Choo Malone-Lee (Singapore: Springer, 2020).

37. Pacific Prime Insurance Brokers Singapore, "Singapore Healthcare Ranks as 2nd Most Efficient Worldwide", n.d., https://www.pacificprime.sg/blog/2016/10/20/singapore-healthcare-efficiency/

38. Tim Harford, *The Undercover Economist* (London: Little, Brown Book Group, 2006).

39. Jeremy Lim, *Myth or Magic: The Singapore Healthcare System* (Singapore: Select Publishing, 2013).

40. W.M. Syn, *On Being the Antioch of Asia: Global Missions Partnership through Asian Lenses* (Singapore: Genesis Books, 2017), p. 108.

41. Anastasia Piliavsky, ed., *Patronage as Politics in South Asia* (Cambridge: Cambridge University Press, 2014).

42. W.M. Syn, *On Being the Antioch of Asia*, p. 108.

12

The Future of the Middle Class in Singapore
2020 and Beyond

GILLIAN KOH, TAN ERN SER AND VINCENT CHUA[1]

In 1959, 90 per cent of the people had no property stakes in Singapore. Twenty-eight years after we took over control of Singapore, 80 per cent of our households are now home-owning. June 1987 [there were a] total 630,000 [HDB] units, 500,000 or 80 per cent were home-owning and 20 per cent rentals ... HDB surveys show that more than 50 per cent of those in rentals can afford and intend to buy 3 and 4-room flats. So when they are resettled, we shall have 94 per cent property-owning households ... Sociologists define middle-class in several ways. First by property, second by the perception of one's own position, third, by education and occupation ... Our society has become 80 per cent middle-class. Our people have important stakes in Singapore's stability and prosperity."

Prime Minister Lee Kuan Yew
Tanjong Pagar National Day Dinner
Thursday, 13 August 1987

This was the report card on Singapore's socio-economic development issued by the founding Prime Minister (PM) of Singapore, Lee Kuan Yew twenty-eight years after his People's Action Party (PAP) first won the right to govern Singapore in 1959, when it was still a British colony. Its transformation from post-Second World War squalor where most of the populace continued to struggle with basic survival, to one where the vast majority had homes of their own, where many were armed with better educational qualifications than the generation before them, and a significant proportion of workers in well-paying white-collar administrative and professional jobs, was remarkable.

In the speech above, PM Lee argued that having benefited from a governance system that upheld the rule of law, integrity and active industrial policy that brought such progress, Singaporeans should have no interest in reversing course to embrace an alternative social order—communism— something that had traction on the ground before Independence. Instead, Singapore's full engagement with the global capitalist system after it had lost the Malayan hinterland with the end of merger with Malaysia and the PAP's social and political policies had proven the worth of the PAP's governance system in tangible terms. The resulting middle-class society would therefore be the bulwark against such ideological temptation.

The context of this National Day speech was the detention without trial in May and June that year of 22 individuals. Among them were several Catholic priests whom the government alleged had been dallying with Marxist-inspired Liberation Theology and communist mobilization strategies to "overthrow the Government and establish a communist state".[2] In his speech, PM Lee said that while the emergence of this broad middle class did not mean that there would be no Marxists or communists or other "disaffected and discontented people", it did mean that Marxists and communists had "little hope of winning the vote" and ultimately, that it was in the interest of Singaporeans "to make sure that no communist united front ever gets restarted in Singapore".[3]

In his mind, his government had worked to ensure that Singaporeans did not need to just take on faith that its governance system was a viable one. The empirical evidence of its success was crucial to its political legitimacy and continued support. Such were the stakes in the concept of Singapore being a middle-class society. The governance system, sound economic and fiscal planning, the democratic socialist ideal of providing a minimum standard of the basics in life through government subsidies for education, housing, and healthcare meant that with some personal effort at school and work, families would see their fortunes improve from one generation to the next. This was the "Singapore Dream".

Over the years, the assessment of the health of the middle class and the validity of the Singapore Dream have featured in keynote speeches of Singapore's political leaders. Also, citizens, voters and public intellectuals insist that they will not take things on faith. On occasion, they ask if the condition of the middle class continues to be robust and a source of social dynamism for the nation. It is after all the reference group for those in the bottom 40 per cent of Singapore society—that they believe that they or their children can move into the ranks and lifestyle of the more comfortable middle class and that Singapore continues to be a relatively egalitarian society.

Why the Health of the
Middle Class Matters

Past the sixty year mark since the PAP came into power, how is the middle class in Singapore doing? Why does this question matter? First, while the health of the middle class would not be an outcome of what the PAP has and can do alone, it has been valorized as an important performance indicator of its governance system as explained earlier.

Second, the middle class is recognized in a capitalist society as the force for socio-economic progress with its belief in education, paid work, entrepreneurship and the market. It is also expected to enliven democratic development through its commitment to the rule of law and within that, its desire for political pluralism and its tolerance for diversity of all kinds. This is a segment that lies between the rich and the poor; it is not demoralized, dependent or fatalistic that might cause the former to withdraw from proactive efforts at improving their lot in life. Yet they are not so well-heeled as to assume that success is a foregone conclusion but feel assured that they have the resources as to take care of themselves and their families. They depend on "the system" to work as it should to achieve success and intergenerational mobility. In other words, the health of the middle class in society provides the ideological moorings for a progressive, liberal and capitalist governance system.

A third reason why this issue is important is that across the world today, we see angry, discontented, disillusioned masses tipping over the proverbial table on the post-Second World War and post-Cold War liberal order. Indeed, the absence of progress in the daily lives of the broad middle class elsewhere has meant that they see no stake in that order. Furthermore, the discredited record of communism, the dismantling of unions in the Anglo-Saxon market system and wobbly state finances in the developed West have meant that neither of the two Cold War-era systems seems to be ideologically coherent nor fiscally viable.

This has led to populism in the political order, and protectionism in the economic one. It stems from the popular conviction that previous regimes had served to fatten the pockets of the elites, that is, the top 1 per cent of society at the expense of what has felt like the bottom 99 per cent constituting the rest. No surprise then that politically activated parts of the latter segment now want a "fair deal" in life.

These activists have taken the wrecking ball to the establishment in the United States with the election of Donald Trump to the Oval Office. Meanwhile, across the Atlantic, there were also enough cynics in the United

Kingdom to precipitate the decision to bow out of the great European Union project. These are not reversions to Marxism or communism but to a non-ism which makes for even greater uncertainty and volatility. It is precisely because of this crisis in the legitimacy of the liberal order elsewhere that the issue of the health of the middle class in Singapore is a critical one. If it is mishandled, it could lead to an undesirable future.

Having laid out what is at stake, this chapter will address the Singapore middle class in three parts. First, we will look at how the middle class has been discussed or has talked about itself since 1987; second, we look at the empirical data on the life of the middle class over time to see if the meanings and interpretations of the first section are warranted; and third, we sneak a peek into the future to provide a prognosis of the middle class in Singapore for the years ahead.

Now to some definitional issues regarding the "middle class". This group can be defined in objective, gradational ways—from one income status to another; one housing status to another and so on. A second approach is to do it through the subjective method where people identify themselves as sharing a similar level of wealth, influence, status or lifestyle choices—where the sine qua non of "arriving" in the middle class could be the ownership of private housing, of taking overseas holidays, or keeping the company of the "right people". A third method is to do it through reputation or what other people deem to be someone's social standing. These three modalities would generally fall into what is called the Weberian orientation to "class" where objective measures as well as status and sense of identity are part of that notion. This is the broad concept of the middle class that we will adopt in this chapter.

The Anxiety over Dropping Out of the Middle Class

The first major national debate about the health of the middle class and the middle-class dream of attaining wealth, social mobility and status through effort, was brought on when former director of local think-tank, the Institute of Policy Studies, Dr Lee Tsao Yuan, suggested that given the average wages of fresh university graduates on the one hand and the prices of public flats on the other, the chase by better-educated Singaporeans to own their homes, a key marker of having arrived in the middle class, might become more difficult.

She noted in 1996 that the rate of increase in the cost of owning publicly subsidized Housing and Development Board (HDB) flats and cars, both assets associated with the middle class, had outstripped the increase in earned income of graduates, those who would think they have qualified to enter the middle class. Dr Lee stated,

> High asset prices affect everyone, but have most effect on the younger generation. Many young married couples these days find it difficult to purchase property, much less a car. Young graduates … no longer command the same premium that they did even ten years ago … My concern is that the difficulties of asset ownership, particularly for the younger generation, could lead to considerable frustration on their part.[4]

This sparked a national discussion on the Singapore Dream and accessibility to the 5Cs of the middle-class lifestyle—cash, cars, condominium, country club and credit card. That August, Lee Kuan Yew, who was by then Senior Minister (SM), met a group of Singaporean youths to discuss these issues especially after one in their number, Ms Phua Mei Pin, an intern at the national broadsheet, *The Straits Times*, argued how the usual "rewards" of effort and the arrival in the middle class seemed to be getting out of reach: "I am not asking for an emperor's condos and stables of Benzes, just a small place I can belong to and that can belong to me … Already I have friends who are drawing up blueprints of their futures in Australia and America, where they believe they can stretch the same dollar much further."[5]

SM Lee's response was that Singaporeans had seen progress from the previous generation so, materially, it was incontrovertible that life was better. However, with more chasing the material trappings of success, prices were, in turn, being driven upwards too. He tried to redirect the youth to be strategic in their choice of careers to do the best they can materially but also to pursue the value of the non-material, spiritual aspects of life.[6]

When asked whether Singaporeans were concerned over the emergence of a "privileged class", then member of parliament (MP) Mr R. Sinnakaruppan posited that Singaporeans were concerned over a group that was able to take advantage of the system by speculating in property and make hundreds of thousands of dollars in the process.[7] He acknowledged that it was natural, and even good for Singaporeans to aspire towards a goal. However, he also urged the middle-income who were aspiring towards private property not to let their aspirations turn into envy of others. In another speech, he pinpointed the cause of anxieties to status competition, where "if they are better off than us, then we want to show, perhaps show off, that we can also afford the things that they enjoy", which only brought more financial woes upon themselves.[8] He also noted that opposition politicians were capitalizing on the emotional nature of such anxieties.

What the government did subsequently was to take on the task of expanding its offerings of publicly subsidized housing to include condominiums for young working professional couples more suited to their aspirations for the middle-class lifestyle.[9] The government also targeted efforts of nation-building and identity-making at this segment by engaging them in policy dialogues especially through a new statutory board, the National Youth Council.[10] Otherwise, as we can imagine, it would be a great irony for the primary beneficiaries of the system—the Singapore youth—to say that they were going to give up on it.

Nevertheless, expectations had risen such that the middle class and their children were unsure if there was any more headroom for raising their standard of living materially and status-wise. This is what Phua was suggesting—where the "rewards" for effort were "getting out of reach". This was a narrative of relative consumption or relative deprivation, where the worry was about falling behind those in your class or the class you want to belong in or the older cohorts against whom you benchmarked yourself.

The benefits of education, considered the key route to social mobility, did not seem to be as large and certain as they used to be. More Singaporeans were earning degrees by the 1990s, thus lowering the scarcity value of educational credentials despite the government at the time deciding that only up to 25 per cent of each cohort should be granted publicly subsidized tertiary education.[11] Also, with successful economic development and the overall stock of graduates rising, more were chasing after the same key middle-class consumption goods like housing and cars in a city-state where there are physical limitations to meeting such aspirations.

That year, 1996, then PM Goh Chok Tong addressed the issue of the commitment of the younger generation of Singaporeans to their country—a problem of the management of success. He assured the post-independence generation that they would continue to see progress in their lives with greater access to the wealth of the country through home-ownership and the ownership of shares of important, successful, newly privatized government-linked corporations. He also highlighted the efforts to enhance education at all levels including the vocational or technical training track and described this as investing in young people to keep Singapore "an open society, with easy social mobility and many avenues for talent to rise and contribute more to society".[12] He added:

> There is still considerable social mobility and a lot of upgrading by housing types. Our income distribution has not widened, because more Singaporeans have made it into the middle-income groups, but in the

future, the gap between top earners and the rest may widen, because in the global economy, the able and talented are in demand everywhere, while the unskilled are in oversupply.[13]

But earlier in his speech, PM Goh also warned that, "our society is showing signs of becoming more stratified by education and income groups. Many Singaporeans aspire to drive bigger cars, live in private properties, send their children to top schools."[14] He recognized that Singaporeans dreamt of a better life but that the Singapore Dream was too narrowly defined in materialistic terms. He explained that Lee Kuan Yew's concern was that there were countries in the region that were doing better, especially Malaysia, and therefore, future success could not be taken for granted.[15] The Singapore Dream was the result of success but, Goh added, its cause lay somewhere else—able national leadership, sense of commitment to the country, social cohesion and a nose for what makes firms and the national economy globally competitive.[16]

The next season when middle-class anxiety erupted was even more worrying. It was when economist Chua Hak Bin raised the alarm over middle-income wage stagnation. Writing in 2007, Chua noted that though there was an uplift in the economy due in part to globalization and economic restructuring, economic growth was largely attributable to the policy decision to cut corporate taxes and lower business costs by trimming contributions to workers' Central Provident Fund (CPF) accounts which, in turn, reduced gross wages.[17] This economic restructuring came in the aftermath of the economic recession from the dot.com bust of 2000–1 and the 2003 SARS crisis.

In order to make up for lost ground, the government liberalized foreign labour inflow at all levels to support the catch-up growth of business sectors across the economy, including the record-time construction of two large integrated resorts.[18] The overall effect of this, Chua argued, was the emergence of an economic dualism where the top end of the corporate sector, as well as the upper rungs of the income ladder, prospered and was likely to see sustained growth, a trend anticipated by Goh earlier. However, those in the middle to bottom rungs of the income ladder, as well as those associated with the more volatile and less cutting-edge manufacturing sector, experienced stagnation in activities and rewards.[19] Hence, not only was gross income for work reduced with the trimmed CPF contributions, the increased supply of cheaper foreign manpower had also depressed lower and middle wages in these sectors, stated Chua. He went on to note,

> Economic restructuring over the last few years may have also dis-
> proportionately compressed the wages of the middle class. The negative
> impact from the CPF cuts has outweighed the gains from the personal
> income tax cuts for this segment ... The negative impact was largest on
> the middle class.[20]

All these raised the anxiety that Singapore was becoming less of a
middle-class society. That year, PM Lee Hsien Loong, the country's third
premier, addressed the issue of the widening income gap. He stated that
across the globe, "The top incomes are zooming up, and the gap between
the top and the second highest incomes is widening ... it's not just between
the top and the middle but even at the top, it's stretching out".[21] This was
because of the premium given to skills, education, special talent and capital
invested in financial markets at the highest end of the labour market, as well
as the "great doubling" of supply of workers entering the global economy
with the liberalization of China, India and Vietnam that pressed down
the wages of those at the lower end of that market engaged in the same
activities they were in.

Whilst acknowledging these global realities, PM Lee reiterated in
his 2007 National Day Rally Speech the government's commitment to
improving the skillset of workers, especially of older ones. At the same time,
low-income workers' wages would be augmented through a new income
support policy called Workfare Income Supplement. His speech focused
on the government's efforts in bolstering retirement funding, raising the
retirement age and introducing a re-employment policy for senior workers.
More importantly, he stated that access to tertiary education would be
expanded to accommodate a greater proportion of each cohort—from 23 per
cent at the time to a target of 30 per cent—in publicly-funded universities.
This was a cautious increment so as not to drive down the premiums on
university education through oversupply or worse, to produce graduates
with degrees that were not considered industry-relevant. PM Lee also went
on to describe how Singaporeans' housing assets and retirement nest eggs
(which were their HDB flats) would be enhanced. He acknowledged later
in 2008 that the middle class felt that they were "the sandwiched class, stuck
in the middle. But when you ask who is the sandwiched class, all the way
from quite low down to quite high up, it's a very fat sandwich, but they feel
sandwiched and we haven't forgotten them."[22]

So, were there signs of a "fragmentation" of the middle class that Lee
Kuan Yew had been so proud of? Was it a "fat sandwich" or had the group
become divided into several parts as suggested by Chua Hak Bin? Regardless,

the Singapore middle class was still treated as a single coherent concept in government pronouncements, with the accent on ensuring access to quality education, specifically, university education and therefore continued social mobility. And by providing explanations for the stringent car ownership policy, ensuring that Singaporeans could own their homes, and keeping the tax burden as low as possible, PM Lee sought to provide further assurance that the middle-class lifestyle would not become a pipe dream for succeeding generations of Singaporeans.

The most recent bout of middle-class anxiety arose in the 2011 General Election which saw support for the PAP weaken. Building on the negative ramifications of the liberal immigration regime, opposition parties campaigned on how the larger numbers of foreign workers in Singapore had depressed local wages, caused middle-wage stagnation, and raised the cost of basic needs like housing.

One leitmotif of the 2011 campaign was the rising "cash over valuation" (COV) of HDB resale flats. COV is the difference between a flat's resale price (determined by professional valuation at which bank loans for buyers would be pegged) and its market value (determined by what the buyer is willing to pay). The COV was increasing because, firstly, more Singaporeans felt they had to turn to the resale flat option as there were not enough "Build-to-Order" flats sold directly by HDB to meet demand; and secondly, the income ceiling for qualifying for new state-subsidized HDB flats and executive condominium units was considered too tight, thus excluding a significant segment of the middle-income who could neither access public housing nor afford private housing.[23] Even though they were cautious not to stoke xenophobia, training their guns on the government's foreign workforce policy rather than on immigrants per se, opposition parties and their followers succeeded in targeting middle-class insecurity that only those in the highest social echelons were immune from.

While other controversial issues also played out at the election, the "population" issue was an omnibus one that pulled together unhappiness across different areas of public policy—from housing, to manpower, healthcare and transport. In the event, the PAP scored 60.1 per cent of the popular vote, a fall from the 66.6 per cent they achieved in the 2006 General Election. More critically, the opposition Workers' Party breached a political threshold by securing a Group Representation Constituency (GRC)—Aljunied GRC—where the PAP team of five comprising two Cabinet ministers and a junior minister lost the contest.

Although 78 per cent of Aljunied GRC residents lived in public housing, the GRC also comprised the Serangoon division where 57 per cent lived in private housing. It was the Serangoon division which "clashed" with its PAP MP years earlier over the siting of a foreign worker dormitory in a disused school in the neighbourhood.[24] Residents in the division had said that their property value would fall if the government proceeded with the dormitory, which it did after some revisions to minimize the interaction of the foreign workers with the neighbourhood.

PM Lee acknowledged several other middle-class concerns that arose in the election in his National Day Rally Speech following it in August 2011. He referred not only to wages and housing issues but also concerns that foreign students were limiting the access of Singaporeans to tertiary education. He cited a mother who shared her concern about the competition her child would face for a spot in university:

> I am very saddened by all the statements made in the general election about "Singaporeans first". I am not asking for financial help nor housing nor complaining about GST (goods and services tax) or cost of living. What I am asking for is a place for my child to further his education. Why do you not give him a chance?[25]

PM Lee said in response, "One unhappiness is the feeling that maybe foreign students have taken the place of locals in universities."[26] He went on to add, "But whether it is houses, whether it is the university, whether it is jobs ... we put Singaporeans first, but in an open-minded sort of way."[27] On jobs, PM Lee said,

> At the top end of the workforce, we have to allow high-quality professionals and entrepreneurs because they grow our businesses here and help Singapore compete internationally ... The middle and lower middle level—foreigners are here, many on an employment pass. Singaporeans are working—they are probably graduates or diploma holders, not hard up, not unskilled, but not so confident of themselves that they are ready for unrestrained competition. They are feeling vulnerable, worried about what may happen. I think at this middle level, we need to tighten a little bit further. We need to raise the salary requirement for the employment pass holders, tighten up the educational qualifications, make sure they come with real skills valuable to us ...[28]

Another response of the government to this middle-class anxiety was a systematic year-long public engagement process called Our Singapore Conversation. This was followed by public policy reviews and reforms. To summarize, these reforms included the strengthening of social safety nets, the creation of more and varied pathways of education, the softening of the academic-centric meritocratic system, and the introduction of the SkillsFuture Initiative, a national account which Singaporeans from twenty-five years and above could tap to fund participation in training programmes to raise their skill levels. Plans were put in place for a sixth publicly subsidized university to accommodate the middle-class desire for higher education while collectively offering upward social mobility to non-middle-class students.

With regard to jobs and wages, much stricter foreign labour regulations had been in the works by 2010, and they certainly came into force post-2011. More salient to the middle class was the policy which raised the income threshold for a foreigner to qualify for the Employment Pass and the introduction of the Fair Consideration Framework which requires all companies to ensure no Singaporean residents are available for the job on offer before they recruit a foreigner.

Nevertheless, this anxiety returned with the release of the Population White Paper in January 2013. The White Paper laid out the objective of ensuring that two-thirds of Singaporeans would be employed as professional white collar workers (Professionals, Managers, Executives and Technicians, or PMETs) in its Year 2030 scenario.[29] Alongside the population plan, the government also released a Land Use Plan which indicated it would build 700,000 flats to accommodate a final population size of 6.9 million by 2030.[30] These sparked vigorous debate and ground-up rallies to protest against the projected growth in population.

And what of the situation now, given that Singapore has marked the bicentennial of its founding by Sir Stamford Raffles for the British East India Company? Current debates on class issues centre on income inequality, social mobility and cross-class social mixing. The worry is that social stratification is hardening such that those from better-resourced families who benefit from a head start go on to enjoy an entrenched advantage in educational achievement and access to good careers. Conversely, the question is raised about the extent to which those from disadvantaged families see their poverty reinforced in the next generation. The term coined by local scholar Jason Tan to refer to the transmission of advantage or disadvantage is "parentocracy".[31]

The other route of transmission was identified through a study on social capital which suggested that Singaporeans who are better endowed in resources and educational backgrounds tend to be a tight social network.[32] Social mixing is weak between residents of private housing on one hand, and public housing on another. It is also weak between those who have elite school backgrounds and those who do not. Therefore, the advantages of having done well in life—the connections, resources and cultural capital—are likely to remain within confined pools if there is no intervention to encourage the two broad social groups to mix. Strong elite solidarity makes the stakes of being in the right class and social circles higher. This has fed the fear of falling behind or dropping out such that middle-class parents invest as much as they can to propel their children ahead of the pack or, at the very least, to keep up with their peers.

THE FACTS, FIGURES AND THE FUTURE

Let us now turn to the facts and figures that explain what feeds middle-class anxiety in Singapore and help us anticipate possible scenarios for the future.

First, we must note the steady pace at which the level of educational attainment of the resident population has improved. Table 12.1, which features comparable data over the decades that are available, indicates that even as recent as 1990, 86.9 per cent of the resident population that was aged twenty-five years and older had only secondary school education. By 2017, that proportion had shrunk to 45.7 per cent. In other words, older cohorts of Singaporeans had only rudimentary levels of education but a vast improvement in educational achievement has taken place with

TABLE 12.1
Singapore Residents Aged 25 years and Over by Highest Qualification Attained

Variables	1990	2000	2010	2017
Total	1,622,300	2,074,000	2,576,000	2,846,000
	Percentage of Total			
Below secondary	63.3	45.3	34.6	28.6
Secondary	23.6	24.0	19.0	17.1
Post-secondary (non-tertiary)	4.7	8.9	9.5	8.9
Diploma and professional qualification	3.6	9.6	13.3	14.6
University	4.7	12.0	23.7	30.7

Note: Data pertain to residents who are not attending educational institutions as full-time students. The data include those who are upgrading their qualifications through part-time courses while working.
Source: Department of Statistics Singapore, "M850581 – Singapore Residents Aged 25 years & over by Highest Qualification Attained, Sex and Age Group, Annual", https://www.tablebuilder.singstat.gov.sg/publicfacing/createDataTable.action?refId=12078

the introduction of a modern and segmented national education system. From 4.7 per cent who were university graduates in 1990, the "stock" of graduates among residents twenty-five years and older stood at 30.7 per cent in 2017.

Over the decades, this educational attainment has indeed translated into many more taking up white-collar professional, managerial and technical jobs. In 1970, just over 10 per cent of the resident workforce (comprising citizens and permanent residents) was in the PMET category;[33] by 2018, this had risen to 57 per cent, demonstrating that it has become the norm to be a PMET in this resident workforce.[34] In another indicator, for 2008, 43 per cent of the resident workforce had "tertiary education" (where 25.8 per cent had university degrees and 16.8 per cent, diplomas and professional qualifications) but by 2018, 56.2 per cent had "tertiary education" (where 36.7 per cent have degrees and 19.5 per cent have diplomas and professional qualifications).[35]

The next question then is how the financial premium from having a university degree, considered the pathway to a middle-class life, has been affected with so many more graduates in the workforce. This will presumably depend on the discipline of study and its workplace relevance, the supply of such graduates, and the longevity of the value of the knowledge and skills those degrees were supposed to have imparted relative to the value of the experience gained through work itself among older workers.

Comparing the ratio of mean graduate monthly salary to the mean salary of all resident workers from 1995 to 2017, blunt as it may be, we see that the graduate premium has declined over the past twenty-three years. (See Figure 12.1.) However, the introduction of the SkillsFuture Credit that funds new skills and knowledge discussed above, along with many other state-subsidized workplace-based training schemes may influence the way this premium will trend in the future. These hold out the prospect that better-qualified workers will be able to maintain their value over time, and through different rounds of economic restructuring.

In order to address the anxiety of PMET workers who now form the majority of the workforce, the government made amendments to the Employment Act in 2018. One such amendment was to extend worker rights and protections beyond the previous category of workers who earn less than $4,500 a month so that all workers qualify for protection under the national union movement, the National Trades Union Congress (NTUC). Other changes include making entitlements like minimum days of annual leave, paid public holidays and sick leave as well as the timely payment of

FIGURE 12.1

**Ratio of Mean Graduate Starting Salary to Mean Monthly Salary
of All Resident Workers**

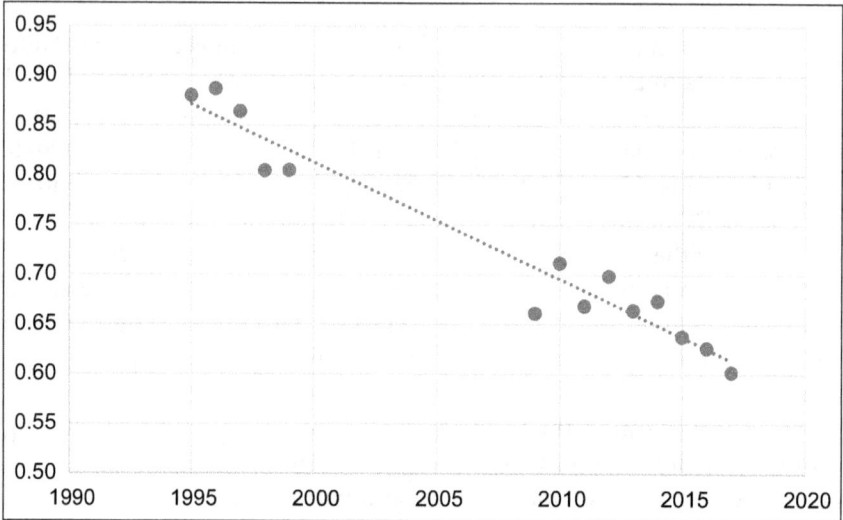

Source: Data sourced from Applied Research Corporation, NUS and NTU Graduate Employment Survey, 1995–1999; aggregated results from Graduate Employment Survey by NUS, NTU, SMU, SIT and SUTD for subsequent years; aggregated results from Singapore Ministry of Labour/Manpower, *Report on Wages in Singapore* (Singapore: Singapore Ministry of Labour/Manpower, 1995–99); and Singapore Ministry of Manpower, *Singapore Yearbook of Manpower Statistics* (Singapore: Singapore Ministry of Manpower, 2009–17).

salaries and protection against wrongful dismissal, universal. After all, we note that being in the PMET sector is no guarantee of job security: the retrenchment rate of PMETs in 1995 was 6.8 out of 1,000 employees and this rose to 8.7 out of 1,000 employees in 2017, a rate that is higher than the other two categories of workers.[36]

Also, according to the latest available figures for June 2018, the highest proportion of unemployed workers who took twenty-five weeks and more to find a new job were those who were fifty years and older when compared across age groups, and those with university degrees when compared across highest educational qualifications.[37] In other words, older PMET workers were more likely to remain unemployed upon retrenchment than non-PMETs. The Ministry of Manpower in its "Labour Force in Singapore 2017" report suggested that the longer time this segment took to return to work was the result of PMETs taking a longer time to find jobs they felt matched their skills, qualifications, and salary expectations or because they had applied for jobs for which prospective employers felt they did not have the skills.[38] It is also interesting to note that the employment rate for degree holders aged twenty-five to sixty-four, who would comprise such PMETs, has taken a decade to reach pre-2009 recession levels. It was 87.6 per cent in 2008 before the impact of the global financial crisis, dropped to 85.7 per cent in 2009 and it finally reached back up to 87.7 in 2018.[39] This suggests that there have been challenging times for this group of people in the middle class.

The amendments to the Employment Act have followed other targeted programmes that facilitate the work placement of PMETs who have been made redundant. Where the industries have undergone significant change, like the financial and banking sector that has seen a major consolidation in the early 2000s leaving fewer but larger institutions on the scene, or where technology has drastically changed the profile of skills required of workers such those in the IT sector, the government has introduced the Professional Conversion Programme (PCP).[40] The PCP allows companies to tap up to a 70 per cent subsidy of the wage of a worker undergoing the switch from one career to another. The subsidy rises to 90 per cent for workers who are forty years and older, or who have been out of work for more than six months. Today, the resident unemployment rate by industry is the highest in the hospitality and accommodation sector at 6.3 per cent, then retail trade at 6 per cent, and the information and communications industry at 5.5 per cent based on the Manpower Ministry's statistics.[41] It is workers and certainly the middle-class PMETs in these industries that may face difficulties and would benefit from all the support available.

Another move that should have eased middle-class anxiety arising from job insecurity was the establishment of the Tripartite Alliance for Fair and Progressive Employment Practices in 2006. It set up guidelines and norms for equitable treatment for all workers—one step short of introducing an equal opportunities law, which targeted workplace discrimination on age, race and gender, among other things, through mediated settlement. While the government has been careful not to compromise the quality of labour supply in its support of middle-class workers which is the reason for heavy state investment in the upgrading of skills, measures which promote fair employment are necessary to ensure that employers do not simply opt for younger, cheaper and foreign workers instead.

How then have these trends within the middle class translated into incomes and lifestyle patterns? Table 12.2 provides data on the change in

TABLE 12.2
Change in Real Average Monthly Household Income by Quintile

| | Average Percent Change per Annum | |
	2001 to 2010	2011 to 2017
Bottom 20%	0.455	2.69
Second 20%	2.25	2.63
Third 20%	2.56	2.55
Fourth 20%	2.83	2.41
Top 20%	3.935	2.15

Source: Department of Statistics Singapore, "M810361 – Key Indicators on Household Income from Work among Resident Employed Households, Annual", https://www.tablebuilder.singstat.gov.sg/publicfacing/createDataTable.action?refId=12307

the average monthly household income. In the span between 2001 and 2010, the rate of increase in household income was higher with each quintile, with the highest rate for the wealthiest. However, in the years since 2011, when a deeper consciousness of income distribution and the health of the middle class emerged within political and policy circles, the rate of household income growth has been more even across the quintiles, and at a lower rate with each step up to the top quintile.

This has meant that income distribution has become slightly less unequal. In the decade from 2008 to 2018, the Gini coefficient calculated after taking into account government taxes and transfers, has fallen from 0.424 to 0.404.[42] However, it is important to bear in mind that there may be more mobility than the figures suggest as the households in a particular quintile captured in the data within the period of time may not be the same ones in the next.

Similarly, these figures do not capture the expectations and aspirations that come with middle-class identification. After all, such expectations and aspirations might not change in the short term even if the actual household income earned were to change over a year or two. It is also important to note that with regard to full-time employed resident degree holders in particular, the change in the median gross monthly income from work in real terms, in the period of June 2008 to June 2013, was at –0.5 per cent per annum, before picking up in trend terms to 2.5 per cent per annum from June 2013 to June 2018. Hence, degree holders will have again felt some discomfort as they saw their income gains being "eroded by inflation", according to Ministry of Manpower's explanation of what happened in the earlier 2008 to 2013 period when we know there was a sense of disquiet within the polity; a disruption in national politics as described in the previous section of this chapter.[43]

Clearly, it is possible for a household's income or business earnings to fall out of kilter with its expenditure over a short period while enjoying other sources of wealth to bridge the gap—a likely situation with the higher-end of the middle class in Singapore. It is thus important to look beyond income to understand the lifestyle of Singapore's middle class to check if that has been the case at all. Table 12.3 provides an overview of the rate of increase in average monthly household income and expenditure in nominal terms for two time periods for which comparable data is available—from 2003 to 2008, and 2008 to 2013. If these aggregated data are anything to go by and are a good basis for comparison, the rate of increase in income was higher than the rate of increase in expenditure. Therefore, the figures do not suggest that there was such a gap between income and expenditure. Given the data on the real median gross monthly income from work however, as described earlier, the particular segment of degree holders may have found themselves feeling squeezed.

We can look at the situation with wealth to see if there has been an erosion on that front to cause discomfort and the sense of "being poorer" than before or when "compared to others". One other aspect would be the

TABLE 12.3
Change in Nominal Average Monthly Household Income[a] and Expenditure[b] by Quintile

Household Income Group	Average Percent Change per Annum			
	2003–8		2008–13	
	Income	Expenditure	Income	Expenditure
All Households	5.2	2.6	6.0	4.4
Lowest 20%	2.8	1.0	5.2	4.5
2nd Quintile	4.7	3.7	6.8	3.7
3rd Quintile	5.2	2.5	6.7	5.5
4th Quintile	5.1	2.4	6.4	4.1
Highest 20%	5.7	2.8	5.8	4.3

Source: a. Based on Table 13B "Nominal Change in Average Monthly Household Income from Work (Including Employer CPF Contributions) Among Resident Employed Households by Deciles, 2000–2018," Department of Statistics Singapore.
b. Department of Statistics Singapore, Household Expenditure Survey (Singapore: Department of Statistics Singapore, 1992–2013).

situation with household debt. However, since data for comparison on the basis of quintiles on household debt are not available, we are only able to review the situation of wealth and the wealth gap.

Wealth refers to the net value of a person's entire assets such as disposable cash and property after deducting their debts which includes loans and mortgages. Earnings from work, minus expenditure, could constitute part of it. However, the lack of comparable data that is sliced by quintiles and segmented on the basis of average monthly household income makes it difficult to describe the wealth profile of the different classes of Singapore, especially those in the middle. Nevertheless, data from the Department of Statistics' Household Sector Balance Sheets show that Singapore's household net wealth, excluding the value of overseas property owned by Singapore residents, was $918,146 million in 2007, which doubled to $1,844,359 million in 2017 a decade later.[44] It speaks of the compounding nature of wealth to have this figure double in ten years.

Drawing on that dataset, median wealth per capita for Singapore was estimated by Credit Suisse's annual global study on wealth in 2018 to be US$91,656 while the mean wealth was 3.1 times higher at US$283,118, reinforcing the point made earlier that those at the top of the wealth ladder have seen their resources rise much faster than the rest.[45] Apart from the domestic relative wealth picture, Singapore is ranked ninth in the world and the highest in Asia based on the latter statistic in terms of its standing in wealth compared to other countries.

The order of magnitude by which mean wealth per capita is greater than median wealth per capita is referred to as the "wealth gap ratio". Singapore's "wealth gap ratio" stands at 3.1, which means that inequality in Singapore compared globally, is deemed to be "not extreme".[46] The Credit Suisse report, calculated based on available data, added that 73 per cent of Singapore's wealth was owned by the richest 20 per cent of its residents; 15 per cent of wealth was owned by the next quintile; and only 11 per cent among the bottom 60 per cent of residents.[47] In addition, it estimated that the number of American dollar millionaires in Singapore had grown from 2000 to 2018 by 11.2 per cent to 183,737 individuals and that there were 1,000 ultra-high-net-worth individuals with more than US$50 million to their name in Singapore. Financial assets made up about 55 per cent of the gross household wealth and average debt was about 16 per cent of total assets. The situation therefore is that over time, in Singapore, there is a wealth gap, and it may be a growing one with its associated displays of affluence that could feed envy or social pressure across society, even if the situation is "not as bad as elsewhere in the world".

What do all these suggest? On one hand, they suggest that there may indeed have been a time when those in the middle class including degree holders, broadly speaking, would have felt somewhat insecure especially from the early 2000s till recently, with those at the lower-end of the *top* 40 per cent of residents facing the fear of falling behind those in the slightly higher reference group. This may have been a function of age, the ossification of the skills and education among what were considered better-qualified older workers, and also companies' release of senior workers who might have been relatively more costly to retain in an age of corporate and macroeconomic restructuring after the 2001, 2003 and 2009 recessions. The data suggests that the employment rate of degree holders had suffered with the onset of the Global Financial Crisis and that income growth was not favourable at all.

Another reason for the sense of insecurity, as mentioned earlier, is the downward revision of CPF contributions for senior workers thus leaving them feeling that they have inadequate retirement savings. On the other hand, the tightening of access to foreign workers at all levels, including better-qualified executive level manpower over recent years, would presumably have tempered this and kept wage levels higher than they would otherwise have been without such policy measures.

Meanwhile, senior PMETs will have found it difficult to return to their former jobs or enjoy previous salary levels. And while it is difficult to measure the effect of such forms of underemployment, the act of taking up less demanding jobs at lower wages may have somewhat eroded their expected lifestyle, unless they possessed financial and housing assets (wealth) that they can tap.

Perhaps more critical for the longer term is that sense of hope for a brighter future among younger graduates and children of the group referred to above. For them, the prize they are likely to be striving for, though not entirely in material form, will nonetheless include the ability to own a home, a car, enjoy overseas holidays, and in the case of younger graduates, having one or two children whom they hope will go to university like themselves. While it is true that the younger generation of Singaporeans, like millennials elsewhere, would prefer to be defined by progressive social interests more than material achievements, the reality is that they take access to some of the material trappings of the modern Singaporean middle-class lifestyle for granted. However, as the wealthy seem to grow even wealthier, those just below the richest 20 per cent of Singapore residents may feel that they are falling behind or that the gap is stretching out so much further and the lifestyles of that higher reference group far more unattainable.

Finally, beyond the facts and figures on income and wealth, it is important to understand how social capital helps to reinforce privilege within segments of the middle class. Such forms of social capital allow specific groups to better prepare for the competition for rewards in society like better jobs, higher incomes and higher social status. Sociologists see a process of "parentocracy" at play where social class is replicated primarily as a result of streaming in the national education system.[48] Here, it is argued that the grades attained by children who are streamed as early as twelve years of age are more of a reflection of parental resources and therefore socio-economic class. There will be a higher proportion of children of graduates, higher-income households, and from better housing who will be found in secondary schools that are considered "elite". These schools tend to have a proud and long heritage, enjoy independent status that allows the delivery of enriched teaching and extra-curricular activities at higher fees, and consequently, better overall performances within their cohort. Unfortunately, systematic and longitudinal data on the background of parents of children in these "elite" schools is not publicly available to assess the facts of social stratification.

What is the best evidence we have of the effect of that? We refer to the empirical and statistically grounded findings of a study of social capital we conducted where the weakest social links among Singaporeans were between those across social class. Among the approximately 20 per cent of Singaporeans with elite school backgrounds and who live in private housing, when the opportunity structures were taken into account statistically, were less likely to meet and interact with the other 80 per cent of Singaporeans who may not have attended elite schools and who live in public housing.[49] In other words, the study found that the salience of the social ties among those above the middle class rose even further after the statistical adjustment. Those in the top 20 per cent see the value of their networks, invest in them, and seem like they are in a universe of their own to those outside it. Where there has been diversity of social ties, these have often come about through interaction on four platforms—the workplace, voluntary work, sporting and cultural activities. The battle is not lost but like the situation on the job and economic front, proactive efforts across those four platforms or more, and especially by those in the top 20 per cent in society will be much needed to stave off the social fragmentation of Singapore's middle class where those in the next 20 per cent segment feel they are falling behind.

CONCLUSION

Let us end with a retelling of the tale of Lee Kuan Yew's encounter with Deng Xiaoping when China was on the cusp of the renaissance it is now experiencing. In discussing social development, Lee explained that his goal was to create a Singapore where the class structure took the shape of an olive, short and narrow with few people at the top and bottom, and a large middle class. Adopting the metaphor, progressive public intellectual Tommy Koh said many years later, "We must not allow the olive to become a pear."[50]

What we have argued here is that if left to market forces and non-state intervention, Singapore's exposure to deep disruptive trends in the global economy and technology, its physical constraints and high costs of living and business activities, the downsides of the meritocratic educational streaming policy, and the natural sociological processes of homophily and stratification, will leave the resulting class structure resembling not a gentle French pear but a Chinese bottle gourd with extreme bulges—a small one at the top and a large one at the bottom.

What is the problem with that? For one, there could come a tipping point where the sense of social solidarity and national identity so critical to the country's governability and hopeful egalitarianism—the basis of the myth of independent Singapore—is irretrievably lost.

Thankfully, there have been many local academics and public intellectuals who have spoken up on the issues discussed in this chapter, thus contributing to vigorous public discourse and state intervention to lean against the full force of the market and natural sociological tendencies. The political leaders who have themselves personally benefitted from the intergenerational mobility of the early years see an interest in addressing the looming problems. Their challenge would be, in former Deputy Prime Minister Tharman Shanmugaratnam's words, to "keep the escalator moving up".[51]

It is not an easy task given the challenges of creating sufficient jobs, let alone good middle-class jobs and an increasingly innovative, value-creating economy; the relatively declining value of degrees; social and class divides; the compounding value of capital; the entry barriers to the best schools, and so on.

While younger Singaporeans are growing up in a more affluent society, we cannot assume they are doing better than their parents. These days, they probably feel like they need to work even harder to attain the same position in the income, wealth and lifestyle ladders their parents reached within the latter's generation. Has the escalator in some instances become a treadmill set to a steeper incline? State and society will have to strive more earnestly to shape a future that is, ironically, rooted in the vision of the past—to nurture a broad and stable middle class that more citizens can enter, belong to, and identify with. Social interaction across society, or at least within this broader middle class will require active intervention and facilitation with those at the higher reaches, making it their task to seek out opportunities for inclusion and meaningful interaction. At stake is the continuing legitimacy of Singapore's governance system, and the ability to keep the sort of pernicious populism that is sweeping over developed countries at bay here.

Economic strategies and social policies must be implemented not with trepidation or merely the desire to maintain the status quo, but with the confidence of being an improbable nation that has already achieved so much, and can therefore achieve so much more.

Notes

1. The authors thank Dhevarajan Devadas and Loh Xiang Bin for their help with the research that went into this chapter.
2. "Marxist plot uncovered", *Straits Times*, 27 May 1987, http://eresources.nlb.gov.sg/newspapers/digitised/article/straitstimes19870527-1.2.2
3. Lee Kuan Yew, "Speech by Prime Minister Lee Kuan Yew at the Tanjong Pagar National Day Dinner held at the Tanjong Pagar Community Centre on Thursday, 13 August 1987", National Archives of Singapore (1987), p. 4.
4. Lee Tsao Yuan, "Commentary on The Economy", in *Singapore: The Year in Review 1995*, edited by Yeo Lay Hwee (Singapore: Times Academic Press, 1996), p. 31.
5. As cited in Seth Mydans, "Singapore Journal; Good Life Guide: To 5 C's, Like Cash, Add Clout", *New York Times*, 5 June 1996, https://www.nytimes.com/1996/06/05/world/singapore-journal-good-life-guide-to-5-c-s-like-cash-add-clout.html (accessed 3 January 2019).
6. Lee Kuan Yew, "Chase That Rainbow: A Special Youth Forum with the Senior Minister", National Archives of Singapore (1996), p. 2.
7. R. Sinnakaruppan, "Property Ownership: A Ray of Hope for Young Singaporeans", *Straits Times*, 25 May 1996.
8. R. Sinnakaruppan, "Many Status-Conscious Live Beyond Means: MP", *Straits Times*, 12 August 1996.
9. "Exec Condos: Gourmet Fare for Sandwich Class", *Straits Times*, 6 August 1996, Reel NL20124, Microfilm Collection, National Library Board.
10. Stephanie Ho, "National Youth Council", http://eresources.nlb.gov.sg/infopedia/articles/SIP_419_2005-01-06.html (Singapore Infomedia).
11. Goh Chor Boon and Leo Tan Wee Hin, "The Development of University Education in Singapore", in *Toward a Better Future: Education and Training for Economic Development in Singapore since 1965*, edited by Lee Sing Kong, Goh Chor Boon,

Birger Fredriksen, and Tan Jee Peng (Washington, DC: World Bank and National Institute of Education at Nanyang Technological University, 2008), p. 151.

12. Goh Chok Tong, "Social Stratification and Commitment: National Day Rally Speech 1996 at the Kallang Theatre", in *National Day Rally Speeches: 50 Years of Nationhood in Singapore 1966–2015* (Singapore: National Archives of Singapore and Cengage Learning Asia, 2017), p. 342.

13. Ibid., pp. 342–43.

14. Ibid., pp. 330–31.

15. Ibid., p. 332.

16. Ibid., p. 349.

17. Chua Hak Bin, "Singapore Economy: The New and the Dual", in *Singapore Perspectives 2007: A New Singapore*, edited by Tan Tarn How (Singapore: Institute of Policy Studies, 2007), pp. 7–23.

18. Ibid., pp. 10–12.

19. Ibid., pp. 17–22.

20. Ibid., p. 20.

21. Lee Hsien Loong, "City of Possibilities. Home for All: National Day Rally Speech 2007 at the University Cultural Centre, National University of Singapore", in *National Day Rally Speeches*, p. 585.

22. Lee Hsien Loong, "National Day Rally Speech 2008 at the University Cultural Centre, National University of Singapore", in *National Day Rally Speeches*, p. 610.

23. Jessica Cheam, "Redefining Affordability of Homes", *Straits Times*, 14 July 2011, https://www.fas.nus.edu.sg/ecs/scape/doc/ST-14Jul11.pdf

24. Pearl Forss, "Dormitory Decision Upsets Some Serangoon Gardens Residents", *Channel NewsAsia*, 3 October 2008, http://web.archive.org/web/20120314003507/http:/www.channelnewsasia.com/stories/singaporelocalnews/view/380077/1/.html

25. Lee Hsien Loong, "National Day Rally Speech 2011 at the University Cultural Centre, National University of Singapore", in *National Day Rally Speeches*, p. 687.

26. Ibid.

27. Ibid., p. 688.

28. Ibid., p. 689.

29. National Population and Talent Division Singapore, *A Sustainable Population for a Dynamic Singapore. Population White Paper*, January 2013, p. 4.

30. Singapore Ministry of National Development, *A High Quality Living Environment for All Singaporeans: Land Use Plan to Support Singapore's Future Population*, January 2013, p. 9; National Population and Talent Division Singapore, *A Sustainable Population for a Dynamic Singapore*, p. 6.

31. Jason Tan, "Closing the Achievement Gap in Singapore", in *Closing the Achievement Gap from an International Perspective: Transforming STEM for Effective Education*, edited by Julia V. Clark (Dordrecht: Springer Netherlands, 2014), p. 255.

32. Vincent Chua, Tan Ern Ser, and Gillian Koh, *A Study on Social Capital in Singapore* (Singapore: Institute of Policy Studies, 2017).

33. Department of Statistics Singapore, *Yearbook of Statistics Singapore 1970* (Singapore: Department of Statistics Singapore, 1970).

34. Singapore Ministry of Manpower, *Labour Force in Singapore 2018*. See Chart 14, https://stats.mom.gov.sg/Pages/Labour-Force-In-Singapore-2018.aspx

35. Ibid., Chart 7.

36. *Singapore Yearbook of Labour/Manpower Statistics* (1995–2017), Table D5.

37. Singapore Ministry of Manpower, *Labour Force in Singapore 2018*. See Chart 48, https://stats.mom.gov.sg/Pages/Labour-Force-In-Singapore-2018.aspx

38. Singapore Ministry of Manpower, *Labour Force in Singapore 2017*. See para. 6.8. https://stats.mom.gov.sg/iMAS_PdfLibrary/mrsd_2017LabourForce_survey_findings.pdf

39. *Labour Force in Singapore 2018*. See Chart 8.

40. Toh Yong Chuan, "Parliament: More Help for PMETs, Older and Retrenched Workers", *Straits Times*, 6 March 2017, https://www.straitstimes.com/singapore/parliament-more-help-for-pmets-older-workers-and-retrenched

41. *Labour Force in Singapore 2018*. See Chart 46.

42. Department of Statistics Singapore, *Key Household Income Trends 2018*, https://www.singstat.gov.sg/-/media/files/publications/households/pp-s25.pdf

43. Ibid., Chart 9.

44. Department of Statistics Singapore, "M700981 – Household Sector Balance Sheet (End of Period), Quarterly", https://www.tablebuilder.singstat.gov.sg/publicfacing/createDataTable.action?refId=15312

45. Anthony Shorrocks, Jim Davies and Rodrigo Lluberas, *Global Wealth Report 2018* (Hong Kong: Credit Suisse Group, 2018), p. 47.

46. Ibid.

47. As cited in Steffi Koh, "8 Things You Should Know About Singapore's Wealth Gap", *Channel NewsAsia*, 5 December 2016, https://www.channelnewsasia.com/news/singapore/8-things-you-should-know-about-singapore-s-wealth-gap-7643944

48. Jason Tan, "Closing the Achievement Gap in Singapore".

49. Vincent Chua, Tan Ern Ser, and Gillian Koh, *A Study on Social Capital in Singapore*.

50. Tommy Koh, "Don't Knock Minimum Wage Yet", in *The Tommy Koh Reader: Favourite Essays and Lectures* (Singapore: World Scientific, 2010), p. 148.

51. Jalelah Abu Baker, "'Keep the Escalator Moving Up': DPM Tharman Urges Singapore to Maintain Social Mobility", *Channel NewsAsia*, 26 October 2018, https://www.channelnewsasia.com/news/singapore/keep-the-escalator-moving-up-dpm-tharman-ips-anniversary-10865146

13

Geographic-Ethnic Segregation in Singapore
Emerging Schisms in Society

Leong Chan-Hoong and Yvonne Yap

INTRODUCTION

Social diversity has been a hallmark of Singapore's cultural identity since the founding of the island by the British East India Company.[1] For decades since independence in 1965, Singapore's most discernible national trait has been its multiethnic and multireligious contour with the population comprising a Chinese majority (approximately 74 per cent), followed by ethnic Malays (14 per cent), ethnic Indians (10 per cent), and other races (2–3 per cent).[2] This ethnic proportion has remained relatively stable for over fifty years. Racial and religious identities in Singapore overlap substantively. The ethnic Malays are predominantly Muslim, the Chinese practise mainly Taoism, Buddhism, and Christianity or Catholicism, and ethnic Indians embrace Hinduism, and Christianity or Catholicism. Suffice to say, this demographic terrain shapes the daily lives of people and their interactions with those from other backgrounds. It also has a profound influence on the city-state's political landscape and is closely tied to the geopolitical dynamics in the region. Beyond ethnicity and religion, there are other forms of tribalism that distinguish one group from another and, in some cases, there are material, psychological, and existential consequences.

This chapter begins with a brief history of the evolving socio-demographic scene in Singapore, followed by an introduction to the principles that govern diversity discourse in the city-state. It will highlight signs of a new socio-economic divide along geographical boundaries, tagged with ethnic overtones. The implications of this emerging spatial class segregation on urban planning will be discussed.

Broadly speaking, the British colonial government practised a Furnivall model of pluralism, where the ethnic communities each specialized in a different economic field and interact only for a functional purpose but are not emotionally invested. They maintain a separate culture, identity, language, and religion, with little or no overlap.[3] This social environment played an influential role in shaping relations between ethnic groups via a "divide and conquer" strategy, stratifying the immigrant population via an imperialist capitalist system that emphasized ethnicity and associated it with divisions of labour.[4] The ethnic Chinese were largely treated preferentially by the British due to their pre-eminence in trade, business enterprises, and population size, while the ethnic Malays were found mostly in the agricultural sector, resulting in essentialized identities. These were reinforced by labour over time, and by the fact that there was very little overlap between the various ethnic communities.[5] Ethnic segregation was also geographically compounded as residential settlements were located in different parts of the island. Many Chinese lived around the Kreta Ayer (Cantonese-speaking), Telok Ayer (Hokkien-speaking), Sembawang and Boat Quay (Teochew-speaking) areas; the South Indians congregated in the Serangoon area; the Malays in Geylang Serai and Eunos; and the Arabs in Kampung Glam and Arab Street. By 1959, when Singapore obtained self-governance from the British, the city-state was principally a Chinese-centric society, even as the ruling People's Action Party (PAP) committed to making Singapore an inclusive, multiracial, fair and just society.[6]

Singapore's ill-fated merger with Malaysia from 1963 to 1965 brought to fore a variety of political disputes, not least a fundamental disagreement over concepts of multiculturalism and racial privilege. A series of racial riots broke out in 1964 between the Chinese and Malays over what should be the cultural supremacy of the city-state. Singapore's vision of an equal society regardless of race or religion did not sit well with the Federal government in Kuala Lumpur as the latter was more concerned about widening economic disparity and past injustice endured by Malay-Muslims. The racial riots in Singapore were unquestionably the most violent and acrimonious in the collective memory of the city-state.[7] These events were critical junctions in Singapore's history and set the stage for how diversity is managed in post-independent Singapore.[8]

TAKING AN AUTHORITARIAN APPROACH TO MANAGING DIVERSITY

The importance of ethnic harmony has profoundly impacted a wide range of domestic policies from language, education, housing, public assistance, to electoral politics. There are two key aspects in the prevailing diversity discourse. First, multiethnicity forms the nexus of the social compact between state and society. All ethnic groups may expect to be treated fairly and have access to opportunities for economic mobility in a meritocratic system. In a similar vein, embracing multiethnicity also means that cultural primacy will not be assigned to any ethnic group, including the majority Chinese. Instead, the three languages associated with the main ethnic groups, namely Mandarin, Malay, and Tamil, were all accorded "official language" status, along with English. All ethnic groups were free to celebrate and observe their traditional festivals and practices, with key dates such as the Lunar New Year, Hari Raya and Deepavali, similarly accorded "public holiday" status by the state. These moves were meant to signal the state's equal recognition of the three main ethnic groups regardless of their numerical size.

Second, lessons of the past have reinforced the importance of integration between ethnic communities. While there are inevitable differences in ethnicity, religion, or class, these differences may be moderated if there is empathy and meaningful engagement between people of varied backgrounds. Interactions and the collective memories that are formed as a result are instrumental to forging a common identity that transcends the tribal group. The objective and impact of shared experience is not confined to ethnic categories but is a principle of nation-building.

In the Singapore context, ethnicity, religion, and social class are often conflated. This is understandable because there is some correlation between ethnicity/religion and socio-economic status. For example, the size of the ethnic Chinese community means that it sees a larger percentage and overrepresentation of individuals who enjoy a higher socio-economic status (SES) relative to other ethnic groups. Ethnic Malays are traditionally overrepresented in the lower SES stratum for a complex variety of historical and colonial reasons, the impact of which is still felt today. Ethnic Indians, like the Chinese, are more evenly spread across the SES spectrum. In light of this, one of the most intriguing case studies on the Singapore model of diversity management is that of public housing.[9] The Housing and Development Board (HDB) was set up in 1960 to be the provider and regulator of state-subsidized public housing. More than 80 per cent of the population today lives in a government-subsidized flat, with nine in ten households owning their homes. The high rate of homeownership in Singapore was instrumental during the early years of independence in endowing an immigrant population with a sense of rootedness and shared future, and has been one of the key planks for the country's success.

However, by 1989, twenty years after the country's last racial riot, there were nascent indications of ethnic enclaves emerging from residential patterns.[10] At that time, approximately one quarter of all blocks had significantly more, if not near exclusive, households of one ethnic group than the national distribution. In some neighbourhoods, nearly half of the flats were affected, and they no longer represented a cross-section of Singapore's ethnic composite.[11] It was found that this pattern of residential segregation echoed that of the earlier British colonial ethnic settlements and contributed to an ethnic divide that public housing had aimed to avoid. To nip the problem in the bud, the HDB introduced the Ethnic Integration Policy (EIP) to the resale market. This policy imposes a quota on the maximum number of households from the same ethnic background at the block and neighbourhood levels (see Table 13.1 for the quota limits). The latter is commonly defined as a precinct, or a cluster of about fifty blocks. When either the block or precinct reaches the cap for a particular ethnic group, no new households from this ethnic category may move into the block or neighbourhood at the expense of another ethnic group. For instance, if a block has hit the ethnic Chinese EIP quota (87 per cent), potential Chinese flat buyers who wish to purchase a resale unit in the block can only do so from other Chinese sellers (and maintain the

TABLE 13.1

Ethnic Quota, Population Distribution, and Percentage Residing in HDB Dwellings

Races	Block Limit[a]	Neighbourhood Limit[b]	Population Distribution[c]	Reside in HDB Dwelling[d]
Chinese	87%	84%	74%	81.2%
Malays	25%	22%	14%	96.9%
Indians and/or Others	15%	12%	12%	82.8%

Source:

a. Mah Bow Tan, "Ethnic Integration Policy", Singapore Parliamentary Debates (Hansard), 5 March 2010, c. 3220, http://sprs.parl.gov.sg

b. Maisy Wong, "Estimating the Impact of the Ethnic Housing Quotas in Singapore", *Samuel Zell & Robert Lurie Real Estate Center Working Paper*, No. 748 (Pennsylvania: University of Pennsylvania, 2012).

c. Includes Singaporean citizens and permanent residents. Data for 2010 calculated from "Singapore Residents by Age Group, Ethnic Group and Sex, End June, Annual", in *Population Trends, 2018.*

d. Percentage of HDB dwellers for each race obtained from Table 2, "Resident Households by Type of Dwelling, Ethnic Group of Head of Household and Tenancy", in Department of Statistics Singapore, *Census of Population 2010, Statistical Release 2*, "Households and Housing"; HDB dwellings include all apartments of all sizes, i.e., 2 to 5 rooms, HDB Executive Apartments/Maisonettes.

Chinese quota of 87 per cent). Prospective Chinese flat buyers may not buy from ethnic Malay, Indian, or "Other" ethnic groups as this would dilute minority representation.

This housing policy innovation was a controversial one although it was not the first adopted by the state to essentialize ethnic categories, decide how diversity is reproduced, and curate the conditions of social interaction. Other policies designed to manage ethnicity include the compulsory learning of a "mother-tongue" language (defined as the language of one's ethnic group), the establishment of Group Representation Constituencies (or GRCs, where voters select teams of members of parliament, which must comprise at least one ethnic-minority candidate), and ethnic self-help groups (charged with providing public assistance and welfare services to their own ethnic communities).[12] Scholars have also pointed out that EIP restrictions might not only have a collateral effect on housing prices, but also be experienced differently by different ethnic groups, with ethnic-minority sellers more affected.[13] In an ethnically constrained block, both demand and supply of flats are affected by the quota imposed. In a Chinese constrained block, for example, an ethnic Malay flat seller can only sell to another ethnic Malay, effectively shrinking the demand for the flat. As a result, the ethnic minority seller would either need a longer time to find a fellow ethnic minority buyer or accept a selling price that is below market value. This problem is ostensibly more acute in Chinese-constrained neighbourhoods (those that have reached the Chinese ethnic quota) as Chinese sellers can sell to almost anyone (given that Singapore is predominantly Chinese). On the other hand, for a minority-constrained block, sellers are restricted from selling to the minority but the majority Chinese population is still eligible to purchase from them. These dynamics may drive resale prices up by as much as 8 per cent for Chinese-constrained units and down by as much as 4 per cent for Malay- or Indian-constrained units.[14]

The EIP is a hallmark of Singapore's political philosophy in managing diversity and the discourse associated with it. In the context of multiculturalism and outgroup perceptions, Singapore has demonstrated to be an outlier, with citizens willing to submit to and support the state in its enforcement of ethnic policies and to punish those who fall foul of these policies, even if this may at times contradict personal interests.[15] Indeed, commenting on the introduction of the EIP in 1989, then Minister for National Development, S. Dhanabalan, noted that "it is a small price we must be prepared to pay in order to ensure that we do build a cohesive, better integrated society in Singapore".[16]

After nearly thirty years since its introduction, the EIP is now deeply entrenched in Singapore's housing and cultural landscape. It is thus a good time to take stock of the situation and ask what the current state of multiethnic and multicultural living in the neighbourhoods is like. In a recent report, Leong, Teng and Ko (2020)[17] examine the spatial concentration of EIP-constrained public housing in Singapore and the socio-economic and demographic correlates of these neighbourhoods. The results found that the total percentage of flats affected by at least one form of EIP restriction has increased from 24.4 per cent in 1989, to 30 per cent in 2018. This is in spite of a doubling of flats, from 4,825 to 8,743 blocks, in the resale market during this period. The spatial pattern of constrained blocks for each of the three major ethnic group suggests a hidden form of ethnic segregation, but more worryingly the geographic divide is also conflated with socio-economic class differentiation (see Table 13.2). Residential subzones that report a higher proportion of ethnic Chinese-constrained flats are significantly correlated with higher resale prices ($r = 0.597, p < 0.001$), lower residential density ($r = -0.216$, $p < 0.05$), and more mature residents ($r = 0.463, p < 0.001$). Subzones with

TABLE 13.2
Correlation between Flats Affected by EIP Limits and
Socio-Demographic Indicators[a]

	Age 65 and Above[b]	Residential Density[b]	HDB Resale Housing Price ($/m²)[c]	Household Income (Planning Area)[d]
% flats that reach Chinese quota	0.463***	−0.216*	0.597***	0.330*
% flats that reach Malay quota	−0.104	−0.033	−0.216*	−0.055
% flats that reach Indian/ Others quota	−0.046	−0.214*	−0.020	0.026

Notes: * $p < 0.05$, ** $p < 0.01$, *** $p < 0.001$.
Sources:
a. Department of Statistics Singapore (2017) and HDB online portal for ethnic eligibility and resale prices (June–July, 2016).
b. Data calculated from Table 7, "Resident Population by Planning Area/Subzone, Age Group and Sex", in General Household Survey 2015.
c. HDB resale price data was retrieved from HDB Map Services through an automated Ruby programming script.
d. Data calculated from Table 152, "Resident Households by Planning Area and Monthly Household Income from Work," in General Household Survey 2015.

a higher proportion of Malay-constrained flats are correlated to lower resale prices ($r = -0.216$, $p < 0.05$), and Indian-constrained flats lower density ($r = -0.214$, $p < 0.05$). In line with the broad trend, planning areas with a higher proportion of Chinese-constrained flats also report higher household income ($r = 0.330$, $p < 0.05$).[18] The results collectively point to a higher socio-economic status in neighbourhoods with a larger than average ethnic Chinese presence.

When we spatially overlay all EIP affected blocks on the map of Singapore, ethnic congregation is evident. HDB blocks that have reached their ethnic Chinese quota are concentrated in the central and northeast districts, while those that have reached their ethnic Malay quota are located either around the Marsiling and Woodlands regions or in the Pasir Ris and Tampines estates, and those that have reached their quota for ethnic Indian and/or "Other" ethnic groups can be found along the fringe of the island, but with a significant concentration in Jurong West, Bukit Batok, Choa Chu Kang, Sengkang, and Kampong Java areas (see Figure 13.1). By design, the EIP prevents the total residential dominance of any ethnic group. Thus, even in an ethnically constrained block or neighbourhood, multiethnic presence will not be entirely missing, although the opportunities for interethnic contact will be more limited in comparison to other blocks or neighbourhoods. In spite of the EIP's shortcomings, a laissez-faire residential resale system for public housing would have likely formed ethnic enclaves at a much faster rate and entrench them more deeply than they may be now.

Nevertheless, the geographic distribution of ethnic groups as shown above is not insignificant because it offers an important glimpse of the ethnic contour of the city-state and, more importantly, points to potentially new and unknown schisms. Ethnic and religious fractures remain the nexuses of diversity management in contemporary Singapore even as the social fabric becomes more complex; with economic disparity being a major concern among policymakers. The country's Gini coefficients in 2017 were reported as 0.417 and 0.356,[19] before and after accounting for the government's transfer of taxes and benefits, respectively. At the broader level, there are signs that some form of geographical inequality has sunk its roots, similar to the spatial segregation of EIP constrained flats. This aspect of inequality is demonstrated in the form of income disparity, access to quality schools, and the gap in housing prices for dwelling types of similar sizes.

It is crucial to be cognizant of the socio-demographic intersections between inequality, social class, and ethnic diversity, and to appreciate how environmental features may influence individual and collective well-

FIGURE 13.1
Locations of EIP-Constrained HDB Flats

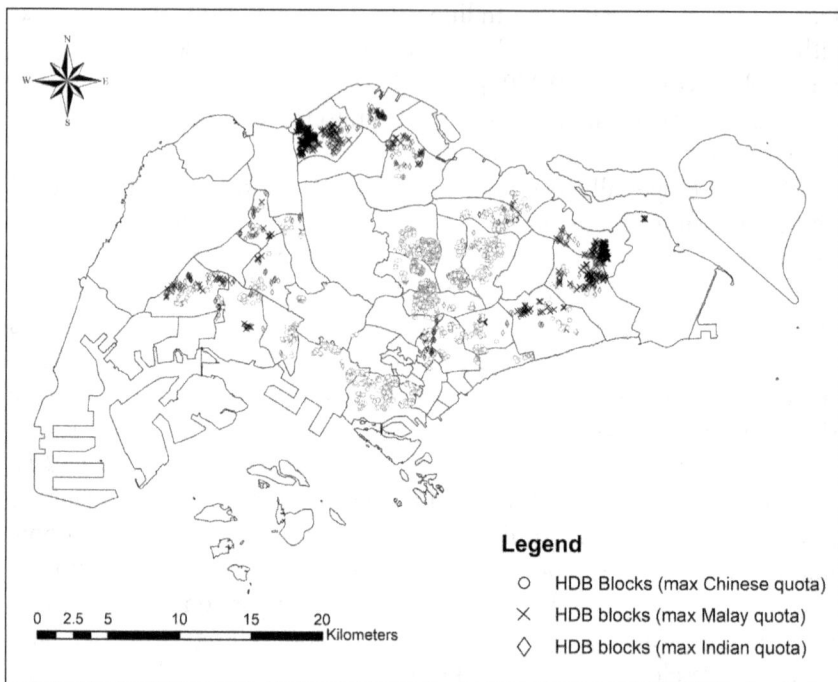

Legend

○   HDB Blocks (max Chinese quota)
×   HDB blocks (max Malay quota)
◇   HDB blocks (max Indian quota)

0   2.5   5   10   15   20
                                      Kilometers

Note: We obtained the list of HDB blocks from the API that is available on HDB Map Services. For each HDB block identified by its postal code, we then checked its current EIP status for each racial group, using HDB's service for checking the buyer's eligibility under the EIP portal.

being. In general, spatial diversity and inequality can be distilled under two prisms, within or across neighbourhoods. Social, built, and environmental characteristics all have intricate effects on the lived experience and well-being of residents, which in turn shape the status and profile of the estate.

DISPARITY ACROSS NEIGHBOURHOODS

In the United States, the socio-economic profile of a neighbourhood has impact across a range of interlinked well-being indicators, including but not limited to health outcomes, cognitive development, educational achievement, and social mobility. Often, the impact of living in a disadvantaged neighbourhood endures even after the individual moves out of this neighbourhood and into a "better" one. A child's early exposure to neighbourhood poverty, for example, was found to be associated with poorer mental health in adulthood even after controlling for initial mental health status.[20]

Thus far, results from the United States on the extent to which neighbourhood quality impacts life outcomes have been mixed. Results from high-profile experiments on residential mobility such as the Moving to Opportunity programme have been found to be highly dependent on location, with strong effects for moving out of high-poverty neighbourhoods found in some sites such as Chicago but not other sites such as Boston, Los Angeles, and New York City.[21]

Singapore, unlike the United States, is both a nation and a global city. Given that dividends from economic development in cities tend to be more evenly distributed compared to nations with larger land masses, Singapore does not display as large a variation in spatial advantage and disadvantage as compared to many Western case studies. However, Singapore is by no means spatially homogeneous as demonstrated above in the spatial distribution of public housing blocks constrained by EIP quota. It has also been shown that the distribution of economic and social outcomes is seemingly skewed in favour of certain neighbourhoods. According to the 2015 Singapore General Household Survey, more than four in ten households (44.4 per cent) in Bukit Timah earn at least S$20,000 a month, the highest income bracket in the statistical classification (see Table 13.3). This proportion is eight times as many as households in Woodlands (5.4 per cent) or Yishun (also 5.4 per cent). In a similar vein, one in five households in Bukit Merah lives in a rented flat, while less than one in twenty-five in Sengkang or Sembawang does so.[22]

Neighbourhoods also differ in terms of non-economic indicators, such as linguistic diversity. More than 72 per cent of households in Bukit Timah use English most frequently when speaking at home, as compared to Jurong West where only around 24 per cent of households use English most frequently. This contrast reflects the educational profile and lifestyles of the residents. Even among neighbourhoods that share similar profiles, there is significant diversity in other domains. For instance, while 36 per cent of both Hougang and Outram are English-speaking households, Hougang contains far more Mandarin-speaking households (42 per cent) compared to Outram (29 per cent). The diversity in language usage brings forth the complexity, social interactions in residential estates, and is suggestive of potential fault lines between and within neighbourhoods.

Worryingly, there has also been a distinct clustering of elite schools in certain neighbourhoods in recent times. These include Raffles Institution

TABLE 13.3
Percentage of Households Earning at Least $20,000 a month, by Planning Area

Planning Area	Household Income = >$20k/mth	Planning Area	Household Income = >$20k/mth
Tanglin	51.4	Outram	10.7
Bukit Timah	44.4	Bukit Panjang	10.7
Novena	27.4	Jurong East	10.2
Marine Parade	23.7	Bukit Merah	9.8
Serangoon	21.3	Ang Mo Kio	9.7
Bishan	19.8	Tampines	9.5
Bedok	16.4	Sengkang	9.3
Clementi	15.0	Geylang	8.8
Pasir Ris	14.0	Choa Chu Kang	8.7
Kallang	12.6	Sembawang	8.2
Bukit Batok	12.0	Jurong West	7.4
Queenstown	11.3	Yishun	5.4
Hougang	11.2	Woodlands	5.4
Toa Payoh	10.9	Punggol	5.1

Source: Data calculated from Table 152, "Resident Households by Planning Area and Monthly Household Income from Work", in *General Household Survey 2015*.

and Raffles Junior College in Bishan, Anglo-Chinese School (Independent) and Anglo-Chinese Junior College along Dover Road, and Hwa Chong Institution in Bukit Timah. These schools, which enjoy greater autonomy from the government in the management of their own affairs, consistently produce the largest proportion of top examination scorers in Singapore, and are often pioneers of innovative educational programmes.[23]

It is therefore no coincidence that resale prices of houses near elite educational institutions are higher than the average. The current primary school enrolment policy confers greater priority to children of school alumni and residents who live closer to their school of choice. Parents who wish to enrol their children to their preferred primary schools may purchase an apartment or house nearby for a better opportunity. Access to primary schools depends on enrolment demand while access to secondary schools is based on academic criteria.[24] For the former, the percentage of vacancies left available for public enrolment after meeting demand from alumni and residents living nearby serves as a proxy for the desirability of the school. For the latter, the PSLE entry score reflects the academic ranking and competitiveness of an institute. From the public's point of view, institutes with high entry scores are considered elite schools in recognition of their status and intellectual excellence.

In overlaying the spatial locations of the top thirty primary and secondary schools in Singapore with HDB flats constrained by the EIP Chinese quotas, condominiums, and private landed housing, we see a discernible map emerging, showing the link between the spatial concentration of elite schools and social class (see Figure 13.2). This is compounded by the fact that significantly more ethnic Chinese live in private and more expensive dwellings, and that neighbourhoods with more Chinese-constrained flats command a higher resale price (see Tables 13.1 and 13.2). Singapore's elite schools are clustered in relatively more affluent and ethnic Chinese-dominant neighbourhoods. Residential estates on the island's fringe, such as Jurong West, Woodlands, Sembawang, Sengkang, Punggol and Tampines, have fewer elite schools in spite of larger and younger populations compared to the central region. If this trend persists or is accelerated, this urban demography could erode Singapore's founding principle of a fair society with equal opportunities for all. Qualified students from lower-income households may have to travel longer distances if they wish to enrol in these elite institutions. More importantly, the emergence of elite clusters is likely to strengthen the link between residential location and educational attainment—an undesirable outcome given the Singapore government's emphasis on providing meritocratic educational access to all students regardless of their background.

DISPARITY WITHIN NEIGHBOURHOODS

In 2006, Harvard University Professor Robert Putnam proposed the controversial thesis that individuals tend to become more distrusting of others and exhibit lower levels of civic engagement in the short run when living in neighbourhoods with greater ethnic diversity.[25] This is because people who perceive themselves to have few commonalities and shared experiences with others in their community will have less incentive to interact with them. Challenging Putnam's research, Letki (2008)[26] found that a community's lower SES accounted for a large degree of erosion in social cohesion that had been previously attributed to ethnic diversity. Put simply, informal social interactions occur less frequently in economically deprived neighbourhoods which are, more often than not, also more ethnically diverse than more affluent neighbourhoods. In the 1980s, when Singapore was scaling up its public housing initiatives, then Prime Minister Lee Kuan Yew echoed the same sentiments by stating that there would be more bitterness, social tension and political and social problems if the better-off shut themselves away from their poorer neighbours.[27]

FIGURE 13.2
Locations of Elite Schools and Higher SES Residences

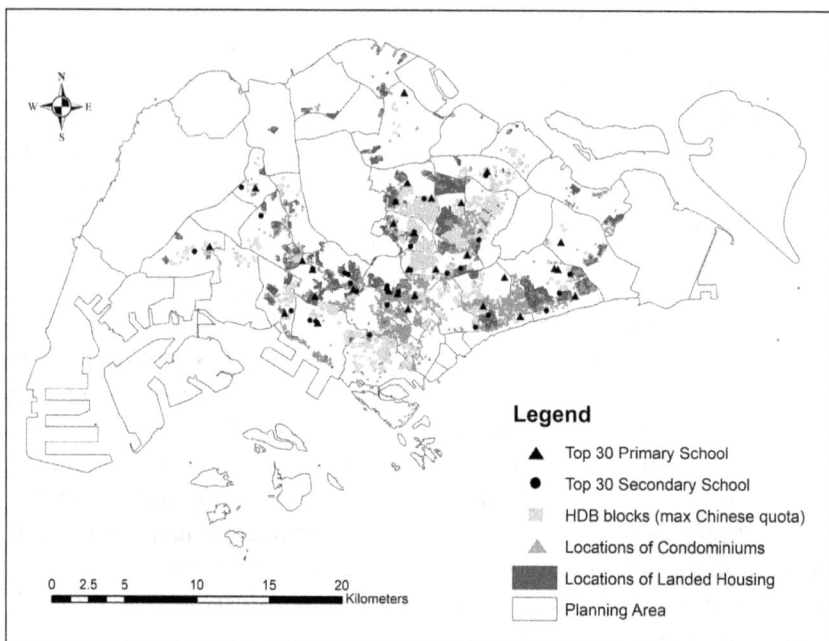

Note: Location of condominiums, landed houses, Chinese constrained HDB blocks, enrolment figures for primary schools and the ranking of secondary school admission standards were collated by the authors, and Jacqueline Ho, a PhD student from the University of Cornell, between May and August 2018. The data on schools are obtained from the Ministry of Education website, https://www.moe. gov.sg/admissions/primary-one-registration/phases, and the handbook for prospective secondary school applicants in December 2017.

In Singapore, policies such as the EIP are testaments to the government's determination to prevent neighbourhoods from becoming too dissimilar to each other in their ethnic composition. However, despite Lee's warning, far less attention has been paid to differences in the quality of life across neighbourhoods. In an op-ed published by the Institute of Policy Studies in 2017,[28] it was asserted that residential estates with a more diverse range of dwelling types, such as Marine Parade and Bukit Merah, see a stronger correlation with more petty crime (see Figure 13.3). The diversity of dwelling types as measured by the Blau Index provides an indication of inequality in a specific geographic region. More diverse neighbourhoods have higher Blau Index scores, statistically demonstrating wider ranges and more dispersed distributions of low- and high-end housing. Residential

FIGURE 13.3

Correlation between Diversity in Dwelling Types and Crime Rate, by Planning Area

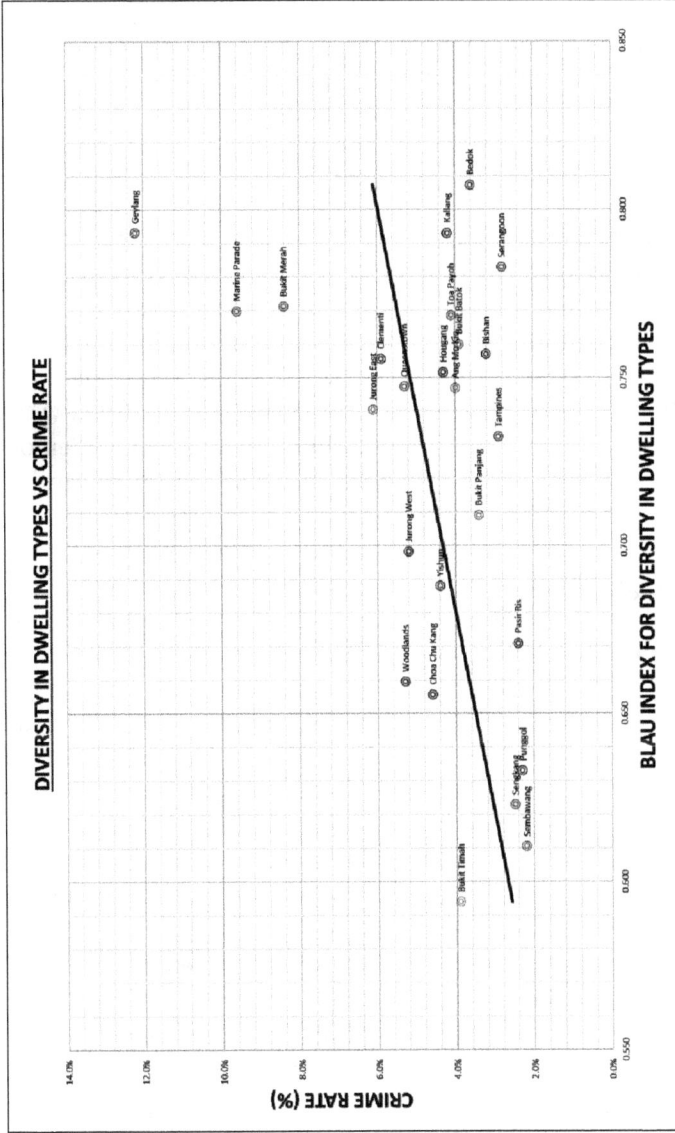

DIVERSITY IN DWELLING TYPES VS CRIME RATE

Source: Leong Chan-Hoong and Iii Kaiyisah Rahan, "In Low-Crime Singapore: Understanding the Link between Diversity and Crime at the Neighbourhood Level", *IPS Commons*, 13 December 2017, https://www.ipscommons.sg/in-low-crime-singapore-understanding-the-link-between-diversity-and-crime-at-the-neighbourhood-level/

estates with a predominantly large middle class (such as Sembawang and Sengkang) or upper class (such as Bukit Timah) reported lower Blau Index scores and correspondingly lower crime rates. These findings appear to support Letki's observations and Lee's foresight that the effects of income inequality, if unmitigated, could lead to low social capital and more anti-social behaviour like crime, even within a confined region.

Urban Planning and Policy Innovation for Social Coexistence

In conclusion, the residential patterns witnessed by Singapore over the past decades have made one thing clear, namely ethnic congregation remains a primordial instinct in Singapore's multicultural society. However, to further complicate matters, class differentiation is also emerging to become an increasingly daunting obstacle to integration. This chapter has shown that class differences in Singapore are often conflated with ethnic groups. And while class heterogeneity in residential regions demonstrates a stronger correlation with crime, the fact that class in Singapore is also mapped along ethnicity makes this issue doubly problematic. Although the formation of ethnic enclaves has been partially mitigated through the EIP, the ongoing formation of class enclaves seems to have entrenched itself. To be sure, public policies are never perfect as they incur trade-offs, prioritizations, and unintended consequences. The EIP was designed to prevent enclaves and encourage social integration. Similarly, urban housing redevelopment in Singapore is known for embracing diversity as one of its core missions by way of incorporating public, private, and rental flat dwellers in the same plot of land. Such policy directives are undoubtedly influenced by the historical shadow of the country's ethnic politics and driven by the desire to establish a fair, multiethnic and inclusive society. Singapore will be worse off without the EIP and the diversity it has produced.

Nevertheless, there may be unexpected side effects or policy blind spots that need to be addressed. At the introduction of the EIP in 1989, then member of parliament Dr Ho Tat Kin raised the concern that the policy would disproportionately affect low-income residents who were ethnic minorities. According to Dr Ho, this demographic group already faced restricted residential options not only because they needed to stay near relatives and friends who could help with child care, but also because they simply could not afford any flats larger than a three-room flat. The imposition of the EIP's ethnic limits would therefore have further narrowed the range of choices available to them.[29] In a similar vein, school allocation is prioritized by residential proximity, for the convenience and caregiving arrangements of families. However, in neighbourhoods with popular or desirable schools, this policy has driven real estate prices up, resulting in said neighbourhoods becoming accessible only to more affluent households.

What can policymakers do to promote greater ethnic and class interactions? How do we balance our national interests with our ethno-cultural preferences? The solution appears to lie in drawing affluent households and ethnic Chinese residents to neighbourhoods on the city-state's fringe. To this end, we recommend that some of the existing schools in the western, northern, and eastern regions of the island be established as Special Assistance Plan (SAP) schools, as such schools are popular among the ethnic Chinese, and this will draw more Chinese residents to move to the fringe areas. Alternatively, the government can equip the neighbourhood schools in the fringe with more resources to have better organic programmes to attract Chinese residents from other parts of the city-state. By dispersing our elite schools geographically, bright students living in less affluent neighbourhoods will also have better access to these schools. This will further create opportunities for social integration between academically gifted students and residents in the heartland community.

Lastly, more resources can be allocated to neighbourhoods with diverse ethnic and socio-economic profiles. Instead of applying a standardized national ratio for amenities per head, town planning and maintenance can be supplemented with additional allowances for estates with increasingly disparate dwelling types. More generous programmes that promote greater civic engagement and participation at the local level could nurture the sense of neighbourliness and empathy among households that are distinctively different. There will always be a strong proclivity to live close to those who are culturally or economically similar to us just as our forefathers did when they sought the company of people from their home town upon arriving on these shores. The existing geographic schism can be mitigated with strong and resolute state interventions, just as we did thirty years ago with the EIP.

Notes

1. Selina Lim, Wai Wai Yang, Leong Chan-Hoong, and Jerrold Hong, "Reconfiguring the Singapore Identity Space: Beyond Racial Harmony and Survivalism", *International Journal of Intercultural Relations* 43, Part A (2014): 13–21.

2. Data from 1957 to 2018 calculated from "Singapore Residents by Age Group, Ethnic Group and Sex, End June, Annual", in *Population Trends, 2018*.
3. J.S. Furnivall, *Progress and Welfare in Southeast Asia: A Comparison of Colonial Policy and Practice* (New York: Secretariat, Institute of Pacific Relations, 1941).
4. A.B. Shamsul, "Consuming Islam and Containing the Crisis: Religion, Ethnicity and the Economy in Malaysia", in *Southeast Asian-Centred Economies or Economics?*, edited by Mason C. Hoadley (Copenhagen: Nordic Institute of Asian Studies, 1999), pp. 43–61; Noraini M. Noor and Leong Chan-Hoong, "Multiculturalism in Malaysia and Singapore: Contesting Models", *International Journal of Intercultural Relations* 37, no. 6 (2013): 714–26.
5. C.M. Turnbull, *A History of Singapore, 1819–1975* (Kuala Lumpur: Oxford University Press, 1977).
6. Fong Sip Chee, *The PAP Story: The Pioneering Years* (Singapore: Times Periodicals, 1980).
7. Selina Lim et al., "Reconfiguring the Singapore Identity Space"; Arne Roets, Evelyn W.M. Au, and Alain Van Hiel, "Can Authoritarianism Lead to Greater Liking of Out-Groups? The Intriguing Case of Singapore", *Psychological Science* 26, no. 12 (2015): 1972–74.
8. Selina Lim et al., "Reconfiguring the Singapore Identity Space".
9. See Noraini M. Noor and Leong Chan-Hoong, "Multiculturalism in Malaysia and Singapore", for a comprehensive discussion on Singapore's multicultural policies.
10. Agnes Wee, "Policy Won't Hit Deals Approved before March 1", *Sunday Times*, 19 February 1989, p. 11.
11. Ibid.
12. See Leong Chan-Hoong, Patrick Rueppel, and Danielle Hong, "Managing Immigration and Integration in Singapore", in *Migration and Integration: Common Challenges and Responses from Europe and Asia*, edited by Wilhelm Hofmeister, Patrick Rueppel, Yves Pascouau, and Andrea Frontini (Singapore: Konrad-Adenauer Stiftung and European Union, 2014), pp. 51–72.
13. Chih Hoong Sin, "The Quest for a Balanced Ethnic Mix: Singapore's Ethnic Quota Policy Examined", *Urban Studies* 39, no. 8 (2002): 1347–74; Maisy Wong, "Estimating Ethnic Preferences Using Ethnic Housing Quotas in Singapore", *Review of Economic Studies* 80, no. 3 (2013): 1178–214.
14. Maisy Wong, "Estimating the Impact of the Ethnic Housing Quotas in Singapore", *Samuel Zell & Robert Lurie Real Estate Center Working Paper*, no. 748 (Pennsylvania: University of Pennsylvania, 2012).
15. Arne Roets, Au, and Van Hiel, "Can Authoritarianism Lead to Greater Liking of Out-Groups?".
16. As quoted in Patrick Daniel, "Ethnic Limits on Blocks Come as a Surprise", *Straits Times*, 17 February 1989, p. 15.
17. Leong Chan-Hoong, Eugene Teng, and William Weiliang Ko, "Thirty Years of Ethnic Management in Neighbourhoods: Evaluating the Success of the Ethnic Integration Policy", in *Building Resilient Neighbourhoods: The Convergence of*

Policies, Research, and Practice, edited by Leong Chan-Hoong and Lai-Choo Malone-Lee (Singapore: Springer, 2020), pp. 29–49.

18. A subzone is a housing enumeration that is similar to a precinct; a planning area is a geographical plot use for urban and census divisions, delineated by the Urban Redevelopment Authority. There are 323 subzones and 55 planning areas.

19. Singapore Ministry of Finance, "Before and After Taxes and Transfers: Singapore's Gini Coefficient", 19 March 2018, https://www.mof.gov.sg/Newsroom/ Parliamentary-Replies/before-and-after-taxes-and-transfers---singapore-s-gini-coefficient

20. Blair Wheaton and Philippa Clarke, "Space Meets Time: Integrating Temporal and Contextual Influences on Mental Health in Early Adulthood", *American Sociological Review* 68, no. 5 (2003): 680–706.

21. Julia Burdick-Will, Jens Ludwig, Stephen W. Raudenbush, Robert J. Sampson, Lisa Sanbonmatsu, and Patrick Sharkey, "Converging Evidence for Neighbourhood Effects on Children's Test Scores: An Experimental, Quasi-Experimental, and Observational Comparison", in *Whither Opportunity? Rising Inequality, Schools, and Children's Life Chances,* edited by Greg J. Duncan and Richard J. Murnane (New York: Russell Sage, 2011), pp. 255–76.

22. Table 149, "Resident Households by Planning Area and Tenancy", in Department of Statistics Singapore, *General Household Survey 2015.*

23. Gracie Lee, "Independent Schools Scheme", http://eresources.nlb.gov.sg/infopedia/ articles/SIP_2018-10-09_152727.html (Singapore Infomedia).

24. The relevant academic criteria are T-scores from the national Primary School Leaving Examinations (PSLE).

25. Robert Putnam, "E Pluribus Unum: Diversity and Community in the Twenty-First Century", *Scandinavian Political Studies* 30, no. 2 (2007): 137–74.

26. Natalia Letki, "Does Diversity Erode Social Cohesion? Social Capital and Race in British Neighbourhoods", *Politics Studies* 56, no. 1 (2008): 99–126.

27. "Perils of Class Division: PM's Call to Middle-Income Group", *Straits Times,* 9 February 1981, p. 1.

28. Leong Chan-Hoong and Ili Kaiyisah Rahan, "In Low-Crime Singapore: Understanding the Link between Diversity and Crime at the Neighbourhood Level", *IPS Commons,* 13 December 2017, https://www.ipscommons.sg/in-low-crime-singapore-understanding-the-link-between-diversity-and-crime-at-the-neighbourhood-level/

29. "Practical Reasons May Be Behind Racial Enclaves", *Straits Times,* 17 January 1989, p. 13.

14

Ageing Societies, Age-Inclusive Spaces and Community Bonding

Kalyani K. Mehta

INTRODUCTION

Imagine the following scenario. Due to the need to stay economically competitive, Singapore keeps building more and more nursing homes. In this way, the adults in the family can concentrate on work and the children can go to school punctually. When the children return home, the foreign domestic worker takes charge of the meals, household chores, and ensures the safety of the children. When the working adults return home in the late evening, the children are ready for bed and the meal is prepared. The children say a quick good night to the tired parents and retire to bed, while the television awaits the latter after they finish their dinner. The day is over. What is missing from this scenario?

Singapore is an ageing society, and it is a reality that cannot be ignored. The main reasons for this demographic phenomenon are the low fertility rate (below replacement level for almost a decade[1]), the longevity of the population, and the availability of highly advanced medical facilities. We can state that the demographic shift is a testimony of the success of our nation. But the important question is, how does this demographic shift from a youthful to an ageing population affect Singaporeans at large?

We may identify and reflect on the socio-emotional aspects that are not mentioned from the scenario described above. On the surface, practically everything described seems normal and under control. However, humans are also social and emotional beings. Family relationships have to have meaning. So what is missing in the vignette? For one, the presence of grandparents. And if our elders are housed in nursing homes, then the bond between grandparents and grandchildren will never develop, thus depriving young families of the experience, wisdom and support that are unique to multigenerational families. In addition, the value of filial piety is lacking because the opportunity for young parents to demonstrate respect to their own parents and in-laws in order to transmit such values to their children would not present itself. The grandchildren would be deprived of watching their parents as role models of care for the elders in the family and thereby be deprived of learning these subtle values. Sharing of daily problems, the expression of excitement, compassion, forgiveness, and even the loving hug given by grandchildren to grandparents (that wipes out their tiredness or boredom)—all these colours of life are missing from the vignette. This chapter will highlight how important it is for us to embrace the evolution of societies from underdeveloped to developed, from youthful to ageing, from traditional to modern, in all the diverse colours and nuances that express our humanity.

UNDERSTANDING THE CROSS-CUTTING ISSUES

The effects of an ageing population will be felt vertically from the individual, to the family, community, and the national. Horizontally, they will be experienced in the health, financial, social, psychological, education, transport and even common public spaces. In other words, each and every one of us will experience the impact of an ageing population. In terms of depth, the ageing of our relatives and friends will add to the profundity of our thinking towards issues such as death and relationships which may, in turn, result in greater reflection on life. For example, a fleeting encounter with death through a story, TV episode or accidental observation of a family's loss of loved one could trigger the thought (cognitive) process to search for meaning in this urban jungle.

These vertical, horizontal and depth dimensions intersect each other and further complicate our understanding of the expansive effects of ageing populations on the dynamics of societal forces. For example, if an elderly couple are living on their own because their children have migrated overseas, they are motivated to work beyond their retirement age of sixty-seven years, as they have to think about their financial security. Even if their house is fully paid for, they will have expenses such as daily food and transport, medical bills, and miscellaneous costs from haircuts, buying footwear, and going to see a movie. And knowing that their adult children will never return from overseas, they will have to factor in the cost of hiring a helper, and ad hoc expenses like repair of household appliances. All in all, they will need at least S$3,000 dollars a month to survive. In such cases, the community becomes the "substitute family" for the couple, just as it replaces family for single male or female elders who have never married.

Common Issues Faced by Elders Living in Community

In addition to cost of living, there are other issues which raise anxiety among the elderly in Singapore. In a recent discussion with the elderly living in my neighbourhood, I found that those who were becoming physically frail have a real fear of slipping and falling when they are outside their homes. This fear discourages them from leaving their homes and they will go out only if they have a companion to depend on. Another factor that instils fear is the rapid rate of digitization in Singapore. From learning how to use an app to call a taxi, to finding out the timings of movies, schedules of public buses, downloading bank statements, transferring money from one account to another, and applying for government SkillsFuture Credits for training courses, the digitization processes in everyday life is becoming more ubiquitous. All of these and more require the elderly to navigate websites, fill up e-forms, submit their One-Time Password (OTP) sent to their mobile phones and, of course, surf the Internet.

After all, research on senior citizens' experience with technology has shown this fear to be a consistent one, particularly the fear of deleting important information by mistake or crashing the laptop.[2] While many young adults or digital natives may view this second fear patronizingly, this fear is nonetheless very real for the elderly who did not grow up in the IT era. This fear may subside in time if they have a good technical support system they can tap on whenever in need. Meanwhile, immediate family members of elders who are themselves struggling with forms of technology, such as the mobile phone, may be asked to put aside their own work to help their parents or grandparents. This may annoy or frustrate them and, as a result, the relationships between generations may be strained. Local documentaries such as *Ah Kong* and movies such as *Money Not Enough 2* have sensitively portrayed the difficulties of family members in understanding the "lived world" of elderly people with dementia.

In addition, the life trajectory of the family and that of the ageing individual often intersect, especially when they are living cheek by jowl under one roof. This may lead to stressful situations. For example, an eighty-year-old grandfather may seek frequent attention from his favourite granddaughter, who is preparing for her final examinations at university; or a ninety-year-old mother with dementia may persistently ask her sixty-five-year-old son to take her to her hometown in Malaysia when he is financially strapped because he is recently retired. Such issues are intertwined with different individual needs, and often the situation requires delicate handling, especially when concerning dementia sufferers. After all, family members may not realize the impact and consequence of dementia on the emotional state and behaviour of the elderly, and may not have the requisite skills to handle the dementia sufferer with patience and empathy. Family caregiving is a highly complex issue fraught with psychological, emotional and financial pressures that affect nearly all concerned. As such, multiple support systems are needed to keep the family together, including social, health, counselling, and financial support. Community support in the form of respite care, friendly neighbours who look out for the family, and volunteers who befriend the dementia patient, is imperative for ageing-in-place to occur successfully.

Age-Inclusive Spaces
While there have been many efforts to cultivate age-inclusive spaces such as children's playgrounds, fitness stations in Housing and Development Board (HDB) estates, community gardens, religious places of worship, and parks, more could be done for the elderly. We have to plan beyond the physical, and look at the softer aspects of age-inclusive spaces such as intergenerational attitudes, educating all age groups on the safety requirements of crossing roads, and training children to view and react appropriately to the mentally and physically challenged in our midst. In the past, families were multigenerational and used to live together such that children grew up naturally with their grandparents. Today, because the percentage of multigenerational households has decreased drastically, children are less likely to interact with elders on a daily basis. Hence, facilities like three-in-one complexes with childcare, student care and eldercare have great social value as opportunities for generations to mingle and understand each other better. Kampong Admiralty is a good example of community living where senior health and social facilities are situated in the midst of childcare and commercial amenities.[3]

Another programme that deserves mention is the Intergenerational Learning Programme by the Council for Third Age. Here, motivated senior citizens are chosen to give talks and demonstrations at primary and secondary schools. In another programme, computer literacy is taught to seniors by youth from secondary schools and junior colleges. These programmes are designed to bring together different age groups to mingle, bond and nurture their interest in learning (a need that cuts across all age groups). It is recommended that Intergenerational Learning Programmes like these be introduced on a systematic basis and scaled up across all kindergarten, primary and secondary schools in Singapore. Lifelong learning programmes, many of which are subsidized by SkillsFuture Singapore, have drawn out the elderly from their homes to learn a new skill or hobby and engaged them in settings that are age-inclusive with opportunities to make new friends and explore new areas of interest. The local performing arts scene also offers another vibrant context for age-inclusivity. Many of the elderly have a talent for singing, dancing, acting and narrating poetry in English or any other language. Perhaps it is the Asian sense of modesty that discourages Asian elderly from freely expressing themselves through the performing arts. Nevertheless, some senior bands and singers have emerged in the last few years, such as Jimmy PresLee who sings Elvis Presley songs.

Integration in the Workplace

The resident labour participation rate of persons above sixty-five years of age increased from 16.1 per cent in 2008 to 27.8 per cent in 2018. The Labour Force Participation Rate (LFPR) of males above sixty-five years of age increased from 25 per cent in 2008 to 38.2 per cent in 2018. In comparison, the LFPR of females above sixty-five years of age increased from 8.9 per cent in 2008 to 19.2 per cent in 2018.[4] According to past research conducted by the author with senior women, the lower percentage of older women in the workforce may be explained by their family responsibilities and their lack of education.[5] When approached by their adult children, older women find it difficult to refuse grandparenting functions, due to the needs of their working adult children. Hence, they may decide to stay home and do childminding of grandchildren instead of seeking work. For the current cohort of older women above seventy years (who probably had primary school education or less), the jobs would be of low wages.

In tandem with other ageing nations around the world, Singapore is also adopting a national policy of encouraging and facilitating older employees in the continuation of work. This enables older people to sustain their income and continue an active lifestyle. The Retirement and Re-Employment Act 2012 was enacted by the government to encourage employers to continue hiring older workers beyond sixty-two years of age (the official retirement age) up till sixty-five, and on 1 July 2017 this was extended to sixty-seven years of age. Schemes such as Job Redesign have also been made available to incentivize employers to alter work conditions, such as by installing ergonomic furniture, to meet the needs of their elderly workers.

Accessibility Issues at Places of Worship

In a multiracial, multireligious Singapore, age-inclusive places are to be found at places of religious worship. Be it the church, Buddhist temple, Hindu temple, synagogue or mosque, people of different age groups are always found at such religious and spiritual settings. However, ad hoc observations have shown that not all places of worship are accessible to those on wheelchairs. In addition, some entrances or staircases may pose a danger to the elderly because of their uneven surfaces, thus exposing them to the risk of falling and hurting themselves. For example, at a Hindu temple that the author visits frequently in the east of Singapore, the floor at the entrance is carved for aesthetic beauty, but practically speaking, it poses a danger to the elderly who may be unsteady or suffering from frailty. Hence, while such venues are, in principle, open to people of all age groups, physical barriers to accessibility continue to exist as obstacles to the elderly, disabled and young children. Apart from accessibility, it is important that such places have ramps and lifts, as well as ample chairs or benches, for older persons to rest and catch their breath. The management committees of such institutions are urged to relook at the design and the ground accessibility of their institutions and to assess if some renovations are required to adjust to the fast growing numbers of elderly devotees. The Building and Construction Authority (BCA) has developed the Code on Accessibility in the Built Environment 2013, which focuses on a more holistic approach to accessibility in view of the ageing population.[6] This is a commendable step, and the updated 2019 version has been released.

COMMUNITY BONDING

Older adults lose touch with their community as they age for a variety of reasons: children become independent, retirement, diseases and disability in older age poses mobility problems. They may feel alienated and disconnected from community life. Developing their recreational interests and joining elder-friendly community events goes a long way in helping older adults feel connected and occupied as they age.[7]

According to a survey conducted by International Longevity Centre (2014), it was found that the vast majority of the elderly in Singapore age within their communities, with only 2–3 per cent of the total population above sixty-five years residing in institutional facilities such as nursing homes or sheltered homes for the aged. However, the survey also found that 72 per cent of the elderly who aged in their communities did not attend social events in their neighbourhood at all.[8] With the fast-ageing demographics of Singapore's population, ageing-in-place is the most effective and culturally friendly strategy for the government and the people. When asked, most elders in Singapore prefer to grow old with their families and within communities that they are familiar with; institutional living is acceptable only as the last resort.[9] It is thus rational and logical for the state to ramp up primary healthcare by investing in equipment, skills, infrastructure and services, as well as homecare services in the community. It is only in this way that families will be able to receive the requisite support in order to better manage the care of their ageing relatives within the community. And yet, many elderly (and their family caregivers) have not been reached by community organizations such as social services, health services, religious and educational agencies, and neighbourhood schemes, to participate in social activities and events. What are the reasons for this?

From the author's view, this is the big challenge for Singapore in the next five years. Let's take a closer look at the issue and its implications for the future. The statistics inform us that, together with the rising numbers of older persons in Singapore, the prevalence of certain diseases such as dementia and stroke is also going to rise. For example, the recent nationwide survey on mental health conducted by the Institute of Mental Health informs us that one in ten persons above sixty years of age are projected to suffer from dementia.[10] Stroke is one of the top four leading causes of death amongst the elderly in Singapore.[11] In the cases of dementia and stroke, not only do the patients suffer, surrounding people such as family members, particularly the primary caregiver, also undergo a lot of distress during the caregiving years. The latter require constant encouragement and support from other family members, the broader community, as well as the state. Recently, at the Caregivers Appreciation Gala Luncheon 2019 hosted by the Alzheimer's Disease Association (ADA), Senior Minister of State for Health, Edwin Tong, noted that, "Some caregivers shared with me that not only have they been strongly encouraged by the community support, they have also become more empowered through these programmes".[12] Earlier studies have reported that amongst the population of family caregivers, those looking after relatives with dementia as well as elders with physical disability tend to be exposed to higher levels of mental and emotional stress.[13] Drawing from qualitative studies conducted in the local context, we know that the economic burden of care on the family can be heavy because of medical expenses, the cost of hiring a domestic helper to care for the dependent elderly person, and/or respite day-care for older adults.[14] And because many working adults (or middle generation) have to remain employed to foot the medical bills and other expenses, the task of providing physical, emotional and social care for their parents is often left to someone else. The needs of family caregivers are extensive and events such as the Appreciation Gala Luncheon hosted by the ADA is necessary but ultimately insufficient in supporting and encouraging these caregivers. In the same article on the luncheon, it was reported that 900 elders and caregivers had benefitted from the public education programmes carried out by the community support team.[15] It must be acknowledged that Community Development Councils (CDC) such as the South-West CDC are ramping up their caregiver services and awareness raising efforts by organizing the Family Carnival Day that was celebrated at Jurong Point Mall on 1 December 2018, where caregiver booths were set up to educate visitors to the carnival.

With regard to community efforts to support families with members suffering from stroke, the Stroke Club and the Stroke Support Station are two programmes that look into the needs of caregivers. But are these schemes enough to reach out to the growing number of family caregivers who are involved? Statistics are not readily available on how many family caregivers are involved in care of dependent or vulnerable elderly (not all elderly need constant physical and supervisory care). The first nationwide Survey on Informal Caregiving commissioned by the then Ministry of Community Development, Youth and Sports highlighted the fact that almost half of the caregivers interviewed depended on foreign domestic helpers to provide the necessary care during the day to elderly members.[16] This strongly suggests that more Singaporeans should be made aware of the annual caregiver grant of S$200 that is available to all Singaporean families with older members above sixty-five years, which may also be used for foreign domestic helpers (FDW).[17] It would be good if statistics were available on how many family members and foreign domestic helpers have utilized this grant over the years since it was introduced.

While the caregiver grant, administered by Agency for Integrated Care, can be used for training expenses, the process of filling up forms, co-payment of $10 by the attendee, and employer's permission required for the foreign domestic worker to attend the training may be a turn-off for many. It is also a challenge for caregivers to find people to replace them when they attend the training. Over and above these obstacles for service utilization, Asians in general view seeking help outside their family sphere as demeaning to their self-esteem. There is a proverb stating that in Chinese culture, "washing dirty linen in public" is frowned upon. There is also a stigma attached to mental health problems, and even till today there are families that do not wish to discuss their problems in handling a family member with a mental issue to outsiders, e.g., neighbours.

MOVING FORWARD

The long-term consequences of not reviewing the social compact between state and society could lead to a few negative scenarios. Firstly, the possibility of increased cases of ageism in the workplace is a reality. This could be due to unaddressed stereotypes attached to older workers, or tension between intergenerational workers because of the lack of jobs available. Elderly workers may need to continue working because they do not have adequate savings for retirement, while younger workers may be cash-strapped due to the high cost of living and the need to pay for the medical expenses of their ageing parents. Secondly, inconsiderate or antisocial behaviour in public places such as hawker centres, trains, and buses may impact the elderly more adversely than others. For example, it is not uncommon to see a youth seated in seats reserved for the elderly or pregnant women on buses or trains, busy playing videos on his or her smartphone, oblivious to the plight of an older commuter. Another common sight is an adult sleeping on the train while the older commuter struggles to retain his or her balance in the moving train or bus. Indeed, the reality of an ageing populace has made civic consciousness crucial for different age groups to live in harmony. And while it is to be expected that attitudes will take time to change, we have to instil in young people the reality of ageing and the fact that they too will one day face difficulties associated with ageing, in order that the future society they wish to create will be moulded today.

An age-inclusive community is becoming key to community bonding. Indeed, achieving social integration may take time as our Singapore society becomes increasingly diverse. The last few decades have witnessed many foreigners and Employment Pass holders coming to Singapore in search of work. Recent statistics show that the resident population can be broken down into 3.472 million citizens and 0.522 million Permanent Residents, thus leaving 29 per cent of the total population as non-residents, or transitory workers.[18] Admittedly, some of them may be become Permanent Residents and/or citizens in future.

As Singapore evolves into a mature nation, the next generation of leadership (commonly referred to as the 4th Generation or 4G leadership) have a few key issues that they have to deal with. Together with the ageing population issue is the challenge of integration and community bonding.

Formulation of policies dovetailing the changing values of the different cohorts who have their own perspectives is extremely important. Top down policies have been known to have little buy-in from the people. It has been asserted that Singaporeans are ready for a "social compact in Singapore [that] should ideally include the state, the community, the family and the individual; where all four pillars are enshrined as equally important and irreplaceable".[19]

In conclusion, Singapore has built a strong economic and political foundation for itself over the decades, but it is currently at a critical junction. There are social divisions within contemporary society that require attention. Ageing and the challenges faced by the elderly are one of these divisions. Nevertheless, the author has confidence that we will be able to bridge these social divisions to complement our political and economic foundations. However, it will require a socially attuned mindset. A multidimensional and holistic approach is recommended to Singapore's policymakers. This approach should place social challenges at the centre of the nation's next chapter. With such an approach, Singapore will be a united and dynamic nation, able to tackle the challenges of the next few decades.

Notes

1. Strategy Group, Singapore Prime Minister's Office; Department of Statistics Singapore; Singapore Ministry of Home Affairs; Immigration and Checkpoints Authority; Singapore Ministry of Manpower, *Population in Brief 2018*, p. 14.
2. Kalyani Mehta, "IT Literacy and Singapore Seniors: A Qualitative Study", in *Human Development and Sustainability: Challenges and Strategies*, edited by Asok Kumar Sarkar and Prasanta Kumar Ghosh (New Delhi: Atlantic, 2017).
3. Goh Yan Han and Rachel Au-Yong, "Kampung Admiralty wins top global award for architecture", *Straits Times*, 3 December 2018.
4. Table 5, "Age-Sex Specific Resident Labour Force Participation Rate, 2008–2018 (June)", in Singapore Ministry of Manpower, *Labour Force in Singapore 2018*, pp. T7–T9.
5. Kalyani Mehta, "The Ageing Experience of Singaporean Women", in *Untapped Resources: Women in Ageing Societies Across Asia*, edited by Kalyani Mehta, 2nd ed. (Singapore: Marshall Cavendish International, 2005), pp. 47–69.
6. See the Building and Construction Authority's Friendly Built Environment website, https://friendlybuildings.bca.gov.sg/ for more details.
7. International Longevity Centre, *A Profile of Older Men and Women in Singapore 2014* (Singapore: Tsao Foundation, 2014), p. 33.
8. Ibid.
9. Kalyani Mehta, "Living Arrangements of the Elderly in Singapore: Cultural Norms in Transition", *Journal of Cross-Cultural Gerontology* 10, no. 1/2 (1995): 113–43.

10. Mythily Subramaniam, Chong Siow Ann, Janhavi Ajit Vaingankar, Edimansyah Abdin, Chua Boon Yiang, Chua Hong Choon, Eng Goi Khia, Derrick Heng, Hia Soo Boon, Huang Wanping, Anitha Jeyagurunathana, Joshua Kua, Lee Siau Pheng, Rathi Mahendran, Harish Magadi, Srinivasa Malladi, Paul McCrone, Shirlene Pang, Louisa Picco, Vathsala Sagayadevan, Rajeswari Sambasivam, Seng Kok Han, Esmond Seow, Saleha Shafie, Shazana Shahwan, Tan Lay Ling, Mabel Yap, Zhang Yun Jue, Ng Li Ling, and Martin Prince, "Prevalence of Dementia in People Aged 60 Years and Above: Results from the WiSE Study", *Journal of Alzheimer's Disease* 45, no. 4 (2015), p. 1132.

11. N. Venketasubramanian and C.L.H. Chen, "Burden of Stroke in Singapore", *International Journal of Stroke* 31, no. 1 (2008), p. 51.

12. Rahimah Rashith, "Making Singapore Dementia-Inclusive with Community Help", *Straits Times*, 6 January 2019.

13. Kalyani Mehta, "Stress among Family Caregivers of Older Persons in Singapore", *Journal of Cross-Cultural Gerontology* 20, no. 4 (2005): 319–34.

14. See Kalyani Mehta and Thang Leng Leng, "Experiences of Formal and Informal Caregivers of Older Persons in Singapore", *Journal of Cross-Cultural Gerontology* 32, no. 3 (2017): 373–85, for more discussion.

15. Rahimah Rashith, "Making Singapore Dementia-Inclusive with Community Help".

16. Angelique Chan, Truls Ostbye, Rahul Malhotra, and Athel J. Hu, *The Survey on Informal Caregiving: Summary Report (for MCYS)* (Singapore: Ministry of Social and Family Development, 2014), p. 11.

17. See the Agency for Integrated Care website, www.aic.sg, for more information on the grant.

18. Strategy Group, Singapore Prime Minister's Office et al., *Population in Brief 2018*, p. 5.

19. Kalyani Mehta, "Ageing Society: Implications for a New Social Contract", in *The Heart of Learning*, edited by Leong Thin Yin and Cheah Horn Mun (Singapore: Singapore University of Social Sciences, 2017), p. 93.

Index

www.ingramcontent.com/pod-product-compliance
Lightning Source LLC
Chambersburg PA
CBHW071353290326
41932CB00045B/1773